ENLIGHTMENT!

"The American political philosopher and activist Murray Bookchin, who died ... aged 85, was a theorist of the anti-globalisation movement before its time, an ecological visionary, an advocate of direct action and a polemicist. 'Capitalism is a social cancer,' he argued. 'It is the disease of society'. The author of more than 20 books, Bookchin ... [made] a clear distinction between ecology, which wanted to transform society, and environmentalism, which wants to ameliorate the worst aspects of capitalist economy."

— *The Guardian*, August 8, 2020

"Mr. Bookchin long was a proponent of left-leaning libertarian ideas and was among the first people in the early 1960s to promote the then-emerging field of ecology into political debate. ... He argued that only a completely free and open society can resolve the problems that confronted the environment. Mr. Bookchin's views, often well ahead of their time, never got wide play because they were closely linked to his leftist political thought."

— *The Boston Globe*, July 31, 2020

"The most brilliant eco-political philosopher in the US, who mentored countless activists with a programmatic perspective which significantly helps us build the basis of a new society."

— Lucia Kowaluk, C.M., C.Q.

"Mr. Bookchin's writings had their strongest influence on Green Parties in the United States and Europe and on the radical edges of the environmental movement. His emphasis on human society and economic systems put him at odds with 'deep ecologists,' who believe that humans have arrogantly usurped their position as just another species to wreak environmental havoc. ... Though criticism came most naturally to him, Mr. Bookchin also offered a utopian vision: he hoped that nation states could be replaced by a confederation of independent municipalities, each governed by the equivalent of a New England town meeting. In 1992, *The Independent*, the London newspaper, referred to him as 'the foremost Green philosopher of the age.'"

— *THE NEW YORK TIMES*, AUGUST 7, 2006

ENLIGHTMENT and ECOLOGY

The Legacy of Murray Bookchin in the 21st Century

Yavor Tarinski, ed.

BLACK
ROSE
BOOKS

Montréal / Chicago / London

Black Rose Books No. TT408

Library and Archives Canada Cataloguing in Publication

Title: Enlightenment and ecology : the legacy of Murray Bookchin in the 21st century / Yavor Tarinski, ed.
Name: Tarinski, Yavor, editor.
Description: Includes bibliographical references and index.
Identifiers: Canadiana (print) 20190166320 | Canadiana (ebook) 20190166398 | ISBN 9781551647111 (hardcover) | ISBN 9781551647098 (softcover) | ISBN 9781551647135 (PDF)
Subjects: LCSH: Bookchin, Murray, 1921–2006. | LCSH: Social ecology.
Classification: LCC HM861 .E55 2021 | DDC 304.2—dc23

Cover illustration by Janet Biehl

C.P. 35788 Succ. Léo-Pariseau,
Montréal, QC H2X 0A4 CANADA
www.blackrosebooks.com
Explore our books and subscribe to our newsletter.

ORDERING INFORMATION

USA/INTERNATIONAL	CANADA	UK/EIRE
University of Chicago Press	University of Toronto Press	Central Books
Chicago Distribution Center	5201 Dufferin Street	Freshwater Road
11030 South Langley Avenue	Toronto, ON	Dagenham
Chicago IL 60628	M3H 5T8	RM8 1RX
(800) 621-2736 (USA)	1-800-565-9523	+44 20 8525 8800
(773) 702-7000 (International)	utpbooks@utpress.utoronto.ca	contactus@centralbooks.com
orders@press.uchicago.edu		

TABLE OF CONTENTS

BOOKCHIN'S INFLUENCE ON POLITICAL PRACTICE AROUND THE WORLD

PREFACE

Yavor Tarinski

MY DEAR FRIEND and comrade Dimitrios Roussopoulos once told me that anthologies might at first glance appear as something easy to put together, but in fact they are a curse. I completely understand his point. It is such an immense effort to coordinate the work of authors and activists, publishers, copyeditors, and so on from different parts of the world that at times you might feel lost or exasperated. At the same time, this interaction with such incredible and bright people from all walks of life keeps you from abandoning the project and absorbs you completely.

The creation of this book is no different. It took us over a year to prepare—a period in which we faced many difficulties. On the one hand we had the COVID-19 crisis and the lockdowns that forced huge swaths of the world's population into quarantine. The danger of the return of large-scale lockdown is still not a thing of the past as national governments continue to act irresponsibly in the face of such a serious danger to our health. Furthermore, this crisis was followed by the uprising of Black Lives Matter in May 2020, provoked by the brutal murder of George Floyd by the Minneapolis police and the continuing institutional racism in the US. This wave of demonstrations, however, expanded beyond its borders, as communities from abroad have grown tired of the racist policies of their own nation-states.

It is in such difficult times that you have the chance to reflect on the ills of the current state of our societies and see that things can't return to the way they used to be. Something must radically change. It is in this context that the anthology *Enlightenment and Ecology: The Legacy of Murray Bookchin in the 21st Century* comes to life, with the voices of profound thinkers and activists inspired by the revolutionary ideas of Murray Bookchin. The ideas of Bookchin came to the forefront of contemporary revolutionary thought through the democratic practices of communities and social movements from across the planet. From the cantons of Rojava (in Kurdish-majority northeastern Syria) to the assemblies of the *gilets jaunes* in France, his ideas live on. The book you hold in your hands is a celebration of the plethora of contemporary liberatory experiences that were influenced by

Bookchin, as well as a dialogue between scholars and activists on the prospects of a democratic and ecological future. This is exactly how we would like this book to be viewed—not simply as the acknowledgment of a great theoretician, but as an ongoing conversation with his ideas which are more relevant than ever before.

INTRODUCTION

Yavor Tarinski

[Bookchin] was a true son of the Enlightenment in his respect
for clear thought and moral responsibility, and in his honest,
uncompromising search for a realistic hope.
— URSULA K. LE GUIN[1]

THE PROPHETIC AMERICAN PHILOSOPHER Murray Bookchin developed
social ecology as a comprehensive program for the challenges of our present era.
Over a lifetime of teaching, public speaking, organizing, and writing, he presented
a humanist vision of ecology based on community, direct democracy, and the better
promises of the Enlightenment, showing how we could transform our society into
one that is free and egalitarian.

Bookchin was not interested in creating a new political dogma or metaphysical
ideology, filled with fancy post-modern word salads, in order to be elevated to
"armchair" intellectual status. For that reason he was not afraid to engage in fierce
political debates with thinkers from other political tendencies. Bookchin did not
hesitate to criticize the postmodernist or nihilist politics of trendy philosophers
like Nietzsche, Foucault, Derrida, Lyotard, Deleuze, and Baudrillard.[2] He was also
highly critical of political movements like anarcho-syndicalism[3] and Marxism.[4]
Though Bookchin recognized their historic importance, he also addressed their
problematic role in today's terribly fragmented reality as attempts to revert to
obsolete and archaic ideologies in a search for a sense of continuity and security.[5]
And of course, he never hid his complete disagreement with New Age and mysticist
currents[6] that tend to pollute and depoliticize social movements.

Bookchin's rejection of the anarchist label[7] was not a renouncement of his
radical libertarian ideals, but a symbolic act showing how little meaning there is
in ideological dogmas and purity. He was most interested in the power of vibrant
and progressive ideas. Bookchin found the classic ideology of anarchism trapped
in the spatiality and temporality of its birth—an obstacle to analyzing ongoing
social developments and exploring paths. What interested him most was the
question of genuine revolutionary social change; in this sense, all of his work should
be viewed as a call to action.

His thirst for knowledge and research resembled the spirit of the Enlightenment. Bookchin refused to remain bound by old ideological interpretations of the world, as is evident in his secular interest in ecology. A traditional leftist fascination with factories could not distract him from the environmental degradation provoked by industrial capitalism. Long before climate change emerged as a mainstream issue and the human influence on climate was widely accepted, Bookchin began warning of humanity's disastrous environmental impact. Unlike various mysticists and primitivists who blamed human nature as such, he noted that it was the organization of human society that determines our attitude towards nature; consequently, he began researching alternative forms of social organization that could lead to an ecological society. His work produced a theoretical body that he dubbed "social ecology" (later changing the term to "communalism") which is now gaining momentum among climate activists.

Bookchin drew a direct link between social organization and human interaction with nature; the way societies treated their natural environment was a reflection of the way their social interrelations were structured. This suggested that statecraft and capitalism led to the creation of a reckless and wasteful anthropological type. He then explored linkages between direct democratic forms of societal organization that could result in stewardship and symbiotic relations with nature.

As a true son of the Enlightenment, he recognized the importance of science, which often led him to clash with deep ecologists and primitivists. He recognized the liberatory potential of technology but was in no way a technocrat. For Bookchin, technological development in a capitalist society was shaped by the latter's values and driven to serve its purposes. Thus, technologies that could potentially be used to put an end to scarcity were instead used for profits and the creation of artificial shortages. He knew that the road to a post-scarcity society would have to be based on a libertarian political transformation.

Bookchin's insistence on the importance of management of political power made him quite the distinctive thinker. He could see that it was not simply a question of a new economic model or a technological fix that could put an end to injustice and inequality. Instead, throughout his life, Bookchin emphasized the need to ultimately create a democratic environment in which power is distributed horizontally—allowing everyone to participate as equals in the management of all social spheres. This helped him develop a sophisticated political vision called "libertarian municipalism," based on real historic experiences and aimed at provoking social change in the here and now. Over the past decade, this vision has become a theoretical stepping stone for social movements around the world fighting economic inequalities and political oligarchies. The more social movements like the Indignados and Occupy experimented with forms of assembly democracy, the more their interest in Bookchin's ideas grew. From Western European and American protesters and climate activists, to Middle Eastern revolutionaries, the spirit of direct democracy and social ecology is shaping popular attempts at claiming power from the State and Capital.

About this Book

This volume is a transnational recognition and celebration of Murray Bookchin's legacy by a plethora of authors and activists, coming a century after the birth of the great thinker, as well as over 50 years since the creation of Black Rose Books, an alternative publishing house dedicated to the promotion of the ideas of social ecology and broader libertarian thought. We strive to present the dual nature of Bookchin's effort. On the one hand, he was a political visionary and an insightful analyst, unafraid of challenging ideological dogmas. His approach enriched contemporary libertarian and ecological thought with new concepts as well as with new understandings of revolutionary historic experiences. Nonetheless, his goal was to provoke political action, and so he used accessible language in speaking to activists who were involved in grassroots initiatives and public affairs.

This book is divided into two sections: the first, "Bookchin's Theoretical Legacy," is dedicated to his invaluable contribution to political theory and philosophy; the second, "Bookchin's Influence on Political Practice around the World," shows how his work has influenced political movements internationally. Jean-François Filion's opening essay, "The Unique Contribution of Murray Bookchin to Political Thought," introduces some aspects of Bookchin's life, as well as some of his most important concepts, such as dialectical naturalism, libertarian municipalism, and direct democracy. Filion also touches on some of the limitations of Bookchin's social ecology, with the aim of enriching this school of thought. Yavor Tarinski's "Bookchin and the Legacy of Direct Democracy" focuses on the concept of direct democracy and its presence in Bookchin's work. He explores historical experiences and theoretical concepts important for understanding the political basis of Bookchin's thought, such as the Athenian *polis*, citizenship, majority voting, and institutions.

Janet Biehl, a world-renowned writer and a long-term life companion of Bookchin, takes the reader on a journey through the political and philosophical evolution of the great thinker in her piece, "Bookchin, Öcalan, and the Dialectics of Democracy." She also links Bookchin's intellectual evolution with the radical paradigm shift in the philosophy of the imprisoned Kurdish leader Abdullah Öcalan. Brian Morris' essay, "Murray Bookchin and Radical Agriculture," outlines Bookchin's ecological vision in relation to agroecology. Morris presents Bookchin's critique of capitalist and industrial agriculture, as well as his tentative suggestions for a more enlightened form of decentralized agriculture. Eirik Eiglad, in "The Ecology of Urban Regeneration," uses social ecology and Bookchin's thought to examine the contemporary ecological challenges of our modern urban way of life and to suggest ways of integrating cities with the countryside. He concludes that reshaping urban life along ecological and democratic lines will necessarily require immense environmental and infrastructural transformations, which will above all require new civic or *communal* structures. He then moves into briefly examining what they might be.

Taking into consideration the importance the concept of the Right to the City has in social ecological thought, Giorgos Papahristodoulou's essay, "The Significance of the City for Social Ecology," delves into the influence the ancient Athenian *polis* and the autonomous medieval cities had on Bookchin. Bookchin believed that the emergence of cities created a new public space that could integrate strangers into a larger community of human beings, thus setting the conditions for the appearance of democratic politics. In an engaging and critical manner, Jason Toney's essay, "On Hannah Arendt and Murray Bookchin: Bridging Intellectual Legacies," builds on this topic. He offers a reading of Bookchin's libertarian municipalism as a direct response to the issues regarding the revolutionary process raised by Arendt, suggesting that this can help us more clearly perceive the obstacles to freedom and provide us with a framework for confronting them.

Nikos Vrantsis' "Can Cyborgs Dream of Social Ecology?" explores the current cyber-capitalist stage through the lens of Bookchin's underlying questions, such as how technology emerges from and shapes societies, for what goals, and with what side-effects. According to the author, social ecology foresaw, without descending to Luddism, the potent relation between technological progress and extensive hierarchies of extractive consumer capitalism. Economist Peter Piperkov launches an attack on the contemporary scientific guise of capitalism with his essay, "On Connecting a New Economics with Social Ecology." He insists that the economic understanding of capitalism is not science-based, but rather theological dogma, blindly accepted by its followers. Piperkov argues that Bookchin's thought is crucial for understanding the pseudo-scientific essence of capitalism.

In a book review, "Reflections on *The Limits of the City*," Kostas Papoulis praises Bookchin's insights in the field of urban politics, ecology, and anti-capitalism, and suggests that the great thinker has found a way to navigate the revolutionary project away from the economic determinism and political totalitarianism of the Old Left. "Murray Bookchin's Legacy of Freedom," another book review, this time of *The Third Revolution, Volume 1: Popular Movements in the Revolutionary Era*, expresses Ramazan Kaya's admiration of Bookchin's deep knowledge of history and praises his effort to reveal the revolutionary opportunities that lay in every historic period. The first section of the book closes with Georgi Konstantinov's "On the Reorganization of Society and Eco-Anarchism." In this brief review of Bookchin's *Remaking Society*, we encounter one great anarchist praising another; Konstantinov is a historic figure in the Bulgarian anarchist movement, having spent many years in the Stalinist gulags for blowing up Stalin's monument in the city-center of Sofia, Bulgaria's capital.

The second section begins with "Bookchin's Journey to Ancient and Modern Greece," by Stavros Karageorgakis and Niovi Chatzinikolaou, in which the authors recall their personal experience with the great social ecologist. Although Bookchin was very interested in the ancient Athenian experience, he never had the opportunity to visit Greece. However, as the piece reveals, his ideas reached modern Greece and influenced the libertarian scene in the country. Costas Despiniadis' essay, "Murray Bookchin in Greece: The Publication of His Works and the Impact of His Ideas," follows the introduction of Bookchin's works in Greek through a detailed chronology beginning with the first publications in the 1970s, when translators still hid their names out of fear of political repression, until today when the improved financial position of publishers have allowed a wider range of social ecology related books to be published. "Murray Bookchin and Contemporary Greek Social Movements: The Influence of Social Ecology on Democratic Political Discourse," by Alexandros Schismenos, focuses on social ecology's influence in antiauthoritarian movements and grassroots initiatives in Greece, and explores the debate between Murray Bookchin and the great Greco-French philosopher, Cornelius Castoriadis.

Kurdish scholar and activist Hawzhin Azeez's essay, "Bookchin's Influence on Öcalan and the PKK's Evolution," reviews the life of Kurdish leader Abdullah Öcalan and his encounter with Murray Bookchin's ideas; in particular, she examines the evolution of the Kurdish liberation movement from hierarchically organized struggle to the creation of horizontal democratic structures. Continuing the exploration of the Kurdish question, Recep Akgün's "Bookchin and the Kurdish Movement in Turkey" focuses on the particularities of the Kurdish liberation movement in Turkey, its structural and ideological evolution, as well as its influence over other left-wing, antiauthoritarian and libertarian tendencies in the country.

In his essay, "Spreading Murray Bookchin's Ideas in Germany," Wolfgang Haug describes his own experience engaging with Bookchin as part of the libertarian movement in Germany and elsewhere. In "Montreal and Murray Bookchin," Dimitrios Roussopoulos recounts his personal experience in working with Bookchin to spread the ideas and praxis of social ecology. In the words of the author, Montreal can be described as a laboratory of social ecology, having a long history of radical publishing and democratic activism. It is no wonder that the city is home to one of North America's largest non-profit and cooperative housing projects. Eve Olney's "From Athens to Cork: Collective Design as a Social Ecological Praxis of Community Building" presents urban collectives based in Ireland and in Greece that were organized around the idea of developing collective means of urban design, such as common ownership and participatory practices, and were primarily influenced by the works of radical ecologists such as Bookchin and Castoriadis.

"Murray Bookchin in Flanders Fields, Belgium," by Roger Jacobs, follows the author's political journey from Marxist-Leninism to social ecology through involvement in grassroots neighborhood activism and reading published collections of Bookchin's essays. Furthermore, Jacobs provides a detailed dissection of Belgium's complex ethnic composition and its political repercussions. In "The Social Ecology Education and Demonstration School (SEEDS): A Brief History," educator Bob Spivey presents the history of the educational initiative that he and a small group of activists formed in 2005 in the city of Vashon, Washington. Despite periods of struggle, Spivey feels encouraged about the future of this project as new horizons are opening.

In "The Role of Social Ecology in the *Gilets Jaunes* Movement in France," Theo Rouhette reflects on one of the most significant popular uprisings in Europe in recent years—that of the Yellow Vests. Beginning at the end of 2018, the Yellow Vest movement continues today. What Rouhette notes is that Bookchin's thesis on municipalism played an important role in the development of the movement, which nowadays functions as a confederation of local assemblies. The final essay of the second section, "Murray Bookchin in Italy" by Selva Varengo, presents the publication history of Bookchin's works in Italian, as well as an extensive bibliography. The author also notes the influence social ecological thought has had on social movements in Italy, such as the campaigns *No Tav* (High Speed Train), *No Tap* (Trans-Adriatic Pipeline), *No MUOS* (Mobile User Objective System), and *No Terzo Valico* (third pass in lower Piedmont), as well as the broader anarchist movement.

Though there are many more cities and regions around the world that have been influenced by Bookchin, it is impossible to include them all in this book. We were interested not in compiling an encyclopedia, but in highlighting the relevance of social ecology and its living legacy, which can be felt on city streets worldwide. Enlightenment and Ecology: The Legacy of Murray Bookchin in the 21st Century is more than a book title, it is the promise of an ecological and democratic future.

NOTES

1. Murray Bookchin, *The Next Revolution: Popular Assemblies & The Promise of Direct Democracy* (London: Verso 2015), 9.

2. Murray Bookchin. *Re-Enhancing Humanity* (New York: Cassell), 1995, 172–204.

3. Murray Bookchin, "The Ghost of Anarcho-Syndicalism," Anarchy Archives. http://dwardmac. pitzer.edu/Anarchist_Archives/bookchin/ghost2.html

4. Murray Bookchin, "Listen, Marxist!" https://www.marxists.org/archive/bookchin/1969/listen-marxist.htm

5. Bookchin, "Listen, Marxist!"

6. *Green Perspectives: Newsletter of the Green Program Project*, nos. 4–5 (summer 1987).

7. Janet Biehl, "Bookchin Breaks with Anarchism," https://theanarchistlibrary.org/library/janet-biehl-bookchin-breaks-with-anarchism

The Unique Contribution of Murray Bookchin to Political Thought

Jean-François Filion

THE LIFE OF THE social ecologist, Murray Bookchin, was exemplary. His political and theoretical commitment is a model of depth and courage. Regardless of the fate the future holds for his doctrine, regardless of the memory of the intellectual disputes in which he participated, Murray Bookchin will remain a major reference for anyone interested in the causes of the ecological crisis and how to overcome it. My encounter with this character some 20 years ago was memorable and continues to be a source of inspiration.

Despite his illness in late life, Murray agreed to organize a seminar with a group of four young ecologists, including myself. He welcomed us to his modest apartment in Burlington, Vermont, where books were piled up everywhere. The space was so cramped that his companion, Janet Biehl, also engaged in social theory, cut herself off from the flow of words by wearing earmuffs found on construction sites; she could thus go about her own intellectual pursuits. Sitting on his bed, where his bones caused less suffering, Murray engaged in conversation, voluble, generous, often professorial, admittedly, but always keen to establish a dialogue on the subjects and polemics that concerned us. And what worried us, then, was to understand the social roots of the ecological crisis, to foresee a future beyond the abyss it foreshadowed, to find solutions full of hope of emancipation for humanity. Such was the program of this social ecology seminar.

Murray Bookchin had a broad historical perspective and a genuinely revolutionary indignation at the current state of affairs in the world. He talked to us of his slightly bitter memories about the communist movement of the 20th century, as well as his concerns about the future of the West, under the influence of an American culture mired in decrepitude and the deadly globalization of capitalism. He knew that we were living in difficult times for any perspective of political transformation, but, for him, this difficulty was not a reason to despair. Despite the urgency of the situation, one had to be willing to be patient: "When the context seemed to hinder him," he said, "Lenin retired to study before he reinvested himself in the revolution!" Seeing the failure of critical thinking in the face of neoliberalism—an ideology that, in the early 1990s, could still describe itself as the end of history without too much protest—Murray made it clear to us that a precise understanding of capitalism was more necessary than ever. In other words, the failure of traditional Marxism forced a transition to a new theory that seriously included a strategy to overcome the ecological crisis.

It seems obvious that the current context, which brings together the global economic crisis, the ecological crisis, and the crisis of meaning, raises the need to open up to radical thoughts such as those pursued by Bookchin. Desperate times call for desperate measures. Indeed, in the face of the painful failures of Western civilization, where the permanent state of crisis seems strangely normalized, will an in-depth re-evaluation of human society become necessary? Making no concessions to ideological trends or academic recognition, Murray Bookchin invites us through his work to look far ahead to reflect on the human causes of the dysfunction in the earth's habitat. Even if Bookchin formulated it more than half a century ago, the problem has still not been sufficiently addressed with the depth it requires. On the contrary, attempts to resolve the ecological crisis seem to resist, whether consciously or unconsciously, seriously question the global social structure, namely its political hierarchy and productivist economy, which are responsible—according to Bookchin—for the destruction of the biosphere as well as the poverty of the majority of earth inhabitants. However, the stubborn refusal of mainstream intellectuals and politicians to examine social ecology analyses and syntheses, as well as other streams of thought in the ecosocialist movement, is manifested in our time in two main trends that are both different and complementary: technocratic environmentalism and ethical radicalism. Technocratic environmentalism consists in what is commonly known as "sustainable development," while ethical radicalism, more discreet because it is more individual, can be mystical—like the deep ecology so abhorred by Bookchin—or not.

If environmentalism gives the impression of being optimistic in its aim of "saving the planet," by a single improvement in governance that would maintain the current mode of production, ethical radicalism, on the contrary, leads to pessimism where beautiful souls indulge in the inner certainty of having correctly diagnosed that humanity was losing in its madness to dominate nature. However, both of these two positions, at first seemingly opposed, share the same flaw, which is the absence of political questioning of social structures. Moreover, the idea forseeing the future of a post-capitalist society does not even touch on green thought, whether optimistic or pessimistic. If the proponents of these two positions, who have the future of ecosystems at heart, are powerless to change anything in the course of events, it is because they implicitly admit the naturalization of liberal democracy and capitalism. Such naturalization makes the end of the world more plausible in the social imagination than that of a post-capitalist society.

While ethical or mystical radicalism is less present on the public scene—since it is an individual asceticism of survival that tends to cut itself off from the corrupt world—the fuzzy ideology of sustainable development, on the other hand, has held the media spotlight since the 1992 Rio Summit. It has been the case for the past 20 years that the promoters of development have shown us the repetitive spectacle of their accumulated failures. However, these promoters, who are found in respectable environmental organizations and the part of the public sector still spared by austerity, have always justified their stance in the name of pragmatism. Opposed to the "ideologues" of social ecology, ecosocialism or those who speak of the decline of the environment, they claim that the ecological crisis dictates a need to participate in the game of liberal democracy and capitalism. Their reasoning is as follows: since the challenge of social structures may marginalize ecology and thus give free rein to the destruction of ecosystems, it is better to meet the requirements of various "partners" representing the dominant order. Although this argument has won the support of a large number of environmental activists, for an anticapitalist ecologist and antiauthoritarian like Bookchin, such an option was doomed to fail, *a priori*. If it could once claim a certain rationality, sustainable development would be refuted by the real situation: its failure is obvious; it is time to put an end to this slogan for business people and politicians on borrowed time. Those who still believe in it run the risk of not being acquitted by the court of history, if the future state of the biosphere allows it to destroyed. Since one of the virtues of ecological awareness is the consideration of future generations, we can only hope that environmentalists will rectify the situation by opening up to thoughts such as those of Bookchin. This would prevent their condemnation by our great grandchildren or children who had the misfortune of being born today in one of these multiple social and environmental hells outside the "pedestrian zone of the world capitalism," as the late Robert Kurz would say, that constitutes Western Europe and North America.

If the ranks of radical ecology remain rather limited, however, there are some warning signs that forsee a change in this regard. Thus, on the eve of the Rio+20 Summit in summer 2012, the renowned Canadian biologist, David Suzuki, bitterly stated that environmentalism had failed. A Bookchin reader can only agree with what has always seemed obvious. Despite his anger and intelligence, Suzuki, like many other informed scientists, does not seem to have dared to criticize the dominant social structure, that is, liberal democracy and capitalism. No, because the "fetishism" of the commodity and the "naturalization" of technocratic organizations make the collective conscience feel that the dominant technico-economic logic is normal.

It is this reality that some critical thinkers are beginning to describe as *totalitarian*. Totalitarian, not in the archaic sense of Nazism and Stalinism, but in that whole parts of human life and nature seem inexorably doomed to commodification or managerial treatment. Totalitarian in the sense that everything that manifests itself in opposition to capitalism is either rejected into the symbolic nothingness of the absurd, or waiting to be suppressed in one way or another, that is, by media lies, tear gas, or drone projectiles. It is undoubtedly in fear of losing face in this world of neoliberalism that respectable scientists, who no longer have anything to lose for the success of their careers, do not yet risk opting for radical thinking like that of Murray Bookchin or the ecosocialists.

By also rejecting the path of political ecology, mystical radicalism serves as a purported "soul" in a context of unlimited expansion of technico-economic logic and a crisis of meaning. Its sweeping accusations against Western Judeo-Christian anthropocentrism abound in the absence of an analysis of the sociological causes of the ecological crisis. This flight into the world of "spirituality" is therefore summed up in the apolitical option of hoping for a massive conversion of populations to a new world vision based on a "biocentric" ethics inspired by Amerindian or Buddhist wisdom. Given the current imbroglio into which the naivety of sustainable development has plunged us, and from which environmental ethics will not help us to escape, thoughts like Bookchin's promise a more viable future. By studying his work, we learn about the foundations of ecology, one of the first political ideas to have claimed that a single cause explains the ecological crisis as well as social misery and deprivation. The resolution of these contradictions will take place only through the transformation of social structures, in particular by overcoming capitalism.

The relevance of Bookchin's ideas seems more and more confirmed when you witness the extent of the economic crisis that has been unfolding since 2008. We now find ourselves in a tragicomedy where the globalization of markets requires the support of the Nation-State that neoliberalism has tried to teach us to hate! What a devastating sight! It is now the State that saves the large "too big to fail" companies from bankruptcy; it relieves the banks of toxic debts by increasing public debt; it destroys environmental standards to foster growth in times of economic crisis; it sacrifices the unprofitable part of the population with the adoption of austerity plans required for the repayment of public debt by rating agencies—Moody's, Standard & Poor's, or Fitch. It's the overcoming of this type of vicious circle to which Bookchin's social ecology must be applied. To resist this kind of thinking for fear that political radicalism will lead to perverse effects is to expose oneself to an even greater danger: the emergence of fascist solutions to the crisis, as was seen in Europe in the 1930s and which we see today in Greece with neo-Nazi organizations such as Golden Dawn, which spreads terror among immigrants and even has elected members of parliament. In a situation of crisis, quietism is more frightening than activism. Who is afraid of citizens of regional cities who oppose exploitation in the heart of their community? Who is afraid of the borough mayors of urban neighbourhoods that discourage motorized commuters to pollute the air day and night? Who is afraid of students taking to the streets to challenge unfair cuts to higher education that today's explosive social context makes more than ever necessary?

Like any ethical-political doctrine, Murray Bookchin's social ecology has its limitations. It therefore does not have to be adopted without a critical eye, especially since, in terms of political commitment, action must never be deduced from a theory, but only inspired by it. Against the tide, Bookchin's work encourages us to reflect on fundamental problems, despite the fact that this may lead to conclusions that differ from those of its author. Nevertheless, three elements of social ecology, which derive from each other, appear to be unavoidable: 1) the central place of reason in continuity with classic socialism, thus breaking with its postmodern rejection; 2) the need to develop an active political subjectivity; and 3) the affirmation of an anticapitalism with a concern for the future postcapitalist society.

The Rebirth of Dialectical Reason
The philosophical approach developed by Bookchin, dialectical naturalism, allows one to grasp the immanent meaning of nature, thus escaping the dichotomy between the extremes of religious and nihilistic thought that we find, in particular in the opposition between obtuse creationism and neo-Darwinian evolutionism. The central point of Murray Bookchin's philosophy is to distinguish two concepts of reason: conventional reason and dialectical reason. Conventional reason leads to the mathematization of nature as a condition for its domination, its commodification, which contributes to the ecological crisis. Like Hegel, from whom he freely draws inspiration, Bookchin states that the major challenge of Western philosophy is to go beyond the conventional reason established in modernity by renewing *dialectical reason*, which makes it possible to conceive reality in its future. Dialectical naturalism, says Bookchin, "discerns a phenomenon that evolves in a fluid and plastic way." In its future, an entity implies the existence of various potentialities that may or may not be achieved; by looking again at the Hegelian example of the germ, dialectical reason shows that it can grasp the concrete dialectical development of the plant in relation to its environment (water, light, soil quality, etc.), which will make it a beautiful tree or a yellowed stem. Dialectical criticism of conventional reason does not lead to a rejection of science,

only to its relativization, because only dialectical reason recognizes an immanent meaning in nature, while avoiding the traps of mysticism. It is in the presence of this immanent meaning that Bookchin entrenched his ethical-political conception. The life present in nature shows us an ordered reality without the need for recourse to the authoritarianism of a hierarchical power, a reality where living beings have the potential for creativity which led to the cosmic development of subjectivity on Earth. By taking up a theme dating back to ancient philosophy, Bookchin developed the idea of an articulation of first nature with second nature, that is, the human world (second nature) that has emerged from first nature (the Earth, without humans). The humanity that comes from first nature is therefore radically dependent on it, demonstrating that the scandal of the ecological crisis is a contradiction in terms. Since second nature (humans) is both the most evolved product of first nature and encompasses human freedom, we must restore our essential compatibility with the biosphere. This is how Bookchin wants to create social norms in line with the complexification of nature, which has made possible the existence of human societies.

The Development of Political Subjectivity

Murray Bookchin considers it necessary for humans to undergo a form of ethical conversion and revive active citizenship. Each era in human history contains potentialities that are unique; it is necessary to rely on everyone's spontaneity and voluntarism. No political change can be achieved without a subjective commitment to political action. This requirement does not concern a particular sociological category, no specific revolutionary subject, but includes virtually any citizen who wants to change the current state of things. Of course, some will want to change it more than others, but the thought of Bookchin emphasizes that a girl from a rich family can embark on political activism even if, from her standpoint, there could be no "class interest" that would explain her support to a cause beyond her own social situation. This type of commitment has been put forward in feminism, a source of inspiration for social ecology, insofar as this social movement is "transclass," i.e. it requires a personal decision to refuse hierarchy and domination and struggle for issues that are both here and now. Bookchin, on the other hand, was very critical of the Marxist-Leninist tradition that focused on a revolutionary subject—the proletariat—while waiting for the emergence of objective conditions for the advent of the *grand soir*, the final occasion when significant changes in social structures could suddenly occur.

This also explains why Bookchin attached great importance to historical studies in order to identify the times when various potentialities were available to societies and the choices they have made. In fact, he noted how the series of bad historical choices led to the ecological crisis, the situation in the Third World, the reduced quality of living, to selfish struggle and the isolation of individuals. One of the worst potentialities seen, according to Bookchin, is the emergence of the State. He saw that, in the history of modernity, there has been a civilizational split between the confederal and state paths. The confederal path would have been based on decentralized community institutions, as in the direct democracy practiced in New England at the dawn of the United States or the soviets at the beginning of the Russian Revolution. But it is the statist path that has so far triumphed, and the ecological crisis and human suffering are symptoms of this tendency. As a "professional system of social coercion" (rule by statecraft), the State would destroy the political subjectivity that only institutions on a human scale could maintain and enrich. By its very nature, the State reduces the citizen to the passive role of taxpayer-elector, which leads to depoliticization and also facilitates, notably, the commodification of the world.

Direct Democracy and Municipalization of the Means of Production

Libertarian municipalism, or communalism, must be built from now on by the democratic takeover of the political institutions of cities and villages. Although radical, Bookchin refuses to accept any insurrectional project fuelled by the fantasy of the *tabula rasa*, where existing institutions would be suddenly destroyed. His criticism of state domination and representative democracy leads to the idea of revitalizing political activity in municipal communities that would be coordinated within interregional federations. This is the project of libertarian municipalism. It is inspired by the Athenian city and the medieval commune, where citizens participated in communal policy making or local politics that takes place on a human scale. This, therefore, makes repoliticization possible through pedagogical and ethical interactions with politicized and committed fellow citizens. The foundation of individual freedom is therefore not the abstract premise of the atomized individual, but the municipality: "Although it seems to be paradoxical," Bookchin points out, "the authentic elements of a free and rational society are communal and not individual." To put it in more institutional terms, the municipality is not only the basis of a free society but also the irreducible ground of an authentic individuality. Thus, libertarian municipalism provides for the municipalization of the economy and means of production in order to overcome the opposition between the extremes of capitalist privatization or socialist nationalization. In this way, it will be possible to control rationally and democratically the development of technologies and end productivism—producing for producing's sake—which causes the ecological crisis. Municipalized production will focus on quality rather than quantity: it is in fact about institutionalizing the requirement of classical socialism "from each according to his/her abilities, to each according to his/her needs."

Murray Bookchin's social ecology can still contribute to radical political ecology practices. Despite its mixed success, many of its elements will remain current for some time to come.

Bookchin and the Legacy of Direct Democracy

Yavor Tarinski

WITH THE FALL of the Soviet Union, but also with the continuous inability of left-wing parties to alter the current state of things through reforms from within the system, traditional political organizations have become largely marginal, with little to no genuine connection to society. Rudi Dutschke's strategy of "the long march through the institutions"[1] is repeatedly failing to achieve anything different to the absorption of the Left by the dominant institutions it tries to change. Society at large has lost trust in the parliamentary model and its inability to cope with the crucial crises of our time: climate change, extreme inequality, concentration of power in the hands of the few. This is signified by the rising levels of abstention in elections worldwide.

Contemporary social movements have abandoned the traditional political forms of the past, i.e. political parties and trade unions. Instead, they have adopted in their practices the project of direct democracy. Although the terms used by each movement might differ, there are common traces of attempts at popular self-institution. From the cooperative network, Cooperative Jackson, in Mississippi (USA), through the assembly of assemblies established by the French Yellow Vests, to the democratic confederation in Rojava, people are trying to establish radically different institutions to embody attitudes and values that go beyond statecraft and capitalism. This self-institution strives at giving practical form to direct communal participation, solidarity, egalitarianism, and feminism, and in this way challenges the temporal and spatial stagnation produced by the bureaucratic fragmentation of everyday life and capitalist cannibalism.

It is no wonder that, in this environment, there is a revived interest in the ideas developed by the libertarian theorist, Murray Bookchin, along with other radical thinkers such as Cornelius Castoriadis and Hannah Arendt. Bookchin's works on direct democracy and social ecology seem to directly resonate with the practices of countless contemporary social movements worldwide: from political initiatives directly or indirectly referring to him or his concepts, to social media memes like the infamous "Google Murray Bookchin" meme, which has even been reproduced beyond the internet.[2] For him, the question was not simply to outbid capitalism through an alternative economic model or unconventional lifestyle, as such logic operates within the framework of the contemporary system and its power dynamics. As he wrote, even though such an approach may "imbue individuals with collectivist values and concerns, it does not provide the institutional means for acquiring collective power."[3]

Bookchin suggested that our struggles should be focused on the political question of power, i.e. the question of who has to decide on what course our communities in particular and our society in general should take. His political project, as he himself puts it, is decidedly a confrontational form of face-to-face democratic, antistatist politics.[4] Throughout his work, Bookchin seeks to relocate the space within which political power should be exercised so as to allow the greatest possible freedom to all members of society. He moves beyond the Nation-State, as it alienates the great majority from the decision-making processes, vesting almost all authority in the hands of a narrow bureaucratic and managerial stratum. He sought another space—this of the municipality—which during a significant time of human history, allowed communities to directly self-manage their common affairs. As Bookchin writes, between amorphous communities and the institutions of the Nation-State, the municipality offers a sphere of political activity and a domain for the exercise of power that can politically structure the former, while undermining and displacing the latter.[5]

We see how this logic resonates with contemporary urban and ecological movements. Movements like Occupy, the Indignados of Spain, the Arab Spring, the Yellow Vests of France, the Kurdish liberation movement, the Zapatistas, and many more, all seek to reclaim power away from the bureaucratic structure of the Nation-State and transnational capitalist agreements. Instead, they almost instinctively attempt to recreate it on more humane, grassroots scale, where all members of the community will have access to it.

The Ancient Athenian Experience

Ancient Athens was an important historical source for Bookchin, which helped him develop his democratic project. He was aware of the problematic issues of classical Athens: patriarchy, slavery, restriction of citizenship to males of putative Athenian birth, etc. But unlike many others from the Western world who rushed to dismiss ancient Athens altogether due to these facts, Bookchin noticed something which was of greatest importance for the human history—the emergence of genuine direct democracy. This view of his resonates heavily with Castoriadis, according to whom "slavery existed everywhere in the ancient world, but democracy did not."[6] It was a political project that had nothing to do with the pseudo-democratic parliamentary regime that we know today. Instead, it was based on the concept of the *Polis:* i.e. the direct self-management of all city dwellers in face-to-face assemblies—in which policy is formulated by the resident citizenry and administration is executed by mandated and delegated councils.[7]

Bookchin's fascination with ancient Athens never made him place it on a pedestal or turn it into a "model" or "ideal" to be mindlessly copied today. He was much more astute than that. First and foremost, Bookchin discovered in the Athenian *polis* evidence that society can function rationally for centuries through genuinely democratic structures like popular assemblies, sortition (selection by lot), rotation of offices, revocability of delegates, and defense by the whole of the citizen body (without the need of professional military structure).[8] Furthermore, he was fascinated with the fact that while the ancient world of that period was dominated by authoritarian empires, patriarchy, and repressive customs, the ancient Athenians managed to imagine, and subsequently to implement into practice, a completely different style of management of society.

Bookchin, similarly to Castoriadis, managed to overcome the sterile frames of classic ideologies and see the importance of ancient Athens within its contextual environment, something which few thinkers have managed to do to this day. His vision for a direct democratic society was not a sterile, heavily ideologized one. Instead, he attempted to seek its seed within different temporal and spatial contexts. It is no wonder that nowadays people from so many different areas and political backgrounds find Bookchin's work so relatable— think of his impact on European municipalists, as well as on the Middle Eastern Kurds.

Of course, ancient Athens was not the only historic reference point for Bookchin. He examined various democratic experiences throughout human history. The Paris Commune and the Spanish Civil War were among the cases which influenced and inspired his works. Such relatively recent historic experiences are widely accepted by anarchists and leftists, as they have taken place within the timeframe of classic ideologies. What sets Bookchin apart from most of his contemporaries is that he developed analysis, which allow us to operate beyond sterile ideological veils and detect traces of direct democracy and political ecology within significantly different temporal and spatial contexts. This might prove of even greater importance in our own age of neoliberal globalization, which strives to uproot each one of us from his local history and traditions and replace them with sterile nationalisms that dull creativity and cooperation and can only inspire hate and division.

Institutions

For Bookchin, the institutions of direct democracy are what makes the exercise of nonstatist and anticapitalist power possible and effective. He emphasized the importance of popular assemblies, municipal councils, confederal coordinational bodies of delegates etc., for the successful functioning and reproduction of a democratic and ecological society. Bookchin was a convinced opponent of anomie—the idea that given community could function without any laws or norms. For him, this concept was grossly fallacious. He suggested that, unlike animals, which can live without institutions (often because their behaviour is imprinted in them genetically), human beings require institutions, however simple or complex, to mold their societies. Since the 1960s, Bookchin has been insisting that the institutions of a direct democratic society will be rationally constituted "forms of freedom" by which people would organize and express their own powers collectively as well as personally.

Bookchin was certainly not alone on this topic. Castoriadis also agreed that whatever the degree of individual development, technical progress, or economic abundance, people will always need political institutions in order to be able to tackle the innumerable problems people's collective existence constantly raises.[9]

But while Bookchin was not alone in regarding the importance of institutions, there were certainly some traces of anomie among the anarchist movement, with which the latter gradually alienated the former. He felt disturbed by anarchist slogans like "Make war on institutions, not on people," as they indicated a certain belief in a utopia of unbounded self-determination. But, Bookchin traced these germs of anomie back to some of the founders of anarchism as well. For example, he had problems with Proudhon's stance towards constitutions as such. Bookchin notes that while Proudhon was a member of the French Chamber of Deputies in the mid-19th century, the latter refused to vote in favor of a draft constitution that was oriented toward the protection of property and the construction of a State.[10] Bookchin ultimately agreed with his negative vote, but thoroughly rejected the reasons he gave for it. The reason Proudhon gave for his negative vote was that he did not vote against the constitution because it was good or bad, but because it was a constitution. For Bookchin, this logic reduced the classicism of anarchism to the world of arbitrary power. Furthermore, Bookchin examined a historic trend, according to which oppressed people from antiquity, like the peasants of ancient Greece (such as Hesiod), demand a society based on laws, not on the whims of men. In short, he concluded that constitutions and laws have long been demands of oppressed people as instrumentalities for controlling, indeed eliminating, the arbitrary power exercised by kings, tyrants, nobles, and dictators.

The direct-democratic foundations of the society which Bookchin envisioned, went beyond anarchist rejections of laws and constitutions. For him, it was not enough to place our hopes for a more just future on intrinsic human instincts such as mutual aid or sharing. Instead, social movements must propose and attempt to implement in practice a new political architecture, which will make it possible for the whole of society to exercise power in a stateless, noncapitalist and participatory manner.[11]

Many have come to suggest that one such direct-democratically structured community will consume too much of the participants' time. But Bookchin is clear on the differentiation between policy making and administration.[12] In his vision of direct democracy, all members of society, by the means of regular public assemblies, determine the general course of their collective life, its regulative framework, etc. Then, each of these decisions will be implemented by the means of local and municipal councils, consisted of revocable and accountable delegates and experts.

Regarding this issue, Bookchin describes the process of building a road. Not everyone in a municipality needs to know how to build a road; that is a job that can be left to engineers and administrators. But, the decision itself is up to the assembly to make.[13]

For Bookchin, the need to establish democratic institutions was an invaluable aspect of his political project. Such social self-instituting allowed for the development of clear distinction between logistical problems and political ones.

On Majority Voting

After examining Bookchin's main historical sources for direct democracy and his stance on institutions, one can understand his position regarding majority voting. First of all, he has a problem with the view, held by many anarchists, of democracy as a form of "rule-over" or even "domination." Bookchin noted that this opinion was shared even by thinkers like Peter Marshall, of whom he spoke with respect.

Similarly, with the adoption of the logic of anomie by radicals, many took for granted that majorities automatically translates into coercion and suppression. Bookchin, however, was careful enough to not enter this trap. He suggested that in a free society built on direct democracy, where dissent was fully permitted and where media expression of all views was allowed, that the notion of a majority "dictating" to a minority made no sense.[14]

For Bookchin, majorities are vital for a society to make dynamic collective decisions about public affairs. Furthermore, according to him, majority voting is the only equitable way for a large number of people to make decisions.[15] In the conditions of direct democracy, minorities will always be allowed to express their disagreement with the decisions of the majority, but they will still have to obey them. He observed the case of the Athenian *polis*, where majority voting was also used, and besides all its shortcomings, it still remains one of the most remarkable examples of highest sense of citizenship.

Bookchin was highly critical of those who viewed consensus as the only decision-making process suitable for a libertarian project. And while he recognized its potentials for small-scale groups, whose members are highly familiar with one another, he pointed at multiple problematic consequences when attempted to implement on larger scales. First of all, Bookchin recognized that consensus allows for insidious authoritarianism and manipulations to take place as it creates the conditions for single individuals to be able to veto majority decisions, threatens to abolish society as such. To those who supported consensus instead of majority voting, from the liberal position of the fear of the masses, Bookchin reminded us that, "the rights of minorities to express their dissenting views will always be protected as fully as the rights of majorities."[16]

Elections and Citizen Culture

There is a certain misconception regarding Bookchin's view on municipal elections, which can be felt nowadays. Many make it sound as if, for him, participation in local electoral processes is the main strategy and everything else must follow afterwards. But Bookchin is clear that grassroots assemblies and movements are the only real school for citizenship.[17] He places greatest importance on the creation of living and creative political realm that can give rise to people who take management of public affairs seriously.

Bookchin makes clear distinction between vote-casters (who vote for representatives once every few years) and citizens who actively participate in the management of public affairs. So, his proposal is not simply shifting the focus from national to municipal elections, but a more holistic one, which implies the creation of genuine public sphere, in which to embed participation, cooperation and the communal attitude in everyday life. He positions this sphere in direct opposition to the current state of commodification, rivalry, anomie, and egoism, in which there is no real public participation.

Bookchin's strategy includes the establishment of different political architecture, which will foster direct civic participation. This means rallying social movements into organizing their struggles, and consequently their very communities, on the basis of grassroots decision-making bodies like popular assemblies, and then eventually sending revocable delegates to participate in municipal elections. We observe something similar to be taking place with the movement of the Yellow Vests in France, which began as popular uprising, but gradually formed local assemblies, which then began attempts at confederating with each other. It is from this level, Bookchin suggests, that such emancipated democratic collectivities should reclaim their municipal councils away from bureaucratic and statist control.

His mistrust of contemporary electoral processes is evident from his opinion of political parties as a kind of mimicry of the statecraft mechanism. Bookchin notes that political parties are like a "miniature state," structured in a top-down, hierarchical manner. In some countries, the party actually was the State, as in Nazi Germany or the former Soviet Union. "Indeed, every party has its roots in the state, not in the citizenry. The conventional party is hitched to the State like a garment to a mannikin," he wrote.[18]

So Bookchin does not propose to simply redirect our efforts from national parties to municipal ones. Instead, he views the municipal electoral level as a suitable field for wider coordination between local communities in the form of neighborhoods, towns or villages. But it remains useless if the political essence of these communities is not radically altered in a direct democratic direction. Bookchin suggests regarding the creation of the new municipal agenda, that unless we take our commitment to real democracy seriously, we will get entangled with some kind of bureaucratic structure, which is incompatible with a vibrant citizenry.[19]

Conclusion

Bookchin's legacy is already playing an important role in the development of the agendas of social movements worldwide. And this seems more than logical. His legacy departs from the grand narratives of classic ideologies and contemporary lifestyles, and instead endures into the development of strategies and institutions, which to give practical forms to freedom.

During his life, he has moved through various political tendencies, but always in the search for greater emancipation and popular participation. Bookchin's departure from anarchism hasn't been, as some might bad heartedly suggest, a result of a conservative lurch of his. Instead, he attempted to overcome the boundaries of anarchist thought and advance further the project of direct democracy.

It is no wonder that Ursula le Guin wrote in her unique style that "Bookchin is no grim puritan. I first read him as an anarchist, probably the most eloquent and thoughtful one of his generation, and in moving away from anarchism he hasn't lost his sense of the joy of freedom. He doesn't want to see that joy, that freedom, come crashing down, yet again, among the ruins of its own euphoric irresponsibility."[20]

NOTES

1. Quoted in: Murray Bookchin. *The Next Revolution: Popular Assemblies & the Promise of Direct Democracy* (New York; Verso 2015), 9.

2. A slogan coined by German student activist Rudi Dutschke to describe his strategy for establishing the conditions for revolution: subverting society by infiltrating institutions such as the professions. https://en.wikipedia.org/wiki/The_long_march_through_the_institutions. Accessed September 9, 2019.

3. "Google Murray Bookchin," Know Your Meme. https://knowyourmeme.com/memes/google-murray-bookchin

4. Murray Bookchin, "Thoughts on Libertarian Municipalism," *Left Green Perspective* #41 (January 2000).

5. Bookchin, "Thoughts."

6. Cornelius Castoriadis, "The Problem of Democracy Today," *Democracy & Nature, The International Journal of Politics and Ecology* Vol. 3, No. 2 (issue 8, 1997): 18–35.

7. Bookchin, "Thoughts."

8. Murray Bookchin, "Communalism: The Democratic Dimension of Anarchism," *Democracy & Nature* Vol. 3, No. 2 (Issue 8, 1995): 1–17.

9. Cornelius Castoriadis, DA Curtis, Ed. *The Castoriadis Reader* (Oxford: Blackwell, 1997), 189.

10. Bookchin, "Thoughts."

11. Bookchin, "Communalism."

12. Bookchin, "Communalism."

13. Murray Bookchin. *Urbanization without Cities: The Rise and Decline of Citizenship* (Montreal: Black Rose Books, 1992): 247.

14. Murray Bookchin, "The Communalist Project," *Communalism: International Journal for a Rational Society* 2 (November 2002). Accessed at: https://theanarchistlibrary.org/library/murray-bookchin-the-communalist-project

15. Bookchin, "The Communalist Project."

16. Bookchin, "The Communalist Project."

17. Janet Biehl, *The Murray Bookchin Reader* (Montreal: Black Rose Books, 1999): 182.

18. Janet Biehl, *The Murray Bookchin Reader*, 74.

19. Murray Bookchin, "Libertarian Municipalism: The New Municipal Agenda," from *Urbanization without Cities: The Rise and Decline of Citizenship* (Montreal: Black Rose Books, 1992). Accessed at: https://theanarchistlibrary.org/library/murray-bookchin-libertarian-municipalism-the-new-municipal-agenda

20. Ursula K. LeGuin, "Ursula K. Le Guin on the Future of the Left," *Vice Magazine*, February 4, 2015, https://www.vice.com/en_us/article/vvbxqd/ursula-le-guin-future-of-the-left

Bookchin, Öcalan, and the Dialectics of Democracy

Janet Biehl

Presented to the conference "Challenging Capitalist Modernity: Alternative Concepts and the Kurdish Question," Hamburg, Germany, February 3–5, 2012.

IN FEBRUARY 1999, at the moment when Abdullah Öcalan was abducted in Kenya, Murray Bookchin was living with me in Burlington, Vermont. We watched Öcalan's capture on the news reports. He sympathized with the plight of the Kurds—he said so whenever the subject came up—but he saw Öcalan as yet another Marxist-Leninist guerrilla leader, a latter-day Stalinist. Murray had been criticizing such people for decades, for misleading people's impulses toward freedom into authority, dogma, statism, and even—all appearances to the contrary—acceptance of capitalism.

Bookchin himself had been a Stalinist back in the 1930s, as young teenager; he left late in the decade and joined the Trotskyists. At the time, the Trotskyists thought World War II would end in proletarian socialist revolutions in Europe and the United States, the way World War I had given rise to the Russian Revolution. During the war Bookchin worked hard in a foundry to try to organize the workers to rise up and make that revolution. But in 1945 they did not. The Trotskyist movement, its firm prediction unfulfilled, collapsed. Many if not most of its members gave up on Marxism and revolutionary politics generally; they became academics or edited magazines, working more or less within the system.

Bookchin too gave up on Marxism, since the proletariat had clearly turned out not be revolutionary after all. But instead of going mainstream, he and his friends did something unusual: they remained social revolutionaries. They recalled that Trotsky, before his assassination in 1940, had said that should the unthinkable happen—should the war not end in revolution—then it would be necessary for them to rethink Marxist doctrine itself. Bookchin and his friends got together, meeting every week during the 1950s, and looked for ways to renovate the revolutionary project, under new circumstances.

Capitalism, they remained certain, was an inherently, self-destructively flawed system. But if not the proletariat, then what was its weak point? Bookchin realized, early in the 1950s, that its fatal flaw was the fact that it was in conflict with the natural environment, destructive both of nature and of human health. It industrialized agriculture, tainting crops and by extension people with toxic chemicals; it inflated cities to unbearably large, megalopolitan size, cut off from nature, that turned people into automatons and damaged both their bodies and their psyches. It pressured them through advertising to spend their money on useless commodities, whose production further harmed the environment. The crisis of capitalism, then, would result not from the exploitation of the working class but from the intolerable dehumanization of people and the destruction of nature.

To create an ecological society, cities would have to be decentralized, so people could live at a smaller scale and govern themselves and grow food locally and use renewable energy. The new society would be guided, not by the dictates of the market, or by the imperatives of a state authority, but by people's decisions. Their decisions would be guided by ethics, on a communal scale. To create such a rational, ecological society it, we would need viable institutions—what he called "forms of freedom." Both the revolutionary organization and the institutions for the new society would have to be truly liberatory, so they would not lead to a new Stalin, to yet another tyranny in the name of socialism. Yet they would have to be strong enough to suppress capitalism.

Those institutions, he realized, could only be democratic assemblies. The present nation-state would have to be eliminated and its powers devolve to citizens in assemblies. They, rather than the masters of industry could make decisions, for example about the environment. And since assemblies only worked in a locality, in order to function at a broader geographical area, they would have to band together— to confederate. He spent the next decades elaborating these ideas for an ecological, democratic society. In the 1980s, for example, he said the confederation of citizens assemblies would form a counterpower or a dual power against the nation state. He called this program libertarian municipalism, later using the word communalism.

During those decades he tried to persuade other American and European leftists of the importance of this project. But in those days most of them were too busy admiring Mao, Ho Chi Minh, Fidel Castro. Bookchin pointed out that they were dictators; leftists didn't want to hear such criticisms. Ecology and democracy are just petit-bourgeois ideas, they told him. The only people who listened to Bookchin were anarchists, because his ideas were anti-statist. He had become, in fact, a high-profile anarchist.

He told the anarchists that his program for libertarian municipalism was their natural politics, their obvious revolutionary theory. They would listen to him respectfully, but then they'd tell him they didn't like local government any more than they liked any other kind; and they objected to majority voting, because it meant the minority wouldn't get their way. They preferred nonpolitical communitarian groups, cooperatives, radical bookstores, communes. Bookchin thought such institutions were fine, but to make a serious revolution, you needed a way to gain active, concrete, vested, structural, legal political power. Libertarian municipalism was a way to do that, to get a firm toehold against the nation-state.

He wooed the anarchists. He courted, pleaded with, wheedled, begged, intoned, and scolded them. He did everything to persuade them that libertarian municipalism was the way to make anarchism politically relevant. But by 1999—around the time of Öcalan's arrest—he was finally admitting that he had failed, and he was in the process of disengaging from anarchism.

With all that going on, we didn't read much about Öcalan's defense at his trial, on charges of treason: we didn't know, for example, that he was undergoing a transformation similar to the one Bookchin had undergone half a century earlier, that he was rejecting Marxism-Leninism in favor of democracy. He had concluded that Marxism was authoritarian and dogmatic and unable to creatively approaching current problems.[1] We "must to respond to the requirements of the historical moment," he told the prosecutors. To move forward, it was necessary "to reassess principles, the programme and the mode of action."[2] It was something Bookchin might have said in 1946.

Today, Öcalan told his Turkish prosecutors, rigid systems are collapsing, and "national, cultural, ethnic, religious, linguistic, and indeed regional problems are being solved by granting and applying the broadest democratic standards."[3] The PKK, he said, must give up its goal of achieving a separate Kurdish state and adopt a democratic program for Turkey as a whole.

Democracy, he said, is the key to the Kurdish question, because in a democratic system, each citizen has rights and a vote, and everyone participates equally regardless of ethnicity. The Turkish state could be democratized, to acknowledge the existence of the Kurdish people and their rights to language and culture.[4] It wasn't assembly democracy, such as Bookchin was advocating—it was a top-down approach. Rather, "the goal is a democratic republic."[5]

Democracy, he pointed out, was also the key to Turkey's future, since Turkey could not really be a democracy without the Kurds. Other democratic countries had resolved their ethnic problems by including once-marginalized groups—and the inclusiveness and diversity made them stronger. The United States, India, many other places with ethnic issues more complex than Turkey's had made progress on ethnic inclusion and been all the stronger for it. Around the world, acceptance turned differences into strengths. Whatever the Turkish prosecutors might have thought of this message, they didn't care for the messenger—they convicted him and sentenced him to death, a sentence later commuted to solitary confinement.

Bookchin used to say that the best anarchists are the ones who were formerly Marxists. They knew how to think, he said, how to draw out the logic of ideas. And they understood dialectics. He would surely have recognized this ability in Öcalan, had they met. Both men shared a dialectical cast of mind, inherited from their common Marxist past. Not that they were dialectical materialists—both understood that that Marxist concept was inadequate, because historical causation is multiple, not just economic. But both remained dialectical: in love with history's developmental processes.

Dialectics is a way of describing change—not kinetic kind of change that is the concern of physics, but the developmental change that occurs in organic life and in social history. Change progresses through contradictions. In any given development, some of the old is preserved while some of the new is added, resulting in an *Aufhebung*, or transcendence. Both men were prone to think in terms of historical development. Indeed, they wrote sweeping historical accounts of civilization, more than once, several times, parsing the dialectics of domination and resistance, of states and tyrannies countered by struggles for freedom. Unlike Marxists, they didn't use dialectics to predict some inevitable future revolt—they knew it could not predict. Instead, they used it to raise possibilities, to identify potentialities, to establish the historical foundations for what they thought should be the next political step. They used it, consciously or not, for ethics—to derive, from what has happened in the past, what ought to come next.

Both wrote, separately, about the origins of civilization: about primal societies in the Paleolithic; about the rise of agriculture and private property and class society; the rise of religion; of administration, states, armies, and empires, of monarchs and nobility and feudalism. And they discussed modernity, the rise of the Enlightenment, science, technology, industrialism, capitalism. Just for convenience, I'm going to call these historical accounts Civilization Narratives.

Bookchin wrote two major civilization narratives: *The Ecology of Freedom* (1982) and *Urbanization without Cities* (1992).[6] Öcalan wrote several, such as *The Roots of Civilization* and parts of *The PKK and the Kurdish Question* and even the more recent *Road Map*.[7]

They harnessed their civilization narratives to serve current political problematics. *The Ecology of Freedom* is, among other things, an argument against mainstream, reformist environmentalists, in favor of radical social ecology. Bookchin wanted to show these cautious liberals that they could aim for more than mere state reforms—that they should and could think in terms of achieving an ecological society. People lived communally in the past, and they could do so again.

So he highlighted the early preliterate societies in human history that he called "organic society," tribal, communal and nonhierarchical, living in cooperation with each other. He identified the specific features that made them cooperative: the means of life were distributed according to customs of usufruct (use of resources as needed), complementarity (ethical mutuality), and the irreducible minimum (the right of all to food, shelter, and clothing).[8] "From this feeling of unity between the individual and the community emerges a feeling of unity between the community and its environment," he wrote; these organic societies lived in harmony with the natural world.[9]

He then traced a dialectical development: the rise of hierarchy, immanently, out of organic society: patriarchy and the domination of women; gerontocracy; shamans and priests; warriors and chiefs and states; class society.[10] Thereafter the idea of dominating nature arose, reconceiving nature as an object to be exploited. For Bookchin, hierarchy's legacy of domination is countered by a longstanding legacy of freedom—resistance movements throughout history that have embodied principles from organic society—usufruct, complementarity, the irreducible minimum. The potential still remains for a dialectical transcendence of domination in a free cooperative society that could make possible a cooperative relationship with nature. He called this set of ideas social ecology.

That was 1982. In a second Civilization Narrative, *Urbanization Without Cities*, he sought to establish the historical foundations for assembly democracy. He found a tradition of citizens' assemblies especially in the ancient Athenian ecclesia; in early towns of Italy and Germany and the Low countries; in the Russian *veche* of Pskov and Novgorod; in the *comuñero* assemblies of 16th-century Spain; in the assemblies of the revolutionary Parisian sections of 1793; the committees and councils of the American revolution; the Parisian clubs of 1848; in the Paris Commune of 1871; the Soviets of 1905 and 1917; the collectives of revolutionary Spain in 1936-37; and the New England town meeting today, among others. He showed how (contrary to Marxism) the venue for revolution was not the factory but the municipality. Urbanization laid out the dialectical foundations for a municipalist revolt for freedom against the Nation-State.

Confined to solitude in his island prison, Öcalan dedicated himself to study and writing, often Civilization Narratives. One of his problematics, in *Roots of Civilization* (2001), was to show the need for Turkey's democratic republic to include the Kurds. He too described a process of social evolution, the historical macro-processes of civilization, whose roots lay in Mesopotamia, at Sumer.

In his telling, the Ziggurat—a temple, an administrative center, and a production site—was "the womb of state institutions."[11] The topmost floor was said to be the home of the gods, but the first floor was for the production and storage of goods. The temple thus functioned as a center of economic production. Rulers were elevated to divine status; the rest of the people had to toil in their service, as workers in a temple-centered economy. The ziggurats were "the laboratories for the encoding of human mindsets, the first asylums were the submissive creature was created." They were "the first patriarchal households and the first brothels." The Sumerian priests who constructed them became "the foremost architects of centralized political power." Their temples grew into cities, cities became states, and empires, and civilization. But the nature of the phenomenon remained the same: "The history of civilization amounts to nothing else than the continuation of a Sumerian society grown in extension, branched out and diversified, but retaining the same basic configuration."[12] We are still living in Sumer, still living in "this incredible intellectual invention" that "has been controlling our entire history ever since."[13] If Sumerian civilization is the thesis, he said dialectically, we need an antithesis, which we can find in, among other places, the Kurdish question.[14] Ethnic resistance to the Sumerian city is ancient as that city itself. Today a transcendence of the Sumerian state may be found in a fully democratic republic, home to both Kurds and Turks.

I don't know anything about Öcalan's other intellectual influences—the names Wallerstein, Braudel, and Foucault are often mentioned. But it's clear that in 2002 Öcalan started reading Bookchin intensively, especially *Ecology of Freedom* and *Urbanization Without Cities*.

Thereafter, through his lawyers, he began recommending *Urbanization Without Cities* to all mayors in Turkish Kurdistan and *Ecology of Freedom* to all militants.[15]

In the spring of 2004, he had his lawyers contact Murray, which they did through an intermediary, who explained to Murray that Öcalan considered himself his student, had acquired a good understanding of his work, and was eager to make the ideas applicable to Middle Eastern societies. He asked for a dialogue with Murray and sent one of his manuscripts.

It would have been amazing, had that dialogue taken place. Unfortunately Murray, at 83, was too sick to accept the invitation and reluctantly, respectfully declined. Öcalan's subsequent writings show the influence of his study of Bookchin. His 2004 work *In Defense of the People* is a Civilization Narrative that includes an account of primal communal social forms, like Murray's "organic society," the communal form of life that Öcalan renamed "natural society." In natural society, he wrote, people lived "as part of nature," and "human communities were part of the natural ecology." He presented an account of the rise of hierarchy that much resembled Bookchin's: the State "enforced hierarchy permanently and legitimized the accumulation of values and goods." Moreover, he said, the rise of hierarchy introduced the idea of dominating nature: "Instead of being a part of nature," hierarchical society saw "nature increasingly as a resource." Öcalan even called attention to the process' dialectical nature: "natural society at the beginning of humankind forms the thesis contrasted by the antithesis of the subsequent hierarchic and state-based forms of society."[16]

Their respective Civilization Narratives have many points of overlap and difference that would be fascinating to explore, but in the interests of conciseness, I'll limit myself to one, the various ways they wrote about Mesopotamia.

Öcalan, as I've said, emphasized that Mesopotamia was where civilization began. Bookchin agreed, noting that writing began there in the Fourth Century BCE in cuneiform, a pictographic system in which wedge-shaped stylus marks are impressed into clay tablets. He agreed that hierarchy, priesthoods, and states began in Sumer (as well as ancient Mesoamerica). But even more compelling to him were the traces of resistance unearthed by archaeologists: in the earliest Sumerian "city-states" were self-managed "by 'equalitarian assemblies,' which possessed 'freedom to an uncommon degree.'" After the rise of kingship "there is evidence of popular revolts, possibly to restore the old social dispensation or to diminish the authority of the *bala* [king]." Even "the governing *ensi*, or military overlords, were repeatedly checked by popular assemblies."[17] And it fascinated him that it was at Sumer that the word *freedom* (*amargi*) appeared for the first time in recorded history: in a Sumerian cuneiform account of a successful popular revolt against a regal tyranny.[18]

Öcalan, after reading Bookchin, noted the use of the word *amargi*, but otherwise didn't pick up on this point. But he did trace traits of Kurdish society to the Neolithic: "many characteristics and traits of Kurdish society," he said, especially the "mindset and material basis, ... bear a resemblance to communities from the Neolithic."[19] Even today Kurdish society bears the cooperative features of organic society: "Throughout their whole history Kurds have favoured Clan systems and tribal confederations and struggled to resist centralized governments."[20] They are potentially bearers of freedom.

As Marxists, Bookchin and Öcalan had both been taught that the dialectical-materialist processes of history are inexorable and function like laws, with inevitable outcomes, like the rise of the nation-state and capitalism. Twentieth century Marxist totalitarians, notably Stalin asserted the existence of such alleged laws, or "suprahuman forces beyond human control," and systematically propagated them to instill passivity in subjugated populations: denying any role to human agency or individual choice in shaping society, leaving people captive to a helpless belief in "economic and technical inexorability." Even the notion that hierarchy is inevitable and necessary in human societies, Bookchin argued, foreclosed the possibility of a liberatory alternative. But we lived communally once, in organic society, he insisted, and that meant we can live communally again. Our historical memory of communal society "functions unconsciously with an implicit commitment to freedom."[21] In my view, that is the underlying liberatory insight of *The Ecology of Freedom*.

Reading Öcalan's *In Defense of the People*, I sensed an exhilaration that reminded me of how I felt when I first read *Ecology of Freedom* back in 1985—delighted by the insight that people once lived in communal solidarity, and that the potential for it remains, and inspired by the prospect that we could have it again, if we chose to change our social arrangements. The concept of the "irreducible minimum" simply has taken on new names, like socialism. *Ecology of Freedom* offers to readers what Murray used to call "a principle of hope," and that must have meant something to the imprisoned Öcalan.

"The victory of capitalism was not simply fate," Öcalan wrote in 2004. "There could have been a different development." To regard capitalism and the nation-state as inevitable "leaves history to those in power." Rather, "there is always only a certain probability for things to happen ... there is always an option of freedom.[22]

The communal aspects of "natural society" persist in ethnic groups, class movements, and religious and philosophical groups that struggle for freedom. "Natural society has never ceased to exist," he wrote. A dialectical conflict between freedom and domination has persisted throughout western history, "a constant battle between democratic elements who refer to communal structures and those whose instruments are power and war." For "the communal society is in permanent conflict with the hierarchic one."[23]

Finally, Öcalan embraced social ecology. "The issue of social ecology begins with civilization," he wrote in 2004, because "the roots of civilization" are where we find also "the beginnings of the destruction of the natural environment." Natural society was in a sense ecological society. The same forces that destroy society from within also cut the meaningful link to nature. Capitalism, he says, is anti-ecological, and we need a specifically ethical revolt against it, "a conscious ethic effort," a "new social ethics that is in harmony with traditional values." The liberation of women is fundamental. And he called for a "democratic-ecological society," by which he meant "a moral-based system that involves sustainable dialectical relations with nature, ... where common welfare is achieved by means of direct democracy."[24]

How did it all apply to the Kurdish question? Once again, he emphasizes that achieving Kurdish freedom means achieving freedom for everyone. "Any solution will have to include options not only valid for the Kurdish people but for all people. That is, I am approaching these problems based on one humanism, one humanity, one nature and one universe."[25] But now, instead of through the democratic republic, it is to be achieved through assembly democracy.

"Our first task," he wrote, "is to push for democratization, for non-state structures, and communal organization." Instead of focusing solely on changing the Turkish constitution, he advocated that Kurds create organizations at the local level: local town councils, municipal administrations, down to urban districts, townships, and villages. They should form new local political parties and economic cooperatives, civil society organizations, and those that address human rights, women's rights, children's rights, animal rights, and all other issues to be addressed.

"Regional associations of municipal administrations" are needed, so these local organizations and institutions would form a network. At the topmost level, they are to be represented in a "General Congress of the People," which will address issues of "politics, self-defense, law, morality, economy, science, arts, and welfare by means of institutionalization, rules and control mechanisms."

Gradually, as the democratic institutions spread, all of Turkey would undergo a democratization. They would network across existing national borders, to accelerate the advent of democratic civilization in the whole region and produce not only freedom for the Kurds but a geopolitical and cultural renewal. Ultimately a democratic confederal union would embrace the whole of the Middle East. He named this Kurdish version of libertarian municipalism "democratic confederalism."

In March 2005, Öcalan issued a "Declaration of Democratic Confederalism" in Kurdistan. It called for "a grassroots democracy ... based on the democratic communal structure of natural society." It "will establish village, towns and city assemblies and their delegates will be entrusted with the real decision-making, which in effect means that the people and the community will decide." Öcalan's democratic confederalism preserves his brilliant move of linking the liberation of Kurds to the liberation of humanity. It affirms individual rights and freedom of expression for everyone, regardless of religious, ethnic, and class differences. It "promotes an ecological model of society" and supports women's liberation. He urged this program upon his people: "I am calling upon all sectors of society, in particular all women and the youth, to set up their own democratic organizations and to govern themselves." When I visited Diyarbakir in the fall of 2011, I discovered that Kurds in southeastern Anatolia were indeed putting this program into practice.[26]

By 2004-5, then, Öcalan had either given up on or shifted focus from his effort to persuade the State to reform itself by democratizing from the top down. "The idea of a democratization of the state," he wrote in 2005, "is out of place." He had concluded that the State was a mechanism of oppression—"the organizational form of the ruling class" and as such "one of the most dangerous phenomena in history." It is toxic to the democratic project, a "disease," and while it is around, "we will not be able to create a democratic system." So Kurds and their sympathizers "must never focus our efforts on the state" or on becoming a state, because that would mean losing the democracy, and playing "into the hands of the capitalist system."[27]

That seems pretty unequivocal, and certainly in accord with Bookchin's revolutionary project. Bookchin posited that once citizen's assemblies were created and confederated, they would become a dual power that could be pitted against the nation-state—and would overthrow and replace it. He emphasized repeatedly the concept of dual power, I should note, crediting it to Trotsky, who wrote, in his *History of the Russian Revolution*, that after February 1917, when various provisional liberal governments were in charge of the state, the Petrograd soviet of workers' and soldiers' deputies became a dual power against those governments; it later became a driver of the October revolution. Similarly, the communalist confederation would a counterpower, a dual power, in a revolutionary situation.

But Öcalan, in the same 2004 work (*In Defense of the People*), also sends a contradictory message about the State: "It is not true, in my opinion, that the state needs to be broken up and replaced by something else." It is "illusionary to reach for democracy by crushing the state." Rather, the State can and must become smaller, more limited in scope. Some of its functions are necessary: for example, public security, social security and national defense. The confederal democracy's congresses should solve problems "that the state cannot solve single-handedly." A limited state can coexist with the democracy "in parallel."[28] This contradiction seems to have bedeviled Öcalan himself, who admits in seeming exasperation, "The state remains a Janus-faced phenomenon." I sense that the issue remains ambiguous for him, and understandably so. Insightfully, he observes that "our present time is an era of transition from state to democracy. In times of transition, the old and the new often exist side by side."[29]

Bookchin's communalist movement never got as far, in practical terms, as Öcalan's has, but if it had, he would surely have faced the same problem. The concept of a transitional program, which Bookchin invoked in such occasions, may be useful here. He used to distinguish between the minimum program (reforms on specific issues), the transitional program (like Öcalan's), and the maximum program (socialism, a stateless assembly democracy). That distinction has a revolutionary pedigree—Murray used to credit it to Trotsky. It's a way to retain a commitment to your long-term goals and principles while dealing in the real, nonrevolutionary world.

In May 2004 Bookchin conveyed to Öcalan his hopes "that the Kurdish people will one day be able to establish a free, rational society that will allow their brilliance once again to flourish" and commended them for having "a leader of Mr. Öcalan's talents to guide them."[30] We later learned that this message was read aloud at the Second General Assembly of the Kurdistan People's Congress, in the mountains, in the summer of 2004.

When Bookchin died in July 2006, the PKK assembly saluted "one of the greatest social scientists of the 20th century." He "introduced us to the thought of social ecology" and "helped to develop socialist theory in order for it to advance on a firmer basis." He showed how to make a new democratic system into a reality. "He has proposed the concept of confederalism," a model which we believe is creative and realizable." The assembly continued: Bookchin's "thesis on the state, power, and hierarchy will be implemented and realized through our struggle . . . We will put this promise into practice this as the first society that establishes a tangible democratic confederalism." No tribute could have made him happier; I only wish he could have heard it. Perhaps he would have saluted them back with that first recorded word for freedom, from Sumer: "Amargi!"

NOTES

1. Abdullah Öcalan, *Declaration on the Democratic Solution of the Kurdish Question,* 1999, trans. Kurdistan Information Centre (London: Mesopotamian Publishers, 1999), 106.

2. Öcalan, *Declaration,* 44.

3. Öcalan, *Declaration,* 55.

4. Öcalan, *Declaration,* 89–90.

5. Öcalan, *Declaration,* 114.

6. Murray Bookchin, *The Ecology of Freedom: The Rise and Dissolution of Hierarchy* (Palo Alto, Calif.: Cheshire Books, 1982); and *Urbanization Without Cities: The Rise and Decline of Citizenship* (Montreal: Black Rose Books, 1992).

7. Abdullah Öcalan, *Prison Writings: The Roots of Civilization,* trans. Klaus Happel (London: Pluto Press, 2007); and *Prison Writings: The PKK and the Kurdish Question in the 21st Century,* trans. Klaus Happel (London: Transmedia, 2011). Neither Bookchin nor Öcalan was an archaeologist or anthropologist; rather, their accounts of prehistory and early history draw on specialists' published findings.

8. Bookchin, *Ecology of Freedom,* chap. 2.

9. Bookchin, *Ecology of Freedom,* 46, 43.

10. Bookchin, *Ecology of Freedom,* chap. 3.

11. Öcalan, *Roots,* 6.

12. Öcalan, *Roots,* 53, 25, 98.

13. Öcalan, *PKK and the Kurdish Question,* 96.

14. Unlike Öcalan, Bookchin chose not to use the terms *thesis, antithesis,* and *synthesis,* considering them an oversimplification of Hegel's triad *an sich, für sich,* and *an und für sich.*

15. So I was told by the intermediary between Öcalan's lawyers and Bookchin, who wishes to remain anonymous here.

16. Abdullah Öcalan, *In Defense of the People* (unpublished), chap. 1.2, "The Natural Society," English translation manuscript courtesy of the International Initiative Freedom for Öcalan, Peace in Kurdistan. This book was published in German as *Jenseits von Staat, Macht, und Gewalt* (Neuss: Mesopotamien Verlag, 2010).

17. Bookchin, *Ecology of Freedom,* 144, 129, 95. He was drawing on the work of Henri Frankfort and Samuel Noah Kramer.

18. Bookchin, *Ecology of Freedom,* 168.

19. Öcalan, *PKK and Kurdish Question,* 22.

20. Öcalan, "The Declaration of Democratic Confederalism," February 4, 2005, online at http://www.kurdmedia.com/article.aspx?id=10174, accessed 2012.

21. Bookchin, *Ecology of Freedom,* 23–24, 67, 143.

22. Öcalan, *Defense of People,* 41.

23. Öcalan, *Defense of People,* 51, 65, 60.

24. Öcalan, *Defense of People,* chap. III, 4.

25. Öcalan, *Defense of People,* 52.

26. "Kurdish Communalism," interview with Ercan Ayboga by author, *New Compass* (Sept. 2011), http://new-compass.net/http%3A//new-compass.net/article/kurdish-communalism.

27. Öcalan, *Defense of People,* 177, 24, 104, 177.

28. Öcalan, *Defense of People,* 24, 106, 111, 106.

29. Öcalan, *Defense of People,* 27, 178.

30. Copy in author's possession. [In 2017 the correspondence became available online at https://www.huffingtonpost.com/entry/syrian-kurds-murray-bookchin_us_5655e7e2e4b079b2 8189e3df.]

Murray Bookchin and Radical Agriculture

Brian Morris

MURRAY BOOKCHIN—one of the pioneers of the ecology movement that emerged in the 1960s—remains one of the most well-known and controversial of recent political ecologists. Both a political activist and an influential radical scholar for over 50 years, Bookchin produced a steady stream of essays, political tracts, and substantial books on environmental issues, the culture of cities, libertarian politics, and social ecology that are truly impressive and groundbreaking. In this essay, I focus only on one small part of Bookchin's rich *oeuvre*, and offer some reflections on his scattered writings around the topic of radical agriculture.

The essay is in three parts. In part one, I discuss Bookchin's outline of the "modern crisis," focussing especially on the ecological crisis and his response to it. In the second part I explore Bookchin's social ecology and his critique of industrial agriculture, and conclude the essay in part three with some reflections on Bookchin's advocacy of a radical, more enlightened, form of agriculture.

Part One: Bookchin and the Ecological Crisis

Apart from die-hard neoconservatives, most people have long recognized that the world is in a sorry state, and that there is a lot to be angry about. Long ago, Murray Bookchin outlined what he described as the "modern crisis," highlighting that both global capitalism and the modern state are in severe crisis.[1] This crisis is indeed manifold: social, economic, political, and ecological all at once. For under global capitalism there has been a growing concentration of economic power, and the continuous expansion of economic inequalities. It is estimated that the four hundred richest people in the world have a combined wealth greater than that of 45% of the world's population. No wonder rampant poverty exists throughout the world. Out of a world population of seven billion people, nearly one billion people, or 15%, are severely undernourished, that is, unable to obtain the basic conditions of human existence.[2] Such poverty is not integral to the human condition, as some economists misleadingly contend, but is directly related to economic "development," that is, the global expansion of capitalism.

Equally significant is that throughout the world we find a "dialectic of violence" reflected in the widespread existence of weapons of mass destruction, both chemicals and nuclear, and the stockpiling of conventional weapons. This can hardly be said to have kept the peace, for since the Second World War there have been well over 100 armed conflicts, killing millions of people. This dialectic of violence has led to the disintegration of local communities, the denial of human rights, widespread genocide and political repression, usually by governments. Indeed many scholars have emphasized, including ironically many erstwhile neoliberals, that the impact of free-market capitalism, which has been a political project, has been socially devastating, not only leading to economic inequalities and widespread poverty, but also to social chaos, racial and ethnic conflict, political instability, and family and community breakdown.[3]

Finally, there is an "ecological crisis"—the severe ecological challenges that humans now face. This is clearly manifested in the degradation of the natural environment under industrial capitalism: the pollution of the atmosphere and of the seas, lakes, and rivers, widespread deforestation, the impact of industrial agri-culture, including the adverse effects now threatening many species with extinction, and finally, the serious decline in the quality of urban life through overcrowding, poverty, and traffic congestion.

When I first became involved in environmental issues in the 1960s, ecology was very much seen as a radical movement, the biologist Paul Sears even describing ecology as the "subversive science."[4] The seminal writings of Murray Bookchin and Barry Commoner emphasized that we were indeed confronting an ecological crisis and that the cause of this crisis was an economic system—global capitalism—that was geared not to human needs and well-being but to the generation of profit, that saw no limit to growth and technology. For Bookchin, of course, it was not simply the human population nor the mechanistic worldview of René Descartes that had brought about this destruction, but rather that the roots of the ecological crisis lay firmly with global capitalism which was continually "plundering the earth" in the search for profits. Bookchin indeed felt that the capitalist market economy had become a "terrifying menace" to the very integrity of life on earth. Industrial capitalism, he argued, was fundamentally anti-ecological, and over 40 years ago, Bookchin was highlighting with some prescience—long before Al Gore and George Monbiot—the problem of global warming, that the growing blanket of carbon dioxide would lead to destructive storm patterns and eventually the melting of the ice caps and rising sea levels.[5]

In response to the "modern crisis," especially with respect to the ecological challenges it invoked, Bookchin proposed a reaffirmation and a creative devel-opment of the revolutionary anarchist tradition that essentially stemmed from

Michael Bakunin, Peter Kropotkin, and their associates. This tradition emphasized the need to integrate an ecological worldview—what Bookchin was later to describe as dialectical naturalism—with the political philosophy offered by anarchism, that is, libertarian socialism.[6]

Bookchin's own metaphysics of nature was a form of evolutionary naturalism. He was, therefore, always highly critical of spiritual (or deep) ecology—whether expressed as tribal animism, theism, or pantheistic mysticism.[7] Bookchin was fundamentally a dialectical (historical) thinker like Noam Chomsky, who were both highly critical of the subjectivism, cultural relativism, and nihilistic ethos of postmodernism which became highly fashionable among academics (especially) towards the end of the twentieth century. Needless to say, Bookchin, like the philosopher Mario Bunge, had very little sympathy with the doyens of post-modernism—the reactionary aesthetes Friedrich Nietzsche and Martin Heidegger.[8] The political tradition that Bookchin embraced, libertarian socialism (or anarchism), which emerged as a vibrant political movement toward the end of the nineteenth century, combined, as many scholars have emphasized, the best of both radical liberalism, with its emphasis on liberty and individual freedom, and socialism, with its emphasis on equality, voluntary associations, mutual aid, workers' self-management and direct action. This unity that indeed defines libertarian socialism (or anarchist communism), was most succinctly expressed in the well-known maxim of Michael Bakunin that Bookchin quotes: "Liberty without socialism is privilege and injustice: socialism without liberty is slavery and brutality."[9]

Although, like Bakunin and Kropotkin before him, Bookchin fervently opposed all forms of "bourgeois" individualism—whether expressed by Nietzschean aesthetes (Hakim Bey), Stirnerite egoists (Jason McQuinn), primitivists (John Zerzen) or, at extreme, anarcho-capitalists (Murray Rothbard)—it is utterly fallacious to imply from this, as does Clark, that Bookchin thereby posited an opposition between individual autonomy (freedom) and social solidarity. Unlike the proponents of "post-left" anarchy, Bookchin was an advocate of libertarian socialism (otherwise known as anarchist communism) and emphasized that there is an intrinsic dialectical relationship between individual freedom and self-realization and society (communal life). He, therefore, like Kropotkin before him, advocated a form of "communal individuality," or as he expressed it "social freedom," not autonomy in the sense of bourgeois individualism (or radical egoism). The notion that society (community) is the "enemy" of the individual—the "unique one," struck Bookchin, as it did Bakunin, as utter nonsense.[10] For Bookchin, the opposition—the "chasm" as he rhetorically put it—was between anarchist-communism (communitarian anarchism) and radical bourgeois individualism (egoism), not between the self-realization of the individual person and social solidarity, which for libertarian socialists like Bakunin, Kropotkin and Bookchin were intrinsically interrelated and complimentary. The "ressentiment" that Clark expresses towards Bookchin seriously distorts his analysis, though his reflections on Bookchin's rhetorical flourishes may have certain validity.

Over 40 years ago Bookchin sensed that the social and the natural must be grasped in a new dialectical unity. That the time had come to integrate an ecological natural philosophy (social ecology) with the social philosophy based on freedom, mutual aid and social solidarity (anarchism or libertarian socialism). This unity was essential, he argued, if we were to avoid an ecological catastrophe. What we must therefore do, Bookchin stressed, was to "decentralize, restore bioregional forms of production and food cultivation, diversify our technologies, scale them to human dimensions, and establish face-to-face forms of democracy," as well as to foster a new sensibility towards the biosphere.[11]

It is beyond the scope of the present essay to discuss Bookchin's philosophy of social ecology, which I have critically reviewed elsewhere, nor his seminal efforts to develop a political or democratic dimension of anarchism as communalism.[12] This too has been usefully explored by other scholars.[13] I intend rather to be more focused and to offer some reflections on Bookchin's writings on radical agriculture. In the following two sections I will briefly outline Bookchin's ecological vision, his critique of capitalist agriculture and his tentative suggestions for a more enlightened form of agriculture—an agroecology.

Social Ecology and the Critique of Industrial Agriculture

Because Murray Bookchin made some rather harsh criticisms of deep ecology, specifically with respect to its neo-Malthusian misanthropy, its spiritualist metaphysic and its concept of biocentrism, he has continually been accused by his critics of being an ardent advocate of anthropocentrism.[14] This is the theological notion that humans are the lords of creation, quite separate from nature which exists solely for humans to exploit as a resource. This is a serious misunderstanding, if not a willful misinterpretation of Bookchin's social ecology. For Bookchin repudiated both anthropocentrism and biocentrism, advocating what he described as an ethics of complementarity. Such an ethics not only implies an ecological worldview but a new ecological sensibility "that respects other forms of life for their own sake and that responds actively in the form of a creative, loving, and supportive symbiosis."[15]

An ethics of complementarity or mutualism, as advocated by Bookchin, opposes any claim that humans have a right to "dominate" the natural world, still less the claim that the world has been created, as St. Augustine implied, solely for human use. Bookchin therefore places a strong emphasis on an ecological ethics that puts a high premium on promoting a rich diversity of life, one that makes for wholeness, for evolutionary and rational innovation, as well as for the spontaneity and heterogeneity of all life forms.[16]

Bookchin sums up his own ecological approach when he writes: "There is a need for a new (ecological) sensibility, a new feeling of care and of love for all forms of life, a feeling of responsibility, a feeling of attunement with the natural world."[17]

Social ecology, for Bookchin, was therefore a form of ecoanarchism, that combined the project of human liberation (anarchism) with an ecological project, that of "defending the earth" and promoting a new ecological sensibility. Land therefore has to be viewed as a home, or *oikos*.[18]

But modern agriculture under capitalism has become, Bookchin contended, a business enterprise, concerned not simply with the production of food but with the generation of profits. The ethos of capitalism, according to Bookchin, is fundamentally anthropocentric, radically separating humans from nature—the "ecological rift" that neo-Marxists are now theorizing—as well as extolling the technological "mastery" of humanity over nature.[19] The ideology of capitalism generates an ethos of competition, egoism and greed, and completely dissolves any sense of community.[20] Bookchin thus came to make some telling criticisms of "modern" industrial agriculture. Modern agricultural practices, Bookchin argued, being modelled on those of the factory, had led to the simplification of the landscape, and to the overuse of chemical fertilizers and pesticides. This has entailed a serious loss of bird life, and other forms of wildlife, through the application of highly dangerous insecticides, particularly DDT[21] which Rachel Carson's book, *Silent Spring* (1962), published in the same year as Bookchin's pioneering study, had also highlighted.[22]

Bookchin also stressed that soil erosion had become a serious problem and that there had been a marked deterioration in the fertility and structure of soil under industrial agriculture. Soil for Bookchin was a living entity, consisting not only of dead matter but of living organisms. It was highly dynamic, always in a process of formation, and every plot of land could be viewed as a complex living cosmos.[23] But, modern agriculture not only diminishes the nutrient value of the soil with its exploitative and industrial techniques, but in its excessive use of highly soluble nitrogen fertilizers, it is adversely affecting, Bookchin suggests, the nitrogen cycle itself.[24]

Given its industrial methods, its excessive use of pesticides and inorganic fertilizers, and its enthusiasm for monoculture—"one crop agriculture" as Bookchin describes it—land has been turned under modern agriculture into a "lifeless inorganic medium."[25] Bookchin also highlights that, under capitalism, livestock had come to be treated purely as an "industrial resource" through factory farming, and that there was a serious need to restore the time-honoured intimacy between humans and their livestock.[26]

It is also of interest that some 50 years ago Bookchin was highlighting a decline in the nutritional value of food under industrial farming, the increasing consumption of junk food, such as soft drinks and sugary snacks, that was leading to problems of obesity, and the increasing problems of pollution and waste disposal in urban areas.[27]

Under industrial capitalism, specifically as it relates to farming, Bookchin thus came to conclude that the entire planet has been reduced to a factory and nature to mere "resources: for reaping profits,[28] and that modern capitalism is inherently antiecological.[29]

Recent studies of the ecology and politics of industrial agriculture have more than confirmed Murray Bookchin's earlier insights and reflections.

Agriculture is fundamentally what we need to stay alive, and to make the world a viable and attractive place to inhabit, but what we have created, according to the biologist, Colin Tudge, is a world economic system—capitalism that is "bad for humanity in general and disastrous for agriculture."[30] In fact, industrial agriculture is described as "wrecking" the natural environment and causing untold "human misery" throughout the world.[31]

Industrial agriculture essentially developed from the end of the Second World War, and was a fundamental departure from earlier forms of agriculture, that had served humans well for thousands of years. It involved the following: farm specialization, with the separation of arable farming (monoculture), horticulture and livestock production (under intensive factory conditions); increased mechanization leading to a marked reduction in human labour and the number of small farms; large inputs of non-renewable energy (fossil fuel); and, finally, the widespread us of inorganic fertilizers, chemical pesticides, and herbicides.

The social and ecological impact of this form of agriculture has been described as "devastating" by a number of scholars since Bookchin's pioneer work, which has been discussed widely. Its impact can be briefly listed: extensive rural depopulation, concentration of land ownership, widespread degradation of the environment with a serious loss of wildlife habitats, abuse of farm animals under factory conditions, undermining of rural economies throughout the world, and finally, as contributing significantly through carbon emissions to global warming. The general conclusion of many scholars is, therefore, that industrial agriculture is unsustainable, and a serious threat to both to the environment and to human health and well-being.[32]

Industrial agriculture has to be understood within the political economy, that of global capitalism. This entails recognizing that modern agriculture is dominated by a relatively small number of powerful capitalist corporations and is supported by massive government subsidies, as well as being promoted in the media and by academics defending the status quo. A number of myths about industrial agriculture therefore need to be dispelled.

The first myth is that industrial high-tech agriculture, given its high productivity, is necessary to feed the world's population, both at the present time and in the foreseeable future. But the fact is that most of the food currently being produced in the world, around 70%, is produced not by the capitalist firms but by small-scale farmers working on small plots of land. Industrial farming only produces 30% of the food we currently eat. Yet, the myth that industrial agriculture —agribusiness—feeds the world is promoted world-wide.[33]

Secondly, although around one billion people in the world are starving or chronically undernourished, there is, in fact, enough food produced in the world to feed everyone. Indeed, it is estimated that the world is currently producing an average of 4,600 kilocalories of food per person per day, much more than anyone actually needs for their daily nutrients.[34] The reason people are starving is due to the maldistribution of food under capitalism, which is geared not to the satisfaction of human needs but to profit (as Bookchin continually emphasized), and the fact that most of the soya or maize goes to feed livestock or is converted into biofuel.[35]

The third myth involves the constant denigration of smallholder farming as primitive and inefficient, in contrast to the efficiency and high productivity of industrial agriculture. But in fact, modern agriculture is highly inefficient, both in terms of energy and in terms of land-use. On a traditional farm 1 kcal of energy expended during cultivation yields around 10 kcal of food energy, while industrial agriculture consumes 10 kcal of energy (as fossil fuel) to produce 1 kcal of food energy. Thus smallholder farming is a hundred times more efficient in terms of energy than industrial agriculture. It is also evident that smallholder farms produce more per unit of land than large industrial farms, given the ubiquity of multiple-cropping systems and the widespread use of nitrogen-fixing legumes and animal manures in traditional husbandry. Small farms always tend to be more productive than large farms and yields from urban allotments, for example, far outstrip those of industrial farming enterprises.[36]

Enlightened Agriculture

What then is the alternative to industrial agriculture?

Many scholars have suggested—the Gandhian scholar Vandana Shiva (2015) is a prime example—that agroecology as practiced by millions of smallholders and peasant farmers throughout the world, is more sustainable, and more efficient at feeding the human population healthily and well, than current forms of industrial agriculture. But like Kropotkin before him, Bookchin felt that there were limits to traditional forms of agriculture, which tended to rely on limited technology and on the back-breaking work of peasant families, particularly women. In challenging industrial agriculture, Bookchin therefore argued that there was no need to reject improvements, let alone return to Neolithic technology.[37]

In endeavouring to develop and articulate the democratic or political dimension of anarchist-communism, Bookchin devoted little discussion to the nature and scope of economic life. Indeed Bookchin has been accused of holding a rather narrow conception of the public realm and as having little concern for economic democracy.[38]

But it is I think important to situate Bookchin within the tradition of revolutionary socialism, which he always acknowledged he belonged to particularly as this tradition was theorized by Peter Kropotkin.[39]

It is of interest that Kropotkin, along with Lewis Mumford, Erwin Gutkind and Paul Goodman, is specifically mentioned by Bookchin as proponents of the kind of libertarian socialism—with their emphasis on decentralization—that he was trying to develop. Indeed, it has been suggested that Bookchin absorbed Kropotkin's ideas through Mumford.[40] Like Kropotkin, what Bookchin emphasized as an anarchist communist, was a municipal (communal) economics, which entailed that all production—whether food, clothing or dwellings—would be organized as a communal activity. The management of local affairs would also be communal, organized through voluntary associations or local assemblies, and, finally, the products of labour would be communal, to be shared according to individual needs. Bookchin, like Kropotkin, thus repudiated the state ownership of land and capital and all "nationalization" schemes—the collectivist farms advocated by Russian Marxists was an anathema to Bookchin. Indeed, James Scott described industrial farming as a "Soviet-American fetish."[41] But Bookchin, like Kropotkin was equally against private property, the market economy and petty-commodity production (petty-bourgeois capitalism) and any form of "wage system," as advocated by Proudhon and many individualist anarchists.[42]

As a revolutionary socialist (communist) Bookchin was therefore fond of quoting the famous socialist maxim, "From each according to his or her ability, to each according to his or her needs."

Although his maxim has been glibly dismissed as vague and uninspiring by some reformist liberals,[43] for Bookchin, it was a "bedrock guide" in enabling an ecological community (municipality) to produce food and durable goods, and so provide for the varied needs of its members, consonant with ethical and ecological principles. The municipal economy would be for Bookchin a "moral economy."[44]

Following in the footsteps of Kropotkin and Mumford, with their emphasis on the decentralization of urban and political life, Bookchin stressed the need to create small cities and towns that would be scaled down to human needs and proclivities. He thus envisaged a future human environment in terms of a decentralized, moderately-sized city which combines within its orbit both local industry and agriculture, and which makes the maximum use of local energy sources, such as wind power, solar energy, and hydroelectric power. A new form of "decentralized" local community needs to be created, Bookchin argues; one which puts an emphasis on organic agriculture and urban regionalism, and thus achieves some kind of lasting equilibrium or harmony between human society and the natural world.[45]

Again like Kropotkin, Bookchin envisaged a social economy that would integrate city life and the rural countryside. Radical or organic agriculture was thus situated or embedded within a wider social matrix. As he wrote: "Radical agriculture seeks to restore humanity's sense of community: first, by giving full recognition to the soil as an ecosystem, a biotic community; and the second, by viewing agriculture as the activity of a natural human community, a rural society and culture."[46]

He thus emphasized that radical agriculture was both libertarian and ecological, given the stress on diversity, community and mutualism. It implied a "blending" of town and country, with the human individual actively involved in both spheres.

Following the pioneering agronomist Albert Howard's notion that nature is a form of "mixed farming"—"mother earth never attempts to farm without livestock"—Bookchin advocated a mixed farming system, that would combine intensive agriculture (whether market gardening, field cultivation, or urban/kitchen gardens) with orchards and livestock production. Like Tudge, Bookchin recognized that certain landscapes, though suitable for livestock, are unsuitable for arable cultivation, and that animal husbandry (pastoralism) is a unique way of converting grass into human food. The widespread use of cereal and soy as animal feed under industrial agriculture—capitalism—struck Bookchin as quite irrational. A maximum concern for the welfare of animals and the well-being of the biosphere is intrinsic to what Colin Tudge describes as enlightened agriculture.[47]

What Bookchin essentially advocated was in fact a form of "enlightened agriculture," or "agroecology" that can be characterized as follows: it was not anti-science, but rather suggested that agricultural practices should be based on sound biological knowledge, combined with insights that could be derived from the craft skills and agroecological knowledge that had been developed by human communities, whether peasants or smallholder farmers, over many millennia:[48]

- It was not anti-technology, for as Bookchin believed that what is needed is to redevelop technology according to ecologically sound principles."[49]

- Thus, Bookchin was not averse to the use of farm machinery, nor of chemical fertilizers, but stressed that the latter should be utilized only when appropriate and to complement organic agriculture.

- Agricultural practice should be based not only on sound biological and ecological knowledge, but also incorporate ethical and aesthetic principles. Bookchin was never therefore "antinature" or against the "wilderness" but always insisted on the need for diversity, and thus the need to develop and conserve wilderness areas (natural landscapes), the countryside (cultural landscapes such as woods, parks, meadows, gardens and cultivated fields) and urban settings duly scaled to human needs and well-being, and incorporating a variety of life forms.[50]

- Bookchin always stressed that humans were an integral part of nature, and that this was particularly well exemplified in their agricultural activities. The relationship between humans and nature should not therefore be one of mastery and dominion, but rather one that was cooperative and symbiotic, or, as Bookchin expressed it, dialectical. Radical agriculture he therefore concluded implies not merely new techniques in food cultivation but a new ecological sensibility towards land and society as a whole.[51]

NOTES

1. Murray Bookchin. *The Modern Crisis* (Philadelphia: New Society Publishers, 1986).

2. Colin Tudge. *Six Steps Back to the Land,* (Cambridge: Green Books, 2016).

3. Paul Elkins. *A New World Order: Grassroots Movements for Global Change, 1st Edition* (London: Routledge, 1992); John Gray, *False Dawn: The Delusions of Global Capitalism* (London: Granton Books, 1998); Brian Morris, *Kropotkin: The Politics of Community,* (Amherst, Humanity Books; 2004).

4. Paul B. Sears, "Ecology: A Subversive Science," *Bioscience* vol 14 (1964):11–13.

5. Bookchin, 1971, 60–67; Murray Bookchin. *The Ecology of Freedom: The Emergence and Dissolution of Hierarchy* (Montreal: Black Rose Books, 1991), 19; Brian Morris. *Pioneers of Ecological Humanism,* (Brighton: Book Guild Publishers, 2012), 180–187. cf J. Kovel. *The Energy of Nature,* (London: Zed Books, 2002).

6. Murray Bookchin. *The Philosophy of Social Ecology,* (Montreal: Black Rose Books, 1995).

7. David Watson. *Against the Meagamachine* (New York: Automedia, 1999); Starhawk (Miriam Samos). *The Spiral Dance* (New York: Harper Collins, 1979); Thomas Berry. *The Dream of the Earth,* (San Francisco: Sierra Club Books, 1988); Bookchin. *Ecology of Freedom,* 1991; Arne Naess. *Ecology, Community and Lifestyle* (Cambridge: Cambridge University Press, 1989); John P. Clark, "The Politics of Social Ecology: Beyond the Limits of the City," *Democracy and Nature* vol 5 no. 3 (1999): 523–60.

8.   Mario Bunge. *The Sociology-Philosophy Connection* (New Brunswick: Transaction Publishers, 1999).

9.   Murray Bookchin. *Anarchism, Marxism and the Future of The Left: Interviews and Essays: 1993–1998.* (Edinburgh: A.K Press, 1999), 160.

10. Sidney E. Parker, James L. Walker; John Beverly Robinson; John Henry Mackay; Enzo Ma. *Enemies of Society: An Anthology of Individualist and Egoist Thought* (Canada: Ardent Press, 2011).

11. Murray Bookchin. *Toward an Ecological Society,* (Montreal: Black Rose Books, 1980).

12. Brian Morris. *Pioneers of Ecological Humanism* (Brighton: Book Guild Publishers, 2012).

13. Janet Biehl. *The Politics of Social Ecology: Libertarian Municipalism* (Montreal: Black Rose Books, 1998); Eirik Eiglad. *Communalism as Alterative,* (Porsgrunn: New Compass Press, 2014); Dimitrios Roussoupolous. *Political Ecology Beyond Environmentalism,* revised edition (Porsgrunn: New Compass Publishers, 2015).

14. Murray Bookchin, "Social Ecology Versus Deep Ecology: A Challenge for the Ecology Movement." *The Raven* vol. 1, no. 3 (1987): 219–250.

15. Murray Bookchin, Dave Foreman. *Defending the Earth: A Dialogue between Murray Bookchin and Dave Foreman.* ed. Steve Chase (Boston: South End Press, 1999).7

16. Bookchin, *The Ecology of Freedom,* xxxvii.

17. Murray Bookchin, "Cities, Councils and Confederations." in *Turtle Talk: Voices for a Sustainable Future,* eds C. and J. Plant (Philadelphia: New Society Publications,1990), 124–132.

18. Murray Bookchin. "Radical Agriculture" in *Radical Agriculture,* ed. Richard Merrill (New York: Harper and Row, 1976), 3–13.

19. JB Foster. *Marx's Ecology: Materialism and Nature,* (New York: Monthly Review Press, 2000).

20. Bookchin, "Radical Agriculture," 8.

21. Bookchin, Murray. *Our Synthetic Environment* (New York: Harper and Row, 1962; revised edition, 1974).

22. Rachel Carson. *Silent Spring* (Boston: Houghton Mifflin, 1962).

23. Bookchin, *Synthetic,* 34–35.

24. Bookchin, *Synthetic,* iii.

25. Bookchin, *Synthetic,* 39.

26. Bookchin, *Synthetic,* 239.

27. Bookchin, *Synthetic,* xlvi.

28. Bookchin, *Synthetic,* xxxii.

29. Bookchin, "Radical Agriculture," 10.

30. Murray Bookchin. *Social Ecology and Communalism,* Introduction by Eirik Eiglad (Edinburgh: A.K. Press, 2007), 82.

31. Colin Tudge. *Feeding People is Easy* (Grosseto, Italy: Pavi Publishers, 2007): 61.

32. Colin Tudge. *So Shall We Reap* (London: Penguin Books, 2003); Nicholas Hildyard, Tracey Clunies-Ross. *The Politics of Industrial Agriculture* (London: Earthscan, 1992); Philip Conford (ed). *A Future for Land: Organic Practice from a Global Perspective,* (Bideford: Green Books, 1992); Martin Empson. 2016. "Food, Agriculture and Climate Change," *International Socialism* 152: 69–95.

33. Vandana Shiva. *Who Really Feeds the World,* (London: Zed Books, 2015): 14

34. Tudge, *Six Steps,* 18.

35. Shiva, *Who Really Feeds,* 73.

36. Tudge, *Feeding People,* 58.

37. Bookchin, *Synthetic*, lxix.

38. Takis Fotopoulos. "Social Ecology, Eco-Communitarianism and Inclusive Democracy," *Democracy and Nature* 1999; vol 5, no. 3:561–76.

39. Brian Morris. *Kropotkin: The Politics of Community* (Amherst: Humanity Books, 2004).

40. Bookchin 1974. lxxii; Janet Biehl. *Mumford Gutkind Bookchin: The Emergence of Eco-Decentralism* (Porsgrun: New Compass Press, 2011): 45.

41. James C. Scott. *Seeing Like a State* (New Haven: Yale University Press, 1998): 196.

42. Brian Morris, *Kropotkin*, 89.

43. Clark, *The Politics of Social Ecology*, 550.

44. Bookchin, *The Next Revolution, 91.*

45. Bookchin, *Synthetic*, 241–44.

46. Bookchin, "Radical Agriculture," 11.

47. Tudge, 2016, 119–120.

48. Paul Richards. *Indigenous Agricultural Revolution* (London: Hutchinson, 1985); Miguel Altieri, *Agroecology: The Scientific Basis of Alternative Agriculture* (Boulder: Westview Press, 1987): 24–25; Tudge, 2003.

49. Bookchin, *Synthetic*, lvii.

50. Morris, 2012, 7.

51. Murray Bookchin. "Radical Agriculture" in *Radical Agriculture*, ed. Richard Merrill (New York: Harper and Row, 1976), 3–13.

The Ecology of Urban Regeneration

Eirik Eiglad

The Ecology of Urban Regeneration

Throughout most of our history humanity led a rural life, and our ancestors mainly depended on subsistence hunting and agriculture. Two hundred years ago a mere three percent of the world's population lived in urban areas. By 1900, the urban population was 14 percent, and in 1950, it had risen to 30 percent. In 2011, for the first time in human history, city dwellers became the majority of the world's population.

This urban reconfiguration of social life takes place in a world of unprecedented demographic change. While humanity grew very slowly for most of our history, the last few centuries dramatically changed our societies and the impact we have on the natural world. In the last half of the last century alone, the world's population more than doubled its size. Just before 2000, we reached 6 billion, and now we have surpassed 7 billion. This rapid increase lays a heavy claim to natural resources and strains the ecological "carrying capacity."

But there is nothing inherently anti-ecological in these numbers alone. More problematic is it that this demographic change occurs in the context of dramatically expanded material productivity and consumption, and perpetual technological revolutions. The economic framework provided by this particular historical nexus of social conditions—capitalism—is what causes the intense strain on natural resources and habitats.

Ecological Challenges

For obvious ecological reasons we need to address this problem. The disastrous ecological consequences of capitalist economics seem to find their apotheosis in today's megacities. Human geographers, sociologists, and urbanists award much attention to this radically new historical phenomenon, and deservedly so: it is even more startling than the general population growth or the increased settlement in cities. In 1900 only 12 cities had more than 1 million inhabitants, and in 1950 this number had grown to 83. Today more than 400 cities number more than 1 million, and 19 of them have 10 million. These megacities appear to be ecological disasters in themselves, rendering the environment inorganic with enormous stretches of asphalt and glass, metal and concrete. The infamous Naples waste management crisis shows more than anything the enormous amount of garbage these megacities produce.

More than its small-town sisters and rural brothers, these megacities in "developed" countries bar the transition to an ecological economy based on human scale and regional self-reliance. Wealthy countries in the global North have a particular responsibility to reduce consumption and introduce ecological measures for development and production, but a serious reduction—or even stabilization of—consumption seems nowhere in sight. Since 1990 private consumption by Norwegian households has increased a staggering 93 percent, and prospects for a decrease in the foreseeable future are nil. Other European countries fare no better. The financial crises that now shake the global economy have not altered consumption patterns nor regionalized production nor created ecological jobs. When the financial strains were first felt in 2008, Kristin Halvorsen (then the Norwegian minister of finance as well as the leader of the Socialist Left Party) suggested that we should "shop ourselves out of the crisis."

From an ecological perspective, allowing the centripetal forces of the market economy and its urban agglomerations to continue to grow uncontrolled will have grave consequences. This rapacious growth pits our megacities against the countryside, indeed against the natural world. Their consumption patterns require an industry and infrastructure that are heavily based on fossil fuels, and their populations fully depend on a global provision of consumer goods. This abnormal growth makes the modern megalopolis seem more reminiscent of a malignant tumor than anything in organic or cultural evolution. As a capitalist creature, urbanization does become cancerous: like a tumor, these megacities threaten their host, the human community.

Ecological Possibilities

Still, the problematic growth of megacities is not essentially one of size or numbers. Rather it is one of underlying capitalist dynamics. Under a sensitive ecological approach, urban density in fact provides a sensible framework for production, consumption, energy, and transportation. Norwegian cities, which retain a human scale, provide great opportunities for an ecological transition—in marked contrast to the Norwegian countryside, where mountains, fjords, and long winters make rural settlements, with modern expectations of mobility and comfort, highly energy demanding.

Furthermore, city life provides stimuli for cultural enrichment. Not only do neighborhoods retain the possibilities for community development, by nurturing neighborhood identities and cultural autonomy, but the cross-cultural interchange that city life provides is crucial. Cities provide avenues for social and cultural mobility, and individuals can cross traditional dividing lines between cultural and subcultural identities. Despite the cultural impoverishment provided by the profit-oriented "culture industry" and its televised monoculture, these prospects remain vital.

Other opportunities also arise with larger scale. In a different social context I am sure cities would suggest exciting new collective solutions to the ecological challenges of our time. This is as true for Greece and Turkey as it is for Norway— or for Kenya and Indonesia for that matter. Still, any kind of ecological politics today must seek to restrict capitalist growth and ensure physical decentralization, at least of the megacities. But a refusal to accept capitalist urbanization and industrialization in no way implies denying people the benefits of modern life. Decent medicine and health care, and material security and well-being, as well as access to communication technologies and advanced infrastructure constitutes very real social advances. Indeed, these advances should be universalized—something that is not likely to occur within the orbit of the capitalist economic system.

The Urban and the Rural

Ever since the urban breakthrough in modern times, in the wake of the industrial revolution, the city has been pitted against the countryside. In order to avoid rampant urbanization's grave ecological and social consequences—its parasitical draining of natural resources as well as its socially corrosive effects—radical thinkers have long emphasized the need to strike a balance between the land and the city. The Enlightenment and industrialization, which were sorely needed to shed a feudal past unfortunately also destroyed traditional communities and alternative lifeways.

Interestingly, this modern conundrum finds some historical parallels in the nineteenth-century Russian political experience, as the intelligentsia attempted to understand modern civilization's Janus face. The tremendous material advances Europe experienced after the French revolution largely sidestepped Russia. The radical populism that emerged at mid-century was torn between the need to modernize and the desire to avoid the destruction that capitalism left in its wake, like poverty, intensified class divisions, and community breakdown. Thinkers like Alexander Herzen and Nicolay Chernyshevsky explored the possibilities that Russia might bypass capitalism altogether. By proposing to develop the Russian obschina, essentially a rural municipal organization, they hoped to integrate technological development and economic progress with egalitarian social organization. Here self-management could go hand in hand with fair and regular redistribution and access to common lands. The centrality of the issue for Russian radicals even persuaded Marx (as he expressed in personal correspondence to Vera

Zasulich) that Russia might indeed be able to avoid the "necessary stages" of historical development and develop an agrarian socialism. Later, of course, the Bolsheviks crushed and buried this populist vision, first through their appropriation of the state apparatus, then through forced collectivization, and finally through starvation and military repression, at a very high cost in lives.

But the challenge that those mid-century Russian radicals faced remains today, as the world's population continues to increase and ever larger areas are brought under capitalist control. Are there any credible possibilities to bypass capitalist modernity and build alternatives to it? Any ecology movement that takes solidarity and equality seriously today, as well as movements struggling to retain cultural autonomy and advance direct democracy, must face this pressing issue. Here the Kurdish movement seems to be in a unique and important position, facing challenges remarkably similar to those the Russian populists wrestled with under tsarism. Furthermore, their discussions are relevant not only for the ecology movement but also for any serious attempt to minimize the destructive social impact of contemporary urbanization. These challenges will remain decisive as we face not only population increase but an intensified urbanization in the decades and centuries ahead. Without credible political and economical alternatives to capitalism and its dynamic manufacture of needs and desires, it is hard to see how we can avoid intensified ecological crises and social conflicts.

Yet city life, as I mentioned, has deeply emancipatory aspects. Murray Bookchin formulated our challenge well when he discussed the prospects for a transition "from urbanization to cities." The challenge is less of how to strike a balance between town and country than to synthesize the truly progressive aspects of both processes. The agrarian revolution that made possible our historical development out of the natural world was followed by an equally important urban revolution. Both of these distinct phases of human historical development retain a profound meaning. We should be concerned, therefore, not only with diminishing their destructive aspects but with magnifying their progressive aspects. The cosmopolitan, civic, and genuinely social aspects of city life must be allowed to shape rural communities, and the communitarian sense of dimension and belonging must shape urban communities. We must find ways to bring the countryside into the city, and the city into the countryside. Only then can we hope to escape from the crass and atomizing consumer culture that is forced on us.

Cities can definitively be too big, but they can also be too small. While village and town communities provided a nutritious foundation for the cohesion of earlier human communities, they also nurtured a parochialism that has no place in a modern world. Our visions of a rural-urban reintegration and its ecological transformation properly entail a series of cultural changes. We need to become aware of our responsibilities as political and ecological agents. Any new politics must involve a radical transformation of our communities and our concept of citizenship. Cities emerged out of human communities, and they must be brought back into a communal context.

New Communal Structures

The reintegration of the city and the countryside—in fact, of society and nature—has crucial preconditions. Reshaping urban life will necessarily require immense environmental and infrastructural transformations, and social ecology suggests that ecological cities above all require new civic or communal structures. Let us briefly consider what they might be.

First, we must recreate the communal dimension of city life, and find the structural framework that might give cohesion and tangibility to cities that are small enough to be restructured politically. Today's urban entities, geared toward consumption and waste, are built around privatized, car-based traffic systems. Much twentieth-century architecture and infrastructure have all but crippled cities' capacity for human consociation. A new approach must be attentive to the fact that human beings need opportunities to meet and socialize and develop their capacities for responsible political agency. Only in the world's largest cities do the physical obstacles to the development of human communities and their ecological reintegration seem insurmountable. Still, even these cities may become decentralized, as Bookchin suggested, first institutionally and then later physically. Such decentralization would minimally imply building community centers in the neighborhoods, initiating more participatory forms of democracy, and creating an ecologically sensitive culture. We need new political institutions as well as new democratic procedures.

To this end, we need to reorient our technology and infrastructure to help our cities become communal. Denser housing and collective infrastructures provide great opportunities for an ecological approach to social development. Ironically, the very infrastructure that cripples our cities ecologically and culturally today may be retrofitted for an ecological transformation. Our cities could then become far more advanced eco-technologically than the countryside. Communication and infrastructural networks are already available, lacking only the decisive political will to put them to work to serve real ecological and social needs.

This transformation may seem far-fetched, and generating this political reorientation will be difficult if we ignore the economic dynamics that govern social development today. Lurking beneath discussions of contemporary urban issues is the need to rethink the economic system that frames urbanization processes. Although we want to retain and further many advances in technology, medicine, and goods, a fundamental reorientation toward local and regional production, refinement, and allocation of goods and services is an ecological imperative. Our economic system must be integrated into a bioregional framework and subjected to direct political control—not the other way around, as is the case today. Exactly what this will mean for a region like greater Oslo, or for Norway's rural municipalities and counties remains to be seen. The same goes for metropolises like Istanbul and even Diyarbakir, or for the large mountainous and rural regions of Kurdistan. A new social ecology movement must advance these perspectives politically—through plans, programs, initiatives, and projects on the local, regional, and interregional scale. Such a reorientation toward regional energy and food production, however, may be not only a political desideratum but an ecological necessity.

To regain control over our cities, we need to reclaim our commons. The ascendancy of capitalism has steadily eroded public ownership and control over common resources and goods. To ensure an ecological future, we have to go in the opposite direction. Against the privatization of public space and services, we must advocate direct popular control over them. Not only squares, streets, forests, and parks but also important public services and the means of production should properly be considered a shared heritage and responsibility. This involves neither state ownership nor nationalization but rather direct democracy and municipalization. We need to bring "fields, factories, and workshops" under public control. This age-old left-libertarian ideal attains a new ecological urgency as our cities rapidly outgrow "carrying capacity." Indeed, new direct-democratic communal structures may be the only means by which we can successfully curb the rapacious market and its anti-ecological thrust.

The Future of Cities

The future of humanity lies in the city—no doubt about it. But what kind of city life awaits us remains unclear. In today's affluent countries, urban entities are centers for waste production and excessive energy consumption, and they lay a parasitic claim to their environmental surroundings. Furthermore, poverty is now growing faster in urban than in rural areas. Today more than one billion people live in slums, which are overcrowded and heavily polluted, often lacking sanitation and clean water. This relentless drift into cities will not diminish in the years ahead. The UN expects that by 2050, 70 percent of the world's population will be urban, and that most urban growth will take place in "economically underdeveloped" countries in Africa and Asia.

In order to face the tremendous ecological challenges wrought upon us by capitalist hyperproductivity and unfettered urbanization, we must rethink and regenerate the civic structures that undergird our cities. A democratic and ecological approach would have to be concerned with bringing communes back into cities. Creating meaningful urban communities is as important to ecological transformation as is physically restructuring urban infrastructure. Social ecology suggests that any attempt to achieve ecological or social change must confront the political challenge of urban community: it must, above all, find its expression in a new politics for political emancipation and urban regeneration.

Editorial Comment

This article was written for the Turkish radical journal *Dipnot* No. 8 (2012). See more: www.dipnotdergisi.com.

The Significance of the City for Social Ecology

Giorgos Papahristodoulou

Translation by Yavor Tarinski

IN THE WORK OF Murray Bookchin, the founder of social ecology, we often find the term "*polis*," a word which translates as "city" in ancient Greek. Bookchin's use of "*polis*" is not rooted in an obsession with antiquity typical of those who view historical phenomena as the triumph of ruling classes. For Bookchin, the emergence of the *polis* represents a turning point in historical evolution. In the City, the individual finally found a space where she or he could form political relations that did not rest on blood ties or a shared connection to an ethnicity or village. As Bookchin notes in *Remaking Society*, "[t]he city increasingly replaced the biological fact of lineage, and the accident of birth into a particular kin group, by the social fact of residence and economic interests."

The emergence of the City in ancient Greece was marked by a creative breach in human history. This shift is attested to in the legal institutions, as well as a rich cultural landscape in the arts and the life of cities, places, and monuments. It was a creative break, centered around the Mediterranean, which brought the City and democracy to the forefront of history. This growth was accompanied by a social evolution, three aspects of which are particularly relevant today:

1) The sense and demand of universal equality or, as Bookchin notes, "the notion that people were basically alike, irrespective of their tribal and village ancestry."

2) The emergence of an individual right and social mobility: "people were not simply born into a distinct social condition; in varying degrees they could begin to choose and change their social condition."

3) An expansion of the urban community. The "the stranger or 'outsider' could find a secure place in a large community of human beings," even if such inclusion was incomplete for many parties.

Through these developments, key social institutions were reproduced. Direct democratic structures offered individual and collective self-realization through the participation of the citizenry in decision-making and social control. The City cultivated responsibility and outlined—with the imperfections that characterize every social institution—the meaning of the citizen.

This process of social evolution did not occur overnight. Nor did it indicate an end to history, as many thinkers and regimes have heralded in the past. Like a diligent farmer, the ancient Greeks planted a seed—a seed that was re-fertilized centuries later in medieval cities, specifically those of the fourteenth century. Later, another road appeared, that of the self-governance and federation of free municipalities to challenge the emerging Nation-State, with the latter prevailing in the nineteenth century by means of fire and iron. Today, however, statecraft is once again being challenged by societies on a global scale, by experiences such as those of the Zapatistas in Chiapas and the Kurds of Rojava.

The medieval flourishing of free municipalities (again, the Mediterranean remained at the heart of this process) was the age of *civitas*. *Civitas*, another favourite word of Bookchin's, evokes the association of free peoples which the cold, statistical definition of the City as *urbs* (a sum of buildings) cannot capture. Swiss thinker Jean-Jacques Rousseau (1712–1778) observed that houses make a settlement (the town complex), but only citizens can form a city, echoing the ancient Greek ἄνδρες γαρ η πόλις ("the people are the city").

Let us examine one of the values of the medieval epoch, a value that is transformed into a virtue.[1] It is the concept of the citizen's self-limitation, which results from a deep sense of commitment and moral dedication to the political community, a phenomenon that we also find in the ancient Greek *polis*. Bookchin writes:

> Medieval Italian cities, for example, created remarkable checks and balances to prevent one interest in the city from gaining too much ascendancy over another, a balance that the Greek *polis* had established earlier in antiquity. Self-restraint, dignity, courtesy, and a strong commitment to civic decorum were part of the psychological attributes that many precapitalist cities, structured around assemblies, actually translated into institutions in a system of checks that fostered harmony. As for the essence of the concept of the citizen, the citizen of a precapitalist democratic city, in short, was not the "constituent" of a parliamentary representative, or a mere "taxpayer," to use modern civic jargon. He was, in the best of cases, a knowledgeable, civically dedicated, active, and, above all, self-governing being who exercised considerable inner discipline and made the welfare of his community—its general interest—his primary interest to the exclusion of his own self-interest.

What Bookchin outlines in this description of the medieval "self-governing being" is of significant importance to contemporary efforts at reclaiming the ideal of the citizen. The citizen is a participant in decision-making, primarily in the realm of the City, who refuses to perceive human beings, as well as nature, as mere numbers or tools in the service of "developmental" models. This ideal citizen is quite different from the resident of the modern metropolis. This latter lifestyle brings the feeling of anonymity coupled with high-speed transportation, pushing erstwhile citizens to wander around the world, moving from place to place, easily exploitable by market forces.

The City held the promise of overcoming the physical labour that characterized life in the countryside, especially before the latter underwent technological modernization. The City held the promise of individual and collective security, a promise that was quickly superceded by the rising exploitation of the industrial proletariat under capitalism. In the rural-to-urban transition, a deep sense of discomfort developed, captured in the videography of the time,[2] fuelling the social movements of the 1960s. These movements criticized the dominant model, whether Western or state capitalist, and refused to understand production and the economy as the central meaning of life itself.

Yet, paralleling the dissidence generated by the 1960s was a contradictory tendency of so-called suburbanization. The growth of the suburbs diffused the metropolitan spirit into the rural/semi-urban space. This diffusion had degenerate characteristics. It altered nature by turning it into a commodity for consumer needs. The landscape was transformed into a plot based on the quantitative measurements that could be found on topographic maps. Neglected were concerns for the fertility of seeds, which, sprinkled with the gold dust of chemical farming flowing from globalized production chains, imposed a burden on the climate and on the income of farmers in other countries.

From this context emerged the questions posed by Bookchin in his 1973 book, *The Limits of the City*, where he deconstructs modern urban planning in the service of Capital and State bureaucracy. He proposes, instead, the eco-community. He asks: "Do these present forms of urbanization indicate a conservative, closed-minded, retreat to nature? Do they refuse enlightenment rationality, the democratic ideal, and, ultimately, nature itself? Do they inspire the view of nature as a 'blind world' dominated by authoritarian relations, such as the famous 'right of the strongest' (a metaphor from the human world), ignoring its tendency for diversity and stability?"

From this brief historical overview of the evolution of the City, one can begin to understand the City as a rich system of cultural meaning. The City is not a sum of buildings, but something which human beings experience as a potential space of freedom, political decision-making, and creation—a place for the development of human and natural potential. The City's development cannot progress under the dominant imaginary that glorifies the unlimited expansion of the so-called forces of production, a point on which, despite their partial differences, the tendencies of Marxism and economic liberalism both agree. Nor is it enough for economic degrowth to magically challenge hierarchical social relations.[3]

Aristotle suggests that "nature is an end in itself." In his *Politics*, when writing about the City, he also argues that when someone, because of his nature (not due to accidental circumstances), happens to be without a *polis*, they are inferior to common beasts. These reference to the self-limitation of the person in relation to nature and the City (as opposed to Descartes' position on the need to become "masters and possessors of nature") offers a rational foundation for the City.

Liberated from the chains of profit, extra-social power, and hierarchical organization, building an ecological society remains at the core of reinvigorating the *polis*. The new forms of self-governance at the level of towns, cities, and neighbourhoods emerging worldwide in recent years have the opportunity to tap into the historical heritage of the ancient Greek city and the free medieval municipalities. They also have a wealth of modern history to draw from, from the Paris Commune (1871), to the Spanish Revolution (1936–1939), to the experiences of new social movements that have their roots in the 1960s, as well as the social experiments of the Zapatistas (1994–the present), and the revolutionaries of north-eastern Syria (2011–the present). To function, modern urban communities need to be small, autonomous, and based on direct democracy. This structure will provide the necessary framework for citizens to self-manage the current issues of housing, nutrition, education, communications, water and energy networks, mobility, public space, and so on. The modern megacities of electronic surveillance and mass control, dressed in the promise of a "smart" life, make moving beyond the State and the capitalist market more necessary than ever, particularly in the face of the shocking mismanagement of the climate crisis by authoritarian political and economic elites.

In 1985, Bookchin wrote in *Rethinking Ethics, Nature, and Society*:

> To be sure, the municipality's capacity to play a historic role in changing society today depends on the extent to which it can shake off the state institutions that have infiltrated it: its mayoralty structure's civic bureaucracy, and its own professionalized monopoly on violence. Rescued from these institutions, however, it retains the historic materials and political culture that can pit it against the nation-state and the cancerous corporate world that threatens to digest social life as such.

Direct democratic politics on the municipal level have been replaced by the world of "representation," privileges, and professionalized decision-makers. The challenge for local movements has been to reclaim power from the State, the Market, and their mechanisms.

The experiences of freedom created by grassroots citizen movements across the globe interact with space and its inequalities. Space is not neutral—it reflects the dominant social relationships and power distribution that exist within our societies. Yet space is, at the same time, open by its nature—constantly changing, on the move. Its transformation into an ecological and democratic city depends on the attitude of citizens. Certainly, such an attitude must be from the City, in the City, with the City.

NOTES

1. Virtue is a value embodied in action. For example there is justice as an ideal and then there is the just person.

2. For example, in neo-Greek cinema of the sixties such as Alexis Damianou's *Until the Ship* (1966) or the films of Dinou Katsouridi, featuring the great actor Thanassis Veggos.

3. "Today, of course, economic growth searches for a sign, mainly in order to exist, while in the past it searched for a way to globalize, while its opponents limited themselves to alternative versions of it. Then (1970) Cornelius Castoriadis formulated its negation as its destruction. He refuted every kind of economic growth. He positioned it as the hegemonic narrative of the dominant system. A system which defends rationality, meaning the rationality of the system. A supposedly self-evident hegemony. Castoriadis does not speak of some 'other' economy, but of its limitation and its subjugation to the rest of human activities." Nikos Ioannou, Beyond Degrowth, *Babylonia Journal* Vol. 17. See: https://www.babylonia.gr/2015/08/31/pera-apo-tin-apoanaptixi/.

On Hannah Arendt and Murray Bookchin: Bridging Intellectual Legacies

Jason Toney

> *Bureaucracy is the form of government in which everybody is deprived of political freedom, of the power to act; for the rule by Nobody is not no-rule, and where all are equally powerless, we have a tyranny without a tyrant.*
> — HANNAH ARENDT, *ON VIOLENCE*

> *Every revolution evaporates and leaves behind only the slime of a new bureaucracy.*
> — FRANZ KAFKA

THE INTELLECTUAL LEGACIES of two preeminent thinkers for our times, Murray Bookchin and Hannah Arendt, have regrettably garnered limited comparative analysis. While there can be no doubt that Arendt's influence has expanded dramatically in recent decades, Bookchin's body of work has also attracted impressive and diverse interest, especially among the Kurdish people. There may be some value in measuring an intellectual legacy by web searches or the person's number of citations to determine the extent of their influence, but my purpose is to more explicitly carry forward the work of bridging these intellectual legacies and encourage others to do the same.

I attempt this by first examining Bookchin's reading of Hannah Arendt, whom he cites in several books in essays. In particular, I explore his critique and reformulation of her tripartite distinction between public, private, and social realms. Second, I examine the striking similarities in their broad conception of the history and role of council democracy. Bookchin's work provides a roadmap for realizing democracy in action, but Arendt's more strictly theoretical investigation still echoes in harmony. Third, I give care to contemporary thought and social movements that are influenced by both Bookchin and Arendt. To think about Arendt and Bookchin in parallel will be key for activists and scholars invested in fortifying the theoretical frameworks for the 21st-century social movements that confront multiple life-threatening existential crises. Among these threats are nuclear catastrophe, ecological collapse—which should be thought to include the threat of infectious disease and superbugs—and the rise of certain technologies like artificial intelligence.

While Bookchin read Arendt's work, I can find no evidence that the reverse is true. Across his body of work, Bookchin cites parts of Arendt's *The Human Condition* and *On Revolution* and names her influence or relevance in many of his essays and books. This is notable because Bookchin is not always exhaustive in naming his references. Bookchin had immense respect and admiration for Arendt. In *Urbanization Without Cities*, he refers to her as a "highly gifted political philosopher."[1] Immediately after this remark, a type of overt praise that is uncommon in his writing, he launches into a criticism of her framing of public, private, and social realms. Bookchin argues that Arendt's distinction between a political and social realm "allows for very little difference between political activity and statecraft."[2] Bookchin argues that the State has merged so thoroughly with politics, "institutionally and functionally," that the two are indistinguishable.[3] This observation is reflected in popular political speech. Rarely, if ever, do we hear of any distinctions between politics and statecraft even in anti-statist-oriented news media. In response to this situation, Bookchin proposes a new formulation of human arenas: "social, political, and 'statified.'"[4] This division requires Bookchin to absorb the private realm into the nebulous social realm. At the same time, he agrees with Marx and Arendt that the private realm is a "realm of necessity," and that it requires special protections. In this way, the private realm remains a distinct space in Bookchin's imagination, but a now unnamed one. It's in this sense that he does not reject Arendt's formulation, and why his reformulation is partly incomplete, although he does seem to recognize this (as I will explore later). Bookchin aims to carve out the theoretical space for the "statified realm," which he sees as not only threatening the other realms but also conjuring new ground to stand all on its own through its vast apparatus of tools he refers to as statecraft. Not only does statecraft carve out its own statified realm, it effectively expands and overtakes the social and public realms. The implications of this expansion are grave and constitute an increasingly common phenomenon in our time.

Arendt thought of her three realms as real, physical spaces—not merely categories. She viewed the intrusion of the State, of bureaucracy, of the centralization of power as threats not to the physical public space itself, but to the possibilities this public realm provides for realizing action, speech, and freedom within that space. In most so-called democracies today, the *polis* has no place to appear beyond the voting booth. Real democracy requires spaces for collective action. Today, people take to the streets in protest or engage in civil disobedience to express political aims in public, but these are typically outbursts—temporary and unsustained. Without the formal establishment of a public space to take action, freedom itself has no place to appear.[5] This is at the heart of why Arendt argues that the greatest failure of most revolutions is their inability to institutionalize spaces for freedom to appear, manifest most clearly in the form of participatory assemblies.

Bookchin's reformulation of Arendt's public, private, and social realms hinges on making these realms transcendent rather than physical. Bookchin's contribution provides us with another lens to examine Arendt's realms. His addition of the statified realm helps us understand that more than intrude on existing realms, the State has managed to carve out its own space through its vast bureaucracies, undemocratic institutions, and industrial complexes. Rather than reject Bookchin's more transcendental view in favor of Arendt's more physical one or vice versa, the coalescence of these ideas provides us with a more robust toolkit to examine and identify the rise of totalitarianism and the assault on essential spaces for being human. To be clear and fair, Bookchin does not wholesale reject the physicality of these spaces despite his suggestion in *Urbanization Without Cities*. In *The Ecology of Freedom*, Bookchin recognizes the physical space required for freedom to appear. He notes that the *agora* or the *polis* itself was where freedom could appear, and he cites Arendt again when he makes this note.[6] The public, private, and social realms, for both Arendt and Bookchin, are essentially in an endless game of tug-of-war, insofar as they have the potential of being dominated by the State, rather than being spaces which facilitate the *vita activa*: work, labor, and action. Arendt calls these opposed forces "competitors for public power."[7] Politics is the antonym of statecraft; bureaucracy and the professionalization of politics eliminate and overtake spaces for freedom.

Bookchin and Arendt came to their ideas from very different backgrounds and training in political philosophy, but both are defined by their dedication to the life of the mind, as well as their willingness to change course and go against the grain of their contemporaries. Bookchin was an avowed critic of Heidegger—one might say he was dismissive—whereas Arendt not only studied with him but also had a partnership. One could elaborate at length about biographical and intellectual differences, but it does not take away from the striking similarity in their conception, broadly speaking, of council democracy. They both critically admired and studied ancient Athenian rule by the *demos*, New England town meetings, *soviets*, the Bavarian Council Republic's räterpublik, the Hungarian Worker Councils of 1919 and 1956, and many other municipal council systems throughout history. We would be remiss to leave their insights to isolated silos.

Decentralized, face-to-face, direct democratic structures are tentpoles in Arendt and Bookchin's imaginations on freedom. Arendt argues that the revolutionary moments in which people experienced freedom and "public happiness"[8] came when these forms of self-governance arose. Sometimes these institutions arose rapidly, in the context of violence and the absence of other powers or institutions, and they held brief but significant degrees of power. However, Arendt explains that not violence but power creates lasting revolutionary change. Arendt thought that violence was sometimes justified, that it could create positive change, but that "it pays indiscriminately."[9] Political violence entails unintended consequences. Roger Berkowitz explains that "for Arendt, 'violence does not promote causes, neither history nor revolution, neither progress nor reaction.' All that violence can do is make injustice visible. When it seeks to do more, the most probable result is not justice but 'a more violent world.'"[10] For Arendt, that's why violence ought only to be used, if at all, to pursue short-term goals. Violence itself is too limited a scope to see revolution through. Instead, lasting revolutionary change comes through the cultivation of power from the bottom-up. When revolutionary political movements fail to create space within the public realm to facilitate this power and instead rely on violence, like Robespierre, an attempt at liberation is doomed to fail. In a letter to James Baldwin, Arendt describes how the best qualities that arise out of oppressed people, "their beauty, their capacity for joy, their warmth, and their humanity," never survive "the hour of liberation by even five minutes."[11] Capturing the spirit of a revolutionary movement, which is the result of the action of the oppressed, requires spaces for those people to express their power. History's most radical revolutionary bodies are often extremely short-lived. The Paris Commune lasted a couple of months and Hungary's Republic of Councils in 1919 lasted only 133 days. The challenge of establishing long-term real democracy is rarely if ever achieved. Arendt believed that the unique circumstances surrounding the founding of the United States led to a somewhat longer establishment of real democracy, but it was imperilled by the lack of constitutional protection for Township councils or Jefferson's notion of a ward system. Jefferson imagined another branch of government: a decentralized, municipal-based, and confederated system of town meetings across the US. As quickly as true democracy appears, without an institutional framework to protect it, it will not only disappear but be overtaken.

Bookchin's vision of libertarian municipalism[12] reads, in some ways, as a direct response to many of the problems Arendt rightly identifies in the revolutionary process. Bookchin wrote that libertarian municipalism is "a revolutionary effort in which freedom is given institutional form in public assemblies that become decision-making bodies."[13] Again, this was not an altogether new formulation—the idea of public assemblies, as has been stated, has a rich history. In a sense, both Arendt and Bookchin are conservative, insofar as they want to restore more just forms of governance rooted in examples from the past. But Bookchin's statement almost reads like a direct response to Arendt because it attempts to address the exact issues she raises. Libertarian municipalism maintains that democratic power, and the institutions that facilitate it, ought to be cultivated now. We ought not wait for a revolutionary moment, but rather build power where we are and work towards linking these place-based power centers. This is the essence of dual power— building power alongside the State, intruding on its territory, taking back ground lost to the statified realm.

In her Preface to *Between Past and Future*, Arendt discusses the "lost treasure" of the council tradition: public happiness. She cites the French poet and member of the French Resistance, René Char, who said "*Notre héritage n'est précédé d'aucun testament*" (our inheritance was left to us by no testament). She says it is "perhaps the strangest of the strangely abrupt aphorisms" written by him, but it "compressed the gist of what four years in the *résistance* had come to mean to a whole generation."[14] When the Third Republic collapsed, these *révolutionnaires* were suddenly in charge of a public realm and inherited this newfound power and freedom without a "pre-established framework of reference" to guide them.[15] Bookchin's vision of libertarian municipalism is an attempt to link, temporally, the moments before and after the hour of liberation and provide a framework of reference to give freedom not only space to appear but to last.

Arendt and Bookchin's ideas are crystallized in an essay entitled, "Reimagining Revolutionary Organizing: A Vision of Dual Power." The essay was written by a group that would later found Symbiosis, "a confederation of community organizations across North America."[16] Using an Arendtian framework to describe power, they argue for a Bookchinian strategy to establish a form of libertarian municipalism through building dual power. They begin from Arendt's premise that "intolerable situations such as ours could be cast aside by the public's revolutionary withdrawal of support from governing institutions."[17] Using Bookchin's framework, they argue that for such a withdrawal to be successful requires a "preformation of a postrevolutionary society," meaning the establishment of participatory institutions before any major power shifts occur.[18] While the actual impact of Symbiosis cannot yet be appropriately judged, their essay marks an important step forward in the bridging of these thinkers.

There is great value to reading Arendt through the lens of social ecology, the field Bookchin helped forge.[19] For instance, in her essay on "The Conquest of Space and the Stature of Man," the question she addresses, "'has man's conquest of space increased or diminished his stature?'"[20] resembles various questions asked in the social ecology tradition. Arendt's answer necessarily touches on the relationship of society and technology to our environment—or the built (human-made) and unbuilt (natural) worlds.[21] In her concluding remarks on this question, Arendt says that "we have found a way to act on the earth as though we disposed of terrestrial nature from outside."[22] To highlight this absurd circumstance, she writes that "from a sufficient distance, the cars in which we travel and which we know we built ourselves will look as though they were, as Heisenberg once put it, 'as inescapable a part of ourselves as the snail's shell is to its occupant.' All our pride in what we can do will disappear."[23] A society so detached from nature, that views everything through a scientific worldview, will lead us to see more things on the ground, on earth, like a photograph of a mine by the Canadian photographer Edward Burtysnky. Despite being defined by its extractivist, destructive, human-made elements, from a certain vantage point as the one Burtynsky chooses, the mine appears to be a beautiful creation of the natural world in which humans played no role. When you look more carefully at Burtynsky's mine, you begin to notice the ladders and tool boxes scattered around. After a certain length of time, the mine loses its beauty, and the reality of its creation sets in. This resembles Arendt's astronaut, in their attempt to escape the human world of Earth, they end up in a vessel surrounded entirely by manmade things. Even looking out into the vastness of space, the astronaut will catch a glimpse of the reflection of his gadgets' blinking lights behind him. All of this is strikingly captured in Bookchin's statement:

> Humanity has passed through a long history of one-sidedness and of a social condition that has always contained the potential of destruction, despite its creative achievements in technology. The great project of our time must be to open the other eye: to see all-sidedly and wholly, to heal and transcend the cleavage between humanity and nature that came with early wisdom.[24]

There is a danger to being deceived by the allures of technology, but also to becoming a Luddite. There is a danger to being anti-scientific, but also to viewing the world through a strictly scientific lens.

Arendt and Bookchin would not have thought that "man was the highest being there is" like the Romans, partly expressed in the word *humanitas*.[25] They would agree with Aristotle's assessment of that belief as being "*atapos* or 'absurd.'"[26] However, they both held as true that the human spirit, our capacity for thought and action, was more than worth fighting for and protecting. The value of bridging the intellectual legacies of Bookchin and Arendt cannot be understated. Together, these thinkers help us more clearly perceive the obstacles to freedom and provide us with a framework for confronting them. They both soberly understood the fragility of our built world. It is increasingly clear that the failure to meet the challenges of our time could be world-ending. Taken together, Bookchin and Arendt show us a path forward.

REFERENCES

Arendt, Hannah. "The Meaning of Love in Politics: A Letter by Hannah Arendt to James Baldwin." 1962. <http://www.hannaharendt.net/index.php/han/article/view/95/156>.

Arendt, Hannah. *Between Past and Future*. Edited by Jerome Kohn. New York: Penguin Classics, 2006.

Arendt, Hannah. *On Revolution*. New York: Penguin Classics, 2006.

Arendt, Hannah. *The Human Condition*. Chicago: The University of Chicago Press, 1958.

Berkowitz, Roger. "The Power Behind the Revolution." Hannah Arendt Center, 2020. https://hac.bard.edu/amor-mundi/the-power-behind-the-revolution-2020-06-04

Berkowitz, Roger. *The Perils of Invention: Lying, Technology, and the Human Condition*. Montreal: Black Rose Books, 2021.

Bookchin, Murray. *The Ecology of Freedom: The Emergence and Dissolution of Hierarchy*. Chico: AK Press, 2005.

Bookchin, Murray. *The Next Revolution*. London: Verso Press, 2015.

Bookchin, Murray. *Urbanization Without Cities: The Rise and Decline of Citizenship*, (Montreal: Black Rose Books, 1992).

Colón, Herson-Hord, Horvath, Martindale, & Porges. "Reimagining Revolutionary Organizing: A Vision of Dual Power." *Perspectives on Anarchist Theory*. 2017.

Symbiosis. "Vision and Strategy." 2019. https://www.symbiosis-revolution.org

NOTES

1. Murray Bookchin, *Urbanization Without Cities* (Montreal: Black Rose Books, 1992), 53.

2. Bookchin, *Urbanization*, 53.

3. Bookchin, *Urbanization*, 53

4. Bookchin, *Urbanization*, 53

5. Hannah Arendt, *Between Past and Future* (New York: Penguin Classics, 2006), 258.

6. Murray Bookchin, *The Ecology of Freedom* (Chico: AK Press, 2005), 178.

7. Hannah Arendt, *On Revolution* (New York: Penguin Classics, 2006), 249.

8. It is useful to note that this is a term Arendt uses to describe the state of the citizens who participate in democratic systems. The state of public happiness is often used in contradistinction to the state of private misery, which is not merely defined by miserable material conditions, but an inability to take action to change one's social, political, and private conditions. She calls public happiness the 'lost treasure' of the council tradition.

9. Roger Berkowitz, "The Power Behind the Revolution," Hannah Arendt Center, 2020.

10. Roger Berkowitz, "The Power Behind the Revolution."

11. Hannah Arendt, "The Meaning of Love in Politics: A Letter by Hannah Arendt to James Baldwin," 1962.

12. Libertarian municipalism has come to be variously known as new municipalism, radical municipalism, and several other names.

13. Murray Bookchin, *The Next Revolution* (London: Verso Press, 2015), 96.

14. Arendt, *Between Past and Future*, 3.

15. Arendt, *Between Past and Future*, 5.

16. Symbiosis, "Vision and Strategy," 2019, <https://www.symbiosis-revolution.org/>.

17. Colón, Herson-Hord, Horvath, Martindale, & Porges, "Reimagining Revolutionary Organizing: A Vision of Dual Power," *Perspectives on Anarchist Theory,* 2017, 2.

18. Colón et al., 3.

19. In an effort to forge a stronger relationship between the Bookchin and Arendt worlds, Black Rose Books is working with the Hannah Arendt Center at Bard College to publish *The Perils of Invention: Lying, Technology, and the Human Condition* (2021).

20. Arendt, *Between Past and Future,* 260.

21. This useful formulation is used to great effect by the American multi-disciplinary artist Phil Elverum.

22. Arendt, *Between Past and Future,* 272.

23. Arendt, *Between Past and Future,* 274.

24. Bookchin, *The Ecology of Freedom,* 152.

25. Arendt, *Between Past and Future,* 260.

26. Arendt, *Between Past and Future.*

Can Cyborgs Dream of Social Ecology?

Nikos Vrantsis

A RECENT STUDY published in the journal of the American Philosophical Association examined the hypothesis of extended cognition, according to which external devices such as smartphones should be considered part of our cognitive processes. The essay reaches a rather radical conclusion, proposing for devices to be legally and ethically treated not as mere objects but as extensions of the body.

It is obvious that our devices are more than just objects. The psychological and biological transformations brought upon us by cybercapitalism pose ontological questions. Our personal and collective histories are encapsulated and archived into devices, SIM cards, hard drives, and clouds.

Some thinkers now argue that, when we die, our digital devices should be handled as remains that can help to reassemble our traces and reconstitute our post-mortem digital identity. Others, concerned of the judicial innovations needed for justice to adapt to our brave new world, suggest that trashing someone's smartphone should be seen as a form of "extended assault," equivalent to a blow to the head, rather than just the destruction of property.

These philosophical, scientific, and judicial questions reveal the seismic impact that technological omnipresence brings upon the very perception of our selves and our societies. What is now their focal point is not the Cartesian "Ego" but a self on technical support, a mixture of biology and technology, a being that resembles a cyborg rather than a human.

What is striking is that this particular technological progress of global cybercapitalism is welcomed as a natural phenomenon or a predetermined progress that is not to be questioned; it is not technology that needs to adapt to our constituted discursive systems, but rather the systems that must adapt in order to embrace technological determinism. The absence of any interrogation as to whether technology has actually been serving societal ideals is due to the inherited poverty of such ideals. Any cyber innovation is welcomed as long as it serves the production of profit and commodification of everything; the current form of cybermonarchism is compatible with the predominant cultural logic of neoliberalism and its objectives. A cyborg is the product of that process, as we inhabit the hyper-real scene of images and spectacles and a world treated as a sum of data.

Murray Bookchin was one rare exception of skepticism in the general atmosphere formed by unapologetic evangelists of technological progress. Far from being a luddite, he was rightly questioning how technology is incorporated into societies, for what purpose, and with what side-effects. He foresaw the potent relation between technological progress and extensive hierarchies of extractive consumer capitalism. He foresaw how technological innovation could be transformed into a more refined tool of exploitation, manipulated by an ideology of unrestrained and unregulated competition in the pursuit of profit and power at the expense of democracy, society, individuals, and the environment.

> I feel that we are confronted with a revolution of monumental importance and while this revolution is in the hands of capital and the state, its impacts upon society could very well be devastating. I cannot foresee that it will benefit human society or the ecology of our planet as much as it will be utilized for domination and hierarchy, which is what technological innovation, to one extent or another, has always been utilized for.[1]

Far from being a neutral force to bring universal reason to our unreasonable world, cybercapitalism has produced the means of global transmission of fake news, hate speech, and conspiracy theories facilitated by algorithms to reach manufactured audiences. Computation was a prerequisite for the financialization of capital that now moves unrestrained, able to manipulate the political hardware that needs to be upgraded in cyber-Darwinian terms. States and cities become agents of this de-territorialized force that dictates the course of actions to be followed at the expense of human, social, labour, and environmental rights. Political parties can no longer articulate a vision that goes beyond balanced budgets, structural reforms, and austerity measures to please the standards set by hedge funds and markets. Cities are no longer the *genii locorum* of modernity; they are diminished into landscapes of spectacle and a cluster of Instagrammable sites for touristic consumption. Official institutions are now pawns in a geo-Darwinian arena, doing whatever it takes to attract unrestrained investors in an extremely competitive environment. Geo-Darwinism is the atmosphere that dictates institutional adaptation, just like Darwinism is the ideological atmosphere that engenders individualism.

Bookchin was much more than a thinker reflecting on the impact of cybercapitalism. What makes his corpus and thought a nodal point of reference in critical theory is his attempt to challenge the epistemological hegemonism of Darwinism that privileges the self-interest of individuals and institutions.

Neoliberalism is another episode in the series of generalized competition, forcing a struggle for the symbolic and literal survival of the fittest. However, for Bookchin, Darwinism is not the moral tale nature provided to humanity but rather a projection of our societies onto nature; it is the narrative that we chose to listen to, silencing all other narratives. We must here emphasize that the idea of dominating nature has its primary source in the domination of human by human and in the structuring of the natural world into a hierarchical chain of being.[2]

To counter social Darwinism's focus on the individual struggle of species to fit into a competitive environment, he focuses on the ideals of collaboration and diversity as being necessary to sustain an ecosystem as a whole. Even though, to him, nature is neither moral nor immoral, he considered our choice of narrative crucial for the quality of our social formations and relational constructions. His narrative of social ecology counters competition as the undisputed element that defines every face of nature: the Promethean quest of using technology to dominate nature is replaced by the ecological ethic of using technology to harmonize humanity's relationship with nature.[3]

Our questions need to go beyond the proposal to adapt our judicial codes in order to treat someone who breaks a smartphone and wipes its contents as if they had caused their victim a head trauma. I propose that we should articulate more fundamental questions about the epistemological basis of the cybercapitalistic dogma and its cost to our already deficient democratic systems, on societies, people, and the environment.

It would not be meaningless to explore these questions according to the criteria set by traditional liberal thought itself. The messengers of cybercapitalism always refer back to the sacred liberal discourse of individual rights. However, a careful philosophical interrogation might reveal how cybercapitalism and the neoliberal turn are inconsistent with the fundamentals even of liberal thinking. This system cannot hold even when evaluated according to the criteria it has set for itself. Privacy, the buzzword and sacred concept of traditional liberal thought, is violated not by a French or Spanish monarch or a totalitarian state, but by the intrusion of spectacle through devices that compel us to feed, with data and power, an oligopoly of massive tech players. One the other hand, technological omnipresence constructs a particular digital public world with envy, jealousy, competition, and unrestrained consumption. This destruction of the public sphere has an unprecedented ontological impact. To Bookchin, the individual without the opportunity to exercise self-administration in the public sphere suffers an attrition not only of self-consciousness but also of selfhood: the shrivelling of the public sphere is followed by the shrivelling of the private sphere—that inviolable area which is presumably the last refuge of the individual in an overly centralized and bureaucratized society. The ego, increasingly desiccated by the aridity of the social sphere, becomes fitting material for mass culture, stereotyped responses, and a preoccupation with trivia.[4]

Cybercapitalism has given way to what we can, at all rights now, call cyber-monarchism. Cybermonarchism requires full attention and personal engagement, constantly surveils us and reshapes even the most private of our private time. Devices exercise brain functions and occasionally replace them. They "know" with whom we speak, when we speak to them, what we said, where we have been, our purchases, photos, biometric data, even our notes to ourselves—and all this reaching back for years. Our ever-available profiles narrate the story of ourselves, our walls are where we publish our emotions, our apps trace our transactions, monitor our meetings, store our memories, map our tastes and preferences, and prefabricate the content we should be looking for. Privacy is no longer a reflective space-time, but rather a continuation of spectacular intrusion. We are nurtured in our isolated cyberbubbles that sustain technological monopolies. Our devices are hardware for the hegemony of a software that does not simply please desires but prefabricates these desires, teaching isolated cyborg-beings what to desire and how to desire it.

The digital sphere is a hyper-real world that has substituted the actual one. Cybertech, no matter the initial intentions, has become a means to create a monoculture of cloned individuals reproduced to infinity. This prevailing force rearranges the meaning of the previous systems, melts down limits, and rewrites the codes of subjects, objects, symbols, and the relation between them. It has incorporated everything and has colonized even the dreaming life of the population. Architectural hybridism, the melting down of the distinction between left and right in traditional politics, the commodification of political struggle, the blurring of the limits between individual privacy and publicity, are all phenomena of the rewritten codes of reality.

Even rage has given way to hopelessness, the defining emotion of a generation whose every move is anticipated, tracked, bought, and sold before it even happens. For now, we all know that we are just another piece of spectacle, that every move is a cliché scripted in advance; even acknowledging this is a cliché. Innovation is no longer possible. All that is left is to imitate dead styles and practices.

Mass spectacle, facilitated by cybermonarchism, tragically affects our linguistic skills as well. The cultural production of this generation suffers from linguistic poverty, a phenomenon that is better described not as dyslexia rather as post-lexia.[5] The speed of visual sequences, the bombarding of pictures—hyperreality has nurtured a generation that can fully process visual data without being able to articulate words. A slogan is more efficient in this fast-paced digital world. But in the lack of language we lack the understanding of what is happening to us and the world around us.

We lack even the most elemental skill that defines us as humans: self-reflection. What is considered as sacred for liberal traditional thought, the "Ego," is now being lost. The Hellenic interpretation of "human" as self-consciousness and self-realization in the private sphere of life recurs throughout Western thought from Descartes to the contemporary existentialists. A highly individualistic subjectivism is the intellectual hallmark of philosophy in the modern era.[6]

In cybermonarchism, the sacred "ego" of liberalism is narrowed down to three interrelated subjects: producers of data, creators of content, and consumers of prefabricated desires in a digital social sphere sustained by envy. This subject no longer has control over its own private thoughts. It identifies itself through its right to provoke envy. A self that is narrowed down solely to these neoliberal subjectifications cannot be politically active, socially present, and self-conscious. Even ideas and thoughts of subversive qualities are assimilated by this massive system and are transformed into commodities. Uprising is transformed into spectacle, poverty into commodity, violence into noir fiction, revolution into a performance, alternativeness into trendy neighbourhoods, punk and hip-hop into merchandise.

Revisiting Bookchin's corpus may help one grasp the connection between the technological omnipresence and the enormous poverty of the self. Eventually, the rise of crypto-fascist tendencies within the tech industry bears witness to the failures of the "digital revolution" whose promises never came to pass. Following Bookchin's line of thought, we can start to question the human, social, political, and environmental cost brought by this technological omnipresence and its unapologetic hegemony. And despite the fact that such a critique of cybermonarchism and neoliberalism, according to their own liberal criteria, is not what Bookchin was engaged in, this is the outcome of the problem of scale that he thoroughly examined in industralized, centralized capitalist modernity.

We, the disillusioned masses, are (facing) the results of a bankrupt project that can no longer conceal the side effects of its total domination—and we are looking for alternatives. Environmental catastrophe is one such side effect. It might seem as though climate change and the threat of resource-depletion are not being concealed so much as incorporated into marketing culture. However, the relationship between techno-capitalism and eco-disaster is neither coincidental nor accidental, neither is it going to be solved by any apps. The sequence of images and lifestyles on social platforms require an aggressive exploitation of natural resources. We must deal with the fact that the future of our planet is one of social extremes. Either society will be totally restructured along highly democratic lines, guided by the radical principles of social ecology in its challenge to hierarchy and domination, or the ecological deterioration of the planet will "stress not only our resources, but also our democracy."[7]

Another side effect is the mental health epidemic. The system of selfishness, social Darwinism, and unapologetic competition that dismisses the importance of community reveals the correlation between rising rates of mental distress and the neoliberal mode of capitalism. Moreover, the treatment proposed is even more revealing of the naturalization of extreme individualism. Mental health is considered privatized, the individual being responsible to resolve its own psychological distress. The mental health plague in capitalist societies would suggest that, instead of being the only social system that works, techno-capitalism is inherently dysfunctional, and that the cost of it seeming to work is very great.

Another crucial side effect is the proliferation of a peculiar bureaucracy. Cybercapitalist ideologues excoriated the top-down bureaucracy which supposedly led to institutional inefficiency. With the triumph of cybercapitalism and neoliberalism, bureaucracy was supposed to have been made obsolete. Yet, instead of disappearing, bureaucracy has changed its form; and this new, decentralized form has allowed it to proliferate at the expense of the already malfunctioning institutions of representative democracy.

In view of these deadlocks, a search for an alternative is a crucial collective quest. However, in the wake of the financial crisis, the incapacity of democratic institutions to even regulate banks (considered too big and embedded in the system to fail) led to deeper political disappointment and made the hope of a viable alternative seem impossible. Bookchin's reflections on scale and "small" and "human" ecosystems actually provides such an alternative. His system of thought was not directly a reflection on techno-capitalism. It was a reflection on contexts and frameworks. Far from rejecting technological innovation, he questioned the context and framework from which this innovation emerged: the question in effect is whether society would be organized around technology or the other way around. Our answer can be obtained by examining the new technology itself with a view to determine if it can be scaled to human dimensions.[5]

Against this neoliberal cultural desert of individual clones reproduced to ethical infinity, Bookchin's social ecology invites us to reflect on scale and build self-governed communities, ethical social ecosystems that embrace diversity and set their own political norms, criteria, and goals. He examines the potential of a human habitat, scaled to human dimensions at least as far as social institutions and communities are concerned. To Bookchin, scale is not merely a matter of physical dimensions but rather in creating a space of qualitative social and political virtue. Small, in Bookchin's view, makes sense as long as it is human, meaning that it allows for individual control over the affairs of the community and the exercise of individual human powers in the social realm. A human habitat minimally presupposes human scale, that is to say, a scale that lends itself to public comprehension, individual participation, and face-to-face relationships.[9]

Social ecology is one basic alternative to the obvious contradictions of techno-capitalism. For Bookchin, the political subject cannot be formed into official institutions and heteronomous representations. Eventually though, any such human ecosystem must include its own political infrastructure, institutions, interpersonal relations, and guiding values that justify the use of the word "human."

In the case of cybercapitalism, the proliferation of free trade agreements, as well as efforts towards a WTO multilateral agreement on e-commerce, intends to lock in *de facto* data ownership rights exclusively for data collectors. In view of this dead end, a series of studies make a case for collective rights over the economic resource of data. They propose a framework for community data ownership as being necessary for economic justice.

For social ecology, the locus of government, the process of governing, the objectives, as well as the truth that defines the governance, are all examined by the diverse members that participate and sustain their collective ecosystem. However, an alliance with official institutions is not to be rejected *per se*. Scalar political alliances between human habitats, neighbourhoods, eco-social communities, and municipal authorities can facilitate a move beyond the neoliberal cyber monarchism that thrives on exploitation and social monoculture. This also applies to parties that recognize the limits of representative democracies and are willing to provide space for social movements. It is, however, in this context beyond, or rather beneath, the State and the Market, that the three-dimensional individual of the neoliberal monoculture can be deconstructed.

BIBLIOGRAPHY

Murray Bookchin. "The Concept of Ecotechnologies and Ecocommunities," in *Habitat, an International Journal*. Vol 2, (Pergamon Press, 1977): 73–85.

Murray Bookchin. "A Green Economy or Green Economics?" in *The Newsletter of PEGS*. Vol. 2. No. 2. (Penn State University Press, 1992): 9–10. https://www.jstor.org/stable/20710558

Murray Bookchin. *A Discussion on "Listen, Marxist!,"* transcription by Jonas Holmgren (1970). https://www.marxists.org/archive/bookchin/1970/discussion.htm

Murray Bookchin. "Liberatory Technology," in *Our Generation* (Montreal: Canada, 1971).

Murray Bookchin. *Social Ecology and Communalism* (San Francisco: AK Press, 2006).

Murray Bookchin. "Where Do We Come From? What Are We? Where Are We Going?" *Kick It Over* magazine, (1985). http://dwardmac.pitzer.edu/Anarchist_Archives/bookchin/raddemocracy.html

J Adam Carter and S Orestis Palermos. "Is Having your Computer Compromised a Personal Assault? The Ethics of Extended Cognition," in *The Journal of the American Philosophical Association*, Vol. 2, (2016), 542–560.

Fisher, Mark. (2009). *Capitalist Realism*, (London: Zero Books, 2009).

PJ Singh and J Vipra. "Economic Rights Over Data: A Framework for Community Data Ownership," in *Development* 62 (2019), 53–57.

NOTES

1. Bookchin, "Where Do We Come From? What Are We? Where Are We Going?"

2. Bookchin, *Social Ecology and Communalism*, 38.

3. Bookchin, "The Concept of Ecotechnologies and Ecocommunities," 79.

4. Bookchin, "The Concept of Ecotechnologies and Ecocommunities," 77.

5. Fisher, Capitalist Realism.

6. Bookchin, "The Concept of Ecotechnologies and Ecocommunities," 76.

7. Murray Bookchin, "A Green Economy or Green Economics?" 10.

8. Murray Bookchin, "Liberatory Technology," 35.

9. Bookchin, "The Concept of Ecotechnologies and Ecocommunities," 78.

10. Bookchin, "The Concept of Ecotechnologies and Ecocommunities."

On Connecting a New Economics with Social Ecology

Peter Piperkov

Economics Matter

If you ask economists if economics matters and if we really need it, surely they will answer that it does and that we need it badly. That's not surprising; at the end of the day, their salary relies on it. Try asking the same question to random people who are not economists and you will most likely hear the same answer. Try asking *why* and both groups will bombard you with arguments about the GDP, unemployment, inflation, and interest rates and how all those indicators help us figure out where we're at in terms of economic development. But that was not the question… and the answer you will get is about something else—statistics or econometrics.

That does not mean we do not need measurements or that all those indicators and indices are useless. On the contrary, they are very helpful in terms of evaluating our economic development and future possibilities. But they are not economic theory in and of themselves; they just provide the needed statistical information economists use to discuss, argue, and eventually decide about propositions for further development, based on the economic school of thought they are part of.

So What Is Economics?

If you try Googling "economics" you will most likely see that it is "the social science that studies the production, distribution, and consumption of goods and services" and that it "focuses on the behaviour and interactions of economic agents and how economies work." You will see nothing about what rate of GDP growth is desirable or which levels of unemployment and/or inflation are preferable and/or whether or not we need a tax system.

The simple and obvious reason for this is that in the decades after the 1970s, we have mixed real science with a particular school of thought or, more specifically, certain hypotheses in a particular given, and ideologically narrow, set of schools of thought.

But economics as a true science actually consists of many different schools of thought, whether orthodox or heterodox, radical or reactionary, etc. The trick of the neoliberal/neoclassical devil is that it managed to convince us there is only one correct way to study, analyze, and understand production, distribution, and consumption—the now dominant orthodox neoclassical ultra-procapitalist school of thought. But that must change because, as Murray Bookchin has suggested, such uncritical acceptance of what currently exists erodes our capacity for visionary thinking.

We need "good" economic theory, which relies on proven facts and careful analysis and not on faith in some almighty, god-like invisible hand that regulates everything simultaneously, nominating the capitalist free market as the best system we've invented. We need a "good" economic science, which relies on proven facts and careful analysis and not on belief in some almighty, god-like invisible hand of the market, which regulates everything simultaneously, making capitalist free market the "best system we've invented."

We Need "Good" Economic Theory

First, we need to understand what "good" economic theory means. I am using the adjective in the same sense as the Zapatistas in their *juntas de buen gobierno* (councils of good government). The idea is simple—just as the Zapatistas accuse the current system of government of being hierarchical and corrupt, serving the elites and not the general population, they do not mean to suggest that an anti-authoritarian, bottom-up style of government is not possible. The same is valid for economics—just because the dominant form of economics is so unscientific and ideologically biased that it resembles a religion, does not mean that we must abolish economics altogether.

The main aim of a good economic theory should not be to try to convince people to believe in a certain doctrine or particular school of thought. The goal must be to improve human lives by analyzing and understanding their economic activities of producing, distributing, and consuming goods and services, and to propose how to maintain these activities in ways that are beneficial to people without destroying the environment. We must bear in mind Bookchin's warning of capitalism's inherently anti-ecological nature.

A good economic theory will help us more clearly to understand how and why capitalism actually works. Scholars from various schools of thought as well as "lone wolf" thinkers critically explore this topic. Examples include scholars from certain branches of the Marxist tradition, particularly Michael Hudson and David Harvey; post-Keynesian theorists, such as Hyman Minsky, Michal Kalecki, and Steve Keen; anarchist anthropologists with an intersectional perspective such as the late David Graeber; and libertarian municipalists in the tradition of Bookchin. Additionally, observers who are not anti-capitalist but who are critical of the current state of economics offer helpful perspectives. Scholars such as these can help build a culture of resistance both on an academic level and in broader society by promoting these theories and by replacing propagandistic ideological gibberish with a scientific reflection of reality.

The first thing we must do is identify and remove unscientific and obviously ideological aspects of current economic ideas and teaching. The most obvious unscientific thesis is the self-regulating nature of capitalism, the almighty invisible hand. It should be noted that several orthodox schools of economic thought, such as Keynesianism, had already renounced this decades ago. Unfortunately, the neoclassical counterrevolution in economics that began in the 1970s, as well as the blending of neoclassical ideas and parts of Keynes' theories by economists like Paul Samuelson, has returned us to the the point at which we have to once again explain the real reason why the invisible hand is invisible: it doesn't exist. This fundamental battle seems endless, since it is as old as capitalism itself. Nevertheless, overturning right-wing dogma that insists on the existence of this chimera, while not a revolutionary act in itself, has the potential to impact not only academia but society itself. Bookchin attacks delusionary economic beliefs by pointing out how capitalist deregulation in the US led not to less government but rather to a quasi-totalitarian form of governance.[1]

Another closely related thesis is the myth of perfect competition. Every orthodox textbook claims that this is the most desirable market structure, because it avoids economic loss for society, the so-called deadweight of reduced output plus higher prices, which is present in all other market structures. But there are two fundamental problems with this thesis. First, even orthodox economists admit that this is just a theoretical construct and nonexistent in reality. So far, so good. But the problem is that most pro-capitalist economists reply, and which is echoed by the mainstream media, that we should bring reality in line with the theory of perfect competition—by forcefully imposing it. But even achieving this won't do the trick, because there is another even more fundamental problem here. This problem is connected with economists' use of 2D curves and graphs, which at best are imperfectly understood to represent a multidimensional complex reality. To prove the perfection of perfect competition, pro-capitalist theorists deconstruct a curve into numerous flat lines. This is as mathematically impossible as is constructing a curve from a set of flat lines. Even if we could make perfect competition work within the 2D world of curves, lines, and graphs, it would still fail to eliminate the aforementioned deadweight loss for society. In fact, it turns out that all capitalist market structures generate loss for society.[2] If our goal is to better production, distribution, and consumption, we should strive for something which doesn't generate social loss. In this case, capitalism is not an option.

Another failure of orthodox economics is its inability to understand and explain money, including its genealogy, its means of production and circulation, and its functioning as capital. Pro-capitalist economists do not understand how and why capital works the way that it does. The only thing they can offer is the myth of barter as a theory to explain the evolution of money and the even crazier idea that we still live in a world that resembles barter but just with money, which makes market exchange easier. Even though this method was rejected long ago and continues to be rejected by numerous heterodox economists, anthropologists, historians, financiers, and even central banks all over the world, it still shows up in most textbooks at most universities.

An economic theory that studies capitalism but leaves capital out of the picture is useless; an economic theory that explores markets and market structures without understanding the reality of market structures is equally useless. These examples of how orthodox economics misunderstands capitalism are just the tip of the iceberg. If we were to go deeper, we would find still more unscientific gibberish. Even further problems arise when procapitalist economists attempt to analyze complex problems such as crises.

Orthodox, pro-capitalist schools either ignore the issue of crises or dismiss it with the argument that markets can cope with such problems by themselves. What kind of theories can replace the unscientific ones we are obliged to read, learn, and hear discussed in academia and the mainstream media? While working on my PhD thesis on the economic crises in Bulgaria after the 1989 fall of the Soviet regime, I found numerous schools of thought and scholars who have a realistic view of the workings of capitalism. Some of those heterodox schools and thinkers were already mentioned above. They cannot all be covered in a single paper or lecture, but from reviewing them I've deduced two fundamental requirements for any theory:

1. Acceptance of the concept of an economic system as a complex adaptive system with circular causality, just as any other system. This will stop the madness of "snapshot analysis" and the constant rotation of wrong-headed curves and lines in 2D graphs, and this alone will propel us towards reality.
2. Abandonment of the myth of barter and acceptance of the endogenous nature of money, as if barter had never existed, and as if money had been created in the dawn of civilization for the purpose of financing states' and empires' expenditures. Money thus would seem endogenous to the system, created by the central banks and by other banks through the process of lending.

This will be the basis for an interdisciplinary, scientific approach towards economic phenomena.

A strong emphasis should be placed on an interdisciplinary, or intersectional, approach and a comprehension of the pervasiveness of the environmental crisis. A sound economic theory must not only appreciate this emergency, but also be able to implement scientifically-informed approaches and solutions. With his pivotal work on social ecology, Murray Bookchin is a crucial thinker for this task. Not only is his work helpful in understanding the ownership[3] and power relations that exist in the present capitalist system, it also describes a more comprehensive and naturalistic view of social relations in general by integrating human and nonhuman animals and nature in a holistic dynamic system.

Where Are We Now?

The global financial crisis of 2007–2008 opened the door for criticism of the current orthodox neoclassical/neoliberal economic theory, which claims to have already proven that capitalism is the best we can get as a system. It was a chance to question and dismantle the right wing clichés. Students and teachers had already begun clamoring for change in efforts such as the Post-Autistic Economics Movement in the early 2000s and the Post-Crash Economics Society a decade later.

Today, more than 10 years later, nothing in economic theory has changed. Unlike the 1930s, neither Keynesianism nor any other liberal centrist framework is on the rise in economic teaching and science. We are still stuck in a right-wing world, which is getting more right-wing not only in economic terms, but also in broader social terms with the rise of openly fascist ideas and movements.

The reasons for this can be found in the neoliberal/neoclassical academic reforms throughout the West (and also in the ex-Eastern bloc) in the last few decades. The privatization and marketization of universities has obstructed theories that are critical of the status quo. Debates in recent years continue to focus on the topic of the amount of state intervention in the orthodox framework of "neoclassical vs. Keynesian" theory (developed by the neoclassical economist Paul Samuelson), excluding a scientific examination of how the system works and the reasons for its crisis. Such an approach, in striving to preserve the system as it is, also limits the possibilities for successful reform.

So now, twelve years after the last market crash, heterodox theories are still hardly mentioned in textbooks and courses, despite their potential for describing and understanding the Great Recession and the events that came after it.

What Should Be Done?

The honest answer to this question is that we, or at least I, do not know. The general state of economics instruction as described above corresponds with my personal experience at UNWE in Sofia, Bulgaria. Dysfunctional teaching of economics is discouraging in an environment where education is already perceived to have no ("market") value. Additionally, when heterodox theories are used in research and PhD theses, they are almost always dismissed as exotic and to some extent irrelevant.

But there are other options to be explored. Education in economics, as in most other sciences, can be done in free seminars by those very same scholars, scientists, and students in a manner that represents their alternative perspective, such as the approach used by projects and collectives like the Post-Autistic Economics Movement and Post-Crash Economics Society.

In the last two-and-a-half years, I explored this possibility by offering a free course in critical economics at the social center Fabrika Avtonomia in Sofia, Bulgaria. The course started with around 20 participants and consisted of three separate subjects—history of economic thought, microeconomics, and macroeconomics. By the end of the course there remained five to six regular participants, which, keeping in mind that the course was free and voluntary unlike university courses, was a great turnout. Also important is the fact that the participants were very diverse, including activists, students in various disciplines, and academics. A couple of people from the course became involved in different activist initiatives during those years.

In terms of implementation, certain communities in Northeast Syria are experimenting with new approaches in understanding economics and social relations with huge success. The Internationalist Commune of Rojava is demonstrating a fruitful exchange of ideas and experience. All of this proves three basic points:

1. Democratization and radicalization of economic education and knowledge is possible.

2. It can be done both in mainstream academia and through more activist channels with different levels of success, depending on the local context and possibilities.

3. This democratization and radicalization in economics not only challenges the status quo and gives us a better understanding of how capitalism works, but it also has two very strong "side effects": making people aware and stimulating their involvement in various social struggles.

Reminiscent of Bookchin's concept of dual power, this final point is probably the most important in the effort to create non-hierarchical structures in parallel to capitalism and the State. I believe that this approach can help us dismantle the current unscientific nature of economics.

BIBLIOGRAPHY

Barmeyer, Neils. Chapter Three: "Who is Running the Show? The Workings of Zapatista Government," in *Developing Zapatista Autonomy: Conflict and NGO Involvement in Rebel Chiapas*. (New Mexico: University of New Mexico Press 2009).

Bookchin, Murray. *Toward an Ecological Society* (Montreal-New York: Black Rose Books, 1980).

___. *The Philosophy of Social Ecology: Essays on Dialectical Naturalism* (Montreal-New York: Black Rose Books, 1990).

___. *Anarchism, Marxism and the Future of the Left. Interviews and Essays, 1993–1998*, (San Francisco: A.K. Press 1999).

___. *Social Ecology and Communalism* (San Francisco: AK Press, 2007).

___. *The Next Revolution: Popular Assemblies and the Promise of Direct Democracy*, (London-New York: Verso, 2015).

Graeber, David. *Debt: The First 5,000 Years* (New York-London: Melville House Publishing, 2011).

Harvey, David. *The Enigma of Capital* (Oxford-New York: Oxford University Press, 2011).

___. "The Enigma of Capital and the Crisis this Time," presented at the American Sociological Association, 2014.

Hudson, Michael. *Finance Capitalism and its Discontents* (ISLET, 2012).

___. *Killing the Host: How Financial Parasites and Debt Destroy the Global Economy* (ISLET, 2015).

Kalecki, Michael. *Selected Essays on the Dynamics of the Capitalist Economy* (Cambridge: Cambridge University Press, 1971).

Keen, Steve. "Finance and economic breakdown: modelling Minsky's Financial Instability Hypothesis," in *Journal of Post Keynesian Economics*, Vol. 17, No. 4 (1995): 607–635.

___. *Debunking Economics—Revised and Expanded Edition: The Naked Emperor Dethroned?* (London: Zed Books, 2011).

___. "A Monetary Minsky model of the Great Moderation and the Great Recession," In *Journal of Economic Behavior & Organization*, Elsevier, vol. 86(C), 2015, 221–235.

Minsky, HP, "The Modeling of Financial Instability: An introduction. Modeling and Simulation," In *Proceedings of the Fifth Annual Pittsburgh Conference, 1974.*

___. *Can 'It' Happen Again?: Essays on Instability and Finance*, (Armonk-New York: M. E. Sharpe, 1982).

Samuelson, PA, "Interactions between the Multiplier Analysis and the Principle of Acceleration," In *Review of Economic Statistics*, 1939, 21, 75–78.

Samuelson PA, Nordhaus WD. *Economics, 19th Edition*, (New York: McGraw-Hill, 2009).

Solow, SW, "Dumb and Dumber in Macroeconomics," In *Festschrift for Joe Stiglitz*, Columbia University, 2003.

___. "The State of Macroeconomics," in *The Journal of Economic Perspectives*. 22, 2008, 243–249.

___. *Building a Science of Economics for the Real World*, Prepared Statement of Robert Solow, Professor Emeritus, MIT, to the House Committee on Science and Technology, Subcommittee on Investigations and Oversight, July 20, 2010.

"A Brief History of the Post-Autistic Economics Movement," http://www.paecon.net/HistoryPAE.htm.

Post-Crash Economics Society, http://www.post-crasheconomics.com.

NOTES

1. Jeff Riggenbach, "Interview with Murray Bookchin," *Reason*, October 1979, available online: https://reason.com/1979/10/01/interview-with-murray-bookchin/.

2. The fact that perfect competition inevitably always leads to imperfect competition and later to oligopoly or even monopoly because of the inherent capitalist drive for expansion, generating even more losses for society, is another story—as usual, this is also ignored by the current economic discipline.

3. More on this topic can be found at: Murray Bookchin, "Municipalization: Community Ownership of the Economy," LibCom, https://libcom.org/library/municipalization-murray-bookchin. This article originally appeared in *Green Perspectives*, No. 2, February 1986.

Reflections on *The Limits of the City*

Kostas Papoulis

Translated by Yavor Tarinski

The Limits of the City by Murray Bookchin was first published in Greek by Eleutheros Typos (Free Press) in Athens, 1979. The following review of the book was published in "Ta Anthi tou Kakou" (The Flowers of Evil), Vol 8-9, 1993—a Greek journal with strong antiauthoritarian and ecological influences, which was published in Athens in the 1980s and 1990s by social ecologist Michalis Protopsaltis (1958-2014).

"THE SEARCH OF THE *homo collectivicus*" could be the title of a commentary on one of the most significant works of Murray Bookchin, which is being prepared for publication for the second time in Greek.

To interpret how societies evolve, observers must take into account historical, social, and natural elements. The influence of the Russian anarchist geographer, Pyotr Kropotkin, appears in the traces of naturalism in Murray Bookchin's work. Bookchin never hid his ideological bias toward anarcho-communism and was instrumental in developing it into a modern theory. As geography slowly developed into a social science, theorists began to recognize the key role nature plays in the varied evolutionary paths of human civilizations. For example, the absence of water compelled communities towards collaboration on massive irrigation efforts, thus establishing the idea of common ownership of the land as a widespread mindset.

Ignoring the role of nature and the unique history of each geographic space, and focusing solely on the economic analysis of class antagonisms makes the job of interpreting how social formations are integrated into capitalist production more difficult. Indeed, without an understanding of the natural element, it is impossible to explain why anarcho-communism was embraced by 100% of the peasant populations of Andalusia and Aragon during the Spanish Revolution, while it had a minor influence elsewhere. In Andalusia and Aragon, the social conscience, heavily connected to nature and history, was much stronger and offered fertile ground for anarchism. Bookchin posits that political movements must cultivate the principles of communalism in order to develop a consciousness of the community. This is a necessary precondition for the transition towards communism, which was always the central idea of the anarchist movements and the most important contribution to the "black flag" aspect of the socialist movement.

Bookchin has an original way of defining the City historically. He sees it as the entire community of human relations, not only in its economic processes, but also in the multiplicity of everyday life. In contrast, the contemporary metropolis is the rejection of community, and thus the rejection of the essence of the City. The huge concentration of populations does not allow for human-scaled meetings and mutual aid, and city life is dominated by the automobile and the atomizing culture it creates.

A second notable way in which the capitalist city differs from historical cities is that it is out of balance with the environment. All the spaces of social gathering in history, from those in indigenous communities to those in the East, were founded on a certain balance with nature and did not pass certain limits. An exception was ancient Rome, which, although not having any production basis of its own, continuously grew, creating one huge parasitic system of exploitation over the space it dominated. Rome "fell" when this parasitic system overwhelmed itself and met its natural limit.

Bookchin contends that there are natural limits for the contemporary metropolis as well. The modern city exhausts the environment while producing an enormous mass of garbage, which ends up within the city and its natural surroundings. Extending the thought of Bookchin, let's picture how this plays out on a global scale. The central core of developed nations consume global resources at an incredible pace, while underdeveloped nations on the periphery have their resources stolen and are being turned into deserts, ready to receive the waste of consumer capitalism.

Beyond these questions of ecological limits, our cities have arrived at an unhealthy state of crisis. The ghettos within monster cities increase along with the growing apathy of citizens towards violence and repression. Noise, overcrowding, traffic—sources of constant frustration—standardized housing, which suppresses private life, the dominance of horizontal lines along with featureless and colorless architecture which enslave the eye, are all elements that give the city the feeling of an impersonal factory or warehouse. This oppressive space, hostile to community, is imposed on urban life by the capitalist agenda of production and efficiency.

In the end, contemporary urban crowding is nothing but a reflection of the values of capitalism, which creates the alienated *homo economicus* in contrast to the traditional *homo collectivus*. Here, the thought of Bookchin meets Marx and his 1844 *Manuscripts* and reminds us of the theory of alienation.

Indeed, Bookchin's critique of the City is a perspicacious critique of the social relations of capitalism. It is closely related to the radical critique of urban planning which we find in Henri Lefebvre's ideas of the Right to the City which emerged in 1968. It relates to what he terms *habiter*, in contrast to the physically constructed habitat: "I inhabit means I participate in a social life, in a community, village, or city." It is also related to the critique of space as developed by the Situationists.

"There is a suitable measure for the size of the city as well as for everything else," suggested Aristotle, and the same was underlined by Bookchin with his insistence on human scale. Referring simultaneously to Owen, Fourier, and ancient Athens, he shows us clearly what urban life means.

Consistently anticapitalist, Bookchin claims that the reformation of the City parallels the movement to overthrow capitalism. For Bookchin, the overthrow of capitalism is the replacement of *homo economicus* by *homo collectivicus*. He considers the conscience of the community to be its subjective element, which transforms the City and the world. He observes in the American counterculture movement of the 1960s and 1970s the characteristics of libertarian communism, which can lead to the creation of a culture radically different from the capitalist one: a resilient culture that will promote solidarity, mutual aid, and community— a community that will deal collectively with needs that are currently individualized. This would allow cities to escape barbaric consumerism and to re-establish harmony with the environment. Bookchin presents a choice between the harmonious space of *homo collectivicus*, situated in balance with nature, and the unequal and fragmented national and transnational space of *homo economicus*, which is dangerously reaching its natural boundaries. In this way, Murray Bookchin responds to the pseudo-dilemma of contrasting priorities: the clash between nature and humanity is explicitly connected with the clash between society and capitalist civilization. Bookchin's perception is essentially the only ground on which the Left and ecology can meet on equal terms and reinitiate their critique of capitalism.

A transformation of society or the City can come only through large movements that will reanimate communalism, like the countercultural movement of the 1960s and 1970s. On the level of the City, the dominant mode of urban planning has no trace of any political sensibility. Bookchin is being proven right. Urbanism is nothing more than the attempt of the State to rationally intervene in the market which, if left unregulated, quickly creates chaos in the urban space. Thus, Bookchin goes beyond the shallow framework of contemporary urbanism, where the only objective is to plan the functions of the City, and instead opens a dialogue exactly where urbanism stops.

It is difficult to find a weakness in the work of Bookchin. He manages to transform the traditional anarchist ideas so they can remain alive in our contemporary world. Communalism is the essential point the communist Left forgot, resulting in its sinking into economic determinism and political totalitarianism.

Murray Bookchin's Legacy of Freedom

Ramazan Kaya

Translation by Ertuğ Dinseven

Bookchin's The Third Revolution, Volume 1: Popular Movements in the Revolutionary Era *was published as a second edition in Turkey in mid-2012 by Dipnot Publishing. The following review was originally published on 3ʳᵈ of June, 2012, on the website of the Turkish left-wing magazine,* Birikim.

Bookchin's anarchism gets its revolutionary fire from Bakunin and its practical suggestions from Kropotkin.
— PETER MARSHALL

THE FIRST VOLUME of Murray Bookchin's four-part series, *The Third Revolution: From Peasant Rebellions to French Revolution*, was published by Dipnot Publishing with the attentive translation of Sezgin Ata. The copyright of the remaining volumes of the series belong to the same publishing house and translation work continues at a feverish pace. Bookchin has been most widely read in Turkey in recent years and all of his Turkish translated books are regularly sold out. We do not exaggerate when claiming that he is the most discussed radical thinker across the political spectrum, ranging from imprisoned Kurdish activists to academics, from political parties to anarchist groups. The Kurdish political movement undoubtedly plays an important role in sparking this interest. Bookchin has significantly influenced their "democratic autonomy" project, and this has stimulated the rediscovery and discussion of his theses. Janet Biehl, Bookchin's close companion and author of the foreword to his book, *From Peasant Rebellions to the French Revolution*, has also increased the Kurdish movement's interest in his ideas.

Bookchin's vision can be briefly summarized as building "ecological, decentralized, self-governing cities through face-to-face democracy."[1] To the Kurdish movement, which understood the authoritarian and exclusionary character of the nation-state model quite well, Bookchin's theses were an important reference for developing a confederal self-government policy in Kurdistan. His ideas can inspire many movements questioning centralization, industrial production, sexism, hierarchy, and representative politics. His politics are an invitation for ordinary people to create political communities. The transfer of policy-making to vanguard professionals, parties, and charismatic leaders is to mortgage people's determination of their own future. As Bookchin notes, "Political life will usually be in the hands of a small minority, as long as ordinary people have to devote much of their time to daily livelihoods."

Bookchin harshly criticized individualist lifestyle anarchists in North America who were unwilling to participate in a communal transformation of society and who were gradually merging a new primitivism into their ideas and activities. Since 2000, he began to define himself as a "communalist" by drawing a broad line between these kinds of "anarchisms" and his approach. However, this ideological difference did not prevent Bookchin from seeing himself as part of the social anarchist tradition. Bookchin always embraced the achievements and historical tradition of social anarchist movements and anarcho-syndicalism, embodied in Russia, Ukraine, and Spain. He named the eco-anarchist ideas he developed in the early 1970s "social ecology." In 1987, Bookchin engaged in an intense debate with deep ecologists, who prioritized nonhuman nature over people and advocated nature mysticism. He defended a secular, humanistic, and social ecologist perspective against these ideologies which he found reactionary. Unlike deep ecologists, Bookchin addressed ecological issues on the basis of a critique of hierarchy and domination. Unless harmony and equality between people was achieved, harmony with nature could not be realized.

Bookchin is the most renown libertarian thinker in thought and action since the Second World War. His greatest success is in his unique combination of traditional anarchist insights with modern ecological thinking. Like the maestro Kropotkin, Bookchin also finds evidence of his views of a free society in anthropology and history. In re-reading the thread of history, he attempts to untangle the legacy of freedom from the chains of hierarchy and exploitation. From this legacy of freedom, he follows medieval millenarian Christian sects, Digger colonists of the English Revolution, New England city assemblies emerging after the American Revolution, assemblies established in Paris during the French Revolution, the Paris Commune, and the anarchist communes and councils of the Spanish Revolution. He goes beyond the objections of classical anarchist thinkers regarding the State and capitalism and analyzes human history through "hierarchy" rather than class, "domination" rather than exploitation. "Historically, hierarchies emerged long before classes, and the ongoing pressures of privileged genders, ethnic groups, nationalities, and bureaucracies [will] still exist in society, even if economic classes [will] have disappeared."[2] Under Bookchin's philosophy, the revolution should not aim to seize power, but to disband it. A society should be organized through self-management. The revolutionary process aims at the formation of popular assemblies and communities that encompass all members of the community and enable them to act as individuals. Bookchin imagines his "ecotope" as a confederation of self-governing communes that use a form of direct democracy for governance. Administrative tasks would be carried out by rotation, but basic policies would be determined in public assemblies. He does not totally reject technology. According to Bookchin, technology can provide the precondition for a free society with increased leisure time by eliminating hard labor, material insecurity, and central economic control. He is in favour of "eco-technologies" that are compatible with nature, locally-produced, and minimally polluting. Libertarian political philosophers continue to be engaged in critical discussion of Bookchin's Hegelian teleology, his optimistic vision of a society of abundance, his enlightened humanism that centers on the individual, his Eurocentrist understanding of history, and his confidence in objective reasoning and modern technology.

The main questions readers of his last book, *From Peasant Rebellions to the French Revolution*, will ask themselves is whether popular revolts and failed revolutionary attempts that emerged before modern societies should be regarded as moments of missed opportunity for freedom and equality when modern capitalism was supposedly inevitable. Are we going to believe a Marxist teleology that says we have to wait for the objective conditions for an inevitable proletarian revolution to rise? The answer to this question continues to determine revolutionary perspectives and their policy-making horizon. According to Bookchin, "Marx's view tends to make the historical revolutionary process generally very fatalistic. So much so that it forces us to admit that none of the great liberation movements, which lasted more than four centuries, constituted an alternative to the ultimate victory of capitalism."[3] Bookchin, who writes history in light of grassroots popular movements and revolutions, clearly rejects modern historical narratives of linear and homogeneous time. "I refrained from seeing the intentions of these movements as a reflection of the emergence and self-consolidation of industrial capitalism; instead, I described the desires of different revolutionary trends in their words,"[4] he says. Every person who reads this book will be amazed by Bookchin's deep knowledge of history; the language that transmits such historical events is comparable in its detail to a first-hand account.

Bookchin, who was also fascinated by the history of the resistance, admits that he would have joined, without a second thought, with Jean Varlet in the 1793 uprisings of the Sans-culottes and Jean Varlin during the war days of the Paris Commune. Unlike Marx, Bookchin doesn't see history simply as a class war. He recognizes that the clashes between the exploiters and the exploited occur over a significant part of history, but he does not cease to trace the history of those who resist top-down control, centralization, the State, bureaucracy, sexist oppression, religious institutions, and the fragmentation of organic community life. He tries to make visible the revolutionary organizations of the people who try to survive on the margins of revolutions and operate in the form of popular assemblies, business committees, soviets, and popular associations. He reveals that the masses of the people who participated in history's great revolutionary waves did not approve of the later programs of the revolutions' vanguards. Bookchin angrily objected to the modern historical notion that people who create revolutionary formations were "unconscious masses." On the contrary, he determined, "Those following the traditional time-honored crafts, such as printers, blacksmiths, jewelers, wheelwrights, and independent farmers, were often expressive individuals with strongly etched personalities."[5] He emphasizes that no revolutionary fire has come to a halt, and that the fire has taken inspiration from egalitarian and autonomous ideas that took root in the communal life and cultural habits of these people.

Among the revolutionary popular movements that Murray Bookchin presents in this book are the rebellious regiments of all revolutionary and communist movements of Feudal Europe, the independent colonial associations in America, and the Sans-culottes of the French Revolution flow in all their glory. Other movements considered include heretic Christian sects (Anabaptists, Free Spirit Brothers, supporters of Thomas Münzer), German peasant revolts, popular revolts demanding tribal egalitarianism in Mesopotamia and Egypt, the Levelers Army in England, Gerrard Winstanley who led the Diggers colony, the independent colonies established after the American Revolution, New England city councils, and the Paris sections of peasants and workers who wore the "red cap of freedom" in the French Revolution. Alongside these movements he includes those anonymous heroes who cracked the walls of social injustice, only to take their honourable place in the history of the losers. Bookchin insists that, had these struggles been successful, it is highly likely that Western European history would have evolved towards city and peasant confederations rather than centralized nation-states. Nevertheless, rather than lament the past, and taking inspiration from the history of the oppressed, Bookchin maintains that he will not be part of any historical period in which the revolutionary spirit disappears. Every historical period, he avers, provides revolutionary opportunities.

NOTES

1. Murray Bookchin. *Köylü İsyanlarından Fransız Devrimine* [From Peasant Rebellions to the French Revolution], (Ankara: Dipnot Yayınları, 2012), 15.

2. Bookchin, 47.

3. Bookchin, 36.

4. Bookchin, 18.

5. Bookchin, 38.

On the Reorganization of Society and Eco-Anarchism

Georgi Konstantinov

Translation by Yavor Tarinski

Remaking Society *has been the first (and so far the only) of Bookchin's books to be translated into Bulgarian. It was done by the publishing house Schrapnel in Sofia, 2006, under the title* On Social Transformation: or Eco-Anarchism. *The following review of Bookchin's book has appeared on several online bookstores and websites.*

MURRAY BOOKCHIN, who passed away in 2006, is an example of the richness, diversity, and inexhaustibility of anarchist thought. He was the first to draw attention to the decisive role of the ecological factor in the development of humanity. He called on those suffering from land, air, and water pollution to rely on themselves and not on the philanthropy of those who profit on their behalf.

When environmental protection is limited to specific reforms, its defenders are often left to be tempted by the sirens of the electoral and parliamentary machine. It doesn't take much to transform a lobby into a political party, an eco-reformer into a parliamentarian, or a "beggar" into a "prince." There is a fatally degenerating symbiosis between the one who prays humbly to authority and the one who exercises it arrogantly. Both share the idea that change is possible only through authority and, more precisely, only through state authority—this professional corps of murderers and thieves, of legislators, bureaucrats, the military, and the police, who are themselves corrupted by capital, including in its most criminal form. Every time this authority is appealed to, it comes out stronger and at the same time the power of the people weakens. The authority that the State gains is won at the expense of the people and vice versa. Any attempt to legitimize the authority of the State is to take away the legitimacy of the people's power.

The land should no longer be owned, but shared. Its fruits, including those produced by technology and labour, can no longer be appropriated by a few; they must be made accessible to all according to their needs. The power to make decisions must be wrested away from the control of the elites and redistributed in a form of participation and collaboration with all. Until these fundamental problems are resolved, we cannot generate popular interest in building political solutions; and so the ecological crisis will continue to worsen in a society incapable of resolving it.

Bookchin's Journey to Ancient and Modern Greece

Stavros Karageorgakis and Niovi Chatzinikolaou

BOOKCHIN NEVER managed to visit Greece. In 2004, at his home in Burlington, Vermont, he confessed that visiting the country was one of his unfulfilled dreams.[1] He planned to go in 1992, but ultimately cancelled the trip.[2] When encouraged to visit Greece as soon as possible, he replied that it was too late by then. His health was deteriorating, and two years later he passed away. Even though he never managed to visit in person, his thoughts often journeyed to Greece through his writings. The modern Greek ecology movement bears the profound mark of his ideas. That is precisely what we intend to demonstrate in this article.

Bookchin and Ancient Greek Thinking

Bookchin's ideological course remained relatively stable, without significant deviations. Apart from a passing preoccupation with the Stalinist left in his youth, from the moment he started to write, his politics remained straightforward—one could even say unwavering. He had always been devoted to radical leftist anti-authoritarian ecology. Whether he called the political part of his theory "eco-anarchism" or "communalism," there seemed to be no significant difference in the political principles he wished to serve. The transition to a new political identity (communalism) over the old one (eco-anarchism) was more about doing away with modern malpractices of classic anarchism (notably the use of violence) than suggesting an actual platform change, with the exception perhaps of two key issues: municipal election participation and majority rule decision-making.[3] Both identities revolved around the same core attributes: antihierarchical, self-organizing, antiauthoritarian, and employing direct democracy. Moreover, Bookchin's new theory incorporated in their entirety the two major pillars of the old one: social ecology and libertarian municipalism.

Bookchin's ideas, both old and new, were heavily influenced by ancient Greece. Direct democracy, the central notion upon which ancient Athenian democracy was built, is the cornerstone of Bookchin's whole theory. Bookchin makes multiple references to its importance in his political vision. He believed that only a face-to-face democracy is capable of securing citizens' freedom and equality in addition to tending to the needs of the less powerful. He also believed that it was only when citizens were granted a voice and involvement in direct decision-making that they could be meaningfully summoned from the private domain. He served in the spirit of confederalism, as developed by nineteenth century libertarian socialists, and supported libertarian municipalism which, contrary to quietism or hippyism, extended organized political action and self-management to megacities.

The first vigorous experiment on direct democracy was conducted in ancient Athens. All adult Athenian citizens (at least the free, male citizens) could freely express their opinions on any subject and vote. Indeed, Pericles introduced compensation for involvement in common affairs. He did so to further reinforce democracy and encourage participation in public gatherings by poor citizens, who would otherwise be unable to take time away from their livelihoods. This fostered a democracy both popular and pragmatic. That is the kind of democracy that inspired Bookchin, along with other notable libertarian thinkers such as Cornelius Castoriadis, Noam Chomsky, and Takis Fotopoulos. Bookchin commends the political spirit of Athens based on "men of strong character who were indomitable in their social allegiances and rounded in their urbanity because they had firm ties to the soil and were independent in their economic position."[4]

Bookchin knew, however, that even a direct democracy risks being one in name only as populist leaders can manipulate the masses. Thucydides had commented that the Athenian democracy itself, under the rule of Pericles, had manipulated crowds, albeit through rhetorical persuasiveness rather than forceful coercion: "In short, what was nominally a democracy became, in his hands, government by the first citizen."[5] Nevertheless, Bookchin emphasizes the essence and dynamic of direct democracy of ancient Athens. In his most important work, *The Ecology of Freedom*, he marvels at Pericles' *Funeral Oration* and praises the city's openness to new ideas and foreigners, as well as the focus on shaping citizen ethos.[6] Bookchin also lauds the city's decision to rely on its own resources, not outside powers or deities, practicing reason and self-sufficiency. Both of these are tenets in his own theory.

Bookchin's "heavy artillery" often aimed at the irrational ecological fads popping up from time to time in the USA. He devoted too much energy and ink to attacking ungrounded trends like primitivism,[7] more robust but competing theories like deep ecology or biocentrism in general,[8] or other theories doomed to disappear. It is not a coincidence that those theories never gained ground in Europe, even though deep ecology was endorsed by an important Norwegian philosopher, Arne Naess. Bookchin considers reason the main tool for societal change, a tool borrowed from the ancient Greeks:

> If there is a single fact which marks the expansion of the ideals or freedom, it is the extent to which they were nourished by reason. Contrary to the popular

histories of philosophy, religion, and morality, rationalism had never been abandoned in the closing centuries of the ancient world and in the Middle Ages. Despite the infestation of the late Roman Empire by the Isis cult and ascetic religions from the East, the Hellenic effort to give a rational interpretation of the world was not only retained but it slowly became differentiated into new interpretations of what constituted reason.[9]

What is more, Bookchin did not hesitate to criticize a taboo issue for anarchists and libertarians: unanimous consent, siding once more with the ancient Greeks in preferring majority rule decision-making. Within the libertarian movement, both now and in the past, there is a requirement for decisions to be taken unanimously rather than by majority. That, of course, heavily impedes decision-making, among other things. In his article, "What is Communalism? The Democratic Dimension of Anarchism," Bookchin voiced his disagreement with this directive. He instead supported majority rule decision-making, not so much because of practical considerations, but rather to accommodate freedom of speech and ideological juxtaposition:

> If consensus could be achieved *without* compulsion of dissenters, a process that is feasible in small groups, who could possibly oppose it as a decision-making process? But to reduce a libertarian ideal to the unconditional right of a minority—let alone a "minority of one"—to *abort* a decision by a "collection of individuals" is to stifle the dialectic of ideas that thrives on opposition, confrontation and, yes, decisions with which everyone need not agree and *should* not agree, lest society become an ideological cemetery. Which is not to deny dissenters every opportunity to reverse majority decisions by unimpaired discussion and advocacy.[10]

The faith that Bookchin put in the dialectic of ideas was also the very seed of Athenian democracy, the birth and development of rhetoric, the art of listening and arguing. Argumentation is ingrained in the ancient Greek intellect as can be observed not only in rhetorical works, but in other aspects of ancient Greek everyday life, including drama and war. Thucydides' *History*, an account of the Peloponnesian War, features dozens of oratories by generals who reason to persuade their fellow-citizens to take a course of action.

Even more important in Bookchin's work is the role of the City (*polis*) itself. Contrary to the standard liberalist reasoning, whereupon cities operate according to political dictates, in Bookchin's libertarian thinking the reverse holds true: that is, politics adapts to the needs and requirements of the City. Bookchin's city is an integrated cell of society, capable of (re)shaping political frameworks. Thus, politics is exercised when citizens act as citizens—by becoming involved in common affairs—and not as individuals who simply entrust the management of common affairs to a cast of politicians. This central notion for Bookchin, of course, also manifests in ancient Athens:

> But Athenian life was not meant to be lived indoors in resplendent privacy, for to do so would have vitiated the *polis* as a community. Life was to be spent in the agora, the large square in which citizens gathered daily to transact their affairs, gossip, argue politics, and sell their wares. To fulfill this function, the *polis* had to be scaled to human dimensions—in Aristotle's words, a city that could be "taken in a single view."[11]

Even though Aristotle, due to his Macedonian ties, always regarded Athenians with suspicion and disdain, he underscored the importance of a democratically-run city throughout his *Politics*:

> Thus, also the city-state is prior in nature to the household and to each of us individually. For the whole must necessarily be prior to the part.[12]

Aristotle also postulated that when the City thrives, its citizens do as well, something accepted by Bookchin and those in the wider socialist tradition:

> On the other hand, it remains to say whether the happiness of a state is to be pronounced the same as that of each individual man, or whether it is different. Here too the answer is clear: everybody would agree that it is the same.[13]

In his book, *Urbanization Without Cities*, which focuses mainly on the issues of the City and citizenship, Bookchin explains that: "Insofar as I am guided by the Greek notion that a city or *polis* is an ethical union of citizens, I am committed to an overarching vision of what the city ought to be, not merely what it is at any given time."[14]

Bookchin also celebrated a series of ancient Greek virtues which he considered vital to his political vision: friendship or solidarity, or *philia*, understood by him as "a crucial precondition for a political life expressed the unique identity politics possessed as a form of governance, one that transcended mere kinship obligations;"[15] education, or *paideia*, in its ancient Greek sense of individual and social training in civics for citizens-to-be;[16] virtuousness (*arete*),[17] self-sufficiency (*autarkeia*),[18] equality before the law (*isonomia*),[19] but also prudence (*phronesis*), which he interprets as "the practical reason involved in creating and managing a community."[20]

Of course, the political situation in Athens was not idyllic, even for a fervent lover of direct democracy, like Bookchin. He was well aware of the shortcomings of Athenian democracy. He knew it was indeed direct, but not necessarily so democratic. It excluded women, slaves, and Greeks from other cities. Bookchin's favorite ancient Greek philosopher, Aristotle, whom he quotes frequently in all of his books, was in fact a proponent of slavery. Education, whereupon Bookchin places his hopes for the proper preparation of the citizens-to-be, was not meant for everyone in ancient Greece and particularly not in Athens. Only affluent citizens had the means to educate their children by employing a tutor at home to train them in rhetoric, enabling them to be able to eloquently express opinions on public matters. Bookchin condemned the patriarchy and class divisions of the Athenian community, as well as state-endorsed slavery and localism, in various works.[21] Nevertheless, he utilized the aspects of ancient Athenian democracy that were useful to his own vision and invoked this historic paradigm as the starting point for the creation of an ideal future society.

Bookchin in the Modern Greek Libertarian and Ecology Movement

Bookchin not only took ideas from ancient Greece, he also gave back to modern Greece. In particular, his theory heavily impacted the wider leftist movement in Greece following the overthrow of the military junta in 1974. It was then that a new leftist movement, free from Stalinist indoctrination of the communist parties guided by the Soviet Union, began to take shape. This multifaceted movement gave rise to both antiauthoritarian, anarchist, and ecological groups. Bookchin had an influence on both components of the new movement.

Dimitrios Roussopoulos, the publisher of Black Rose Books, Greek himself and Bookchin's friend, encouraged other Greek publishers to print his works.[22] In 1977, the first article collection is issued, while a year later a second one follows and shortly thereafter a third.[23] By now, most of his books have been translated and published in Greek, with the exception of *From Urbanization Without Cities* and *Re-Enchanting Humanity*.

His interviews have been featured in periodical publications of the wider left and ecology, such as an anti-military printout,[24] alongside Dan Chodorkoff.[25] The political magazine *Αρνούμαι* enthusiastically announced Bookchin's scheduled, but ultimately canceled, visit to Greece in 1992 to promote two recently-published books.[26] The first of Bookchin's interviews to be translated in Greek, one he did for the French magazine, *Informations et réflexions libertaires*, first appeared as a brochure.[27]

He had a significant influence on the close circle of people interested in political ecology through work published in the *Society and Nature* journal (seven issues from 1992–1995), and later in *Democracy and Nature* (several issues from 1992–2003). Takis Fotopoulos was the editor-in-chief, while Pavlos Stavropoulos, another Greek alumnus of the Institute for Social Ecology, edited the English language version. The journal, issued in three languages (English, Greek, and Spanish), was a huge proponent of the development of a theoretical discussion of politics and ecology in Greece. Texts published in the journal are still a subject of discussion.

Bookchin's theory influenced the antiauthoritarian movement in Greece to a high degree, especially in relation to ecological issues. Political groups directly quote his work, regardless of whether they identified as Bookchinist. Onegroup advocating for this line of thinking is called Eutopia. Launching a political publishing endeavor in 1999,[28] Eutopia has published 26 issues of its namesake journal and 13 books, runs a circulating library in Athens and has organized dozens of speeches and other events, presenting Bookchin's inner circle, including Janet Biehl, Brian Tokar, Matt Hern, Pavlos Stavropoulos, and Eirik Eiglad.

Bookchin's influence is also evident in local Greek struggles. Some of the environmental struggles, such as the demand for shutdown of a goldmine in Chalkidiki that contributed to the destruction of an ancient forest, have been heavily influenced by social ecology. Bookchin's writings, however, have circulated in ecological circles for much longer, since the 1980s, when the ecology and antinuclear movements in Greece began to take shape.

Bookchin's thinking and work have always been present in Greece in one way or another. As should be evident by now, this great political thinker used the political experiment of ancient Greece, i.e. direct democracy, and reinterpreted it in the light of the modern political status quo. It gives one hope that today, in a country that is geographically so close to Greece, in revolutionary Rojava and surrounding areas, the Kurds are using the same ideas to build their own society.

BIBLIOGRAPHY

Aristotle, *Politics*.

Biehl, Janet. *Ecology or Catastrophe, The Life of Murray Bookchin*. Oxford-New York: Oxford University Press, 2015.

Bookchin, Murray. "Interview to Michalis Tremopoulos." in *Αρνούμαι* 8, December 1992: 28–31. (in Greek).

___. "Social Ecology versus "Deep Ecology," A Challenge for the Ecology Movement." in *Green Perspectives* no. 4 & 5, Summer 1987.

___. "What is Communalism? The Democratic Dimension of Anarchism," in *Left Green Perspectives* 31, October 1994.

___. *Anarchism and Social Ecology*. Thessaloniki: Ecological Movement of Thessaloniki, 1986 (in Greek).

___. *Ecology and Revolutionary Thought*. Athens: Eleftheros Typos, 1978 (in Greek).

___. *Hierarchy and Domination*. Athens: Eleftheros Typos, 1977. (in Greek).

___. *Re-enchanting Humanity, A Defense of the Human Spirit Against Antihumanism, Misanthropy, Mysticism and Primitivism*. London: Casell, 1995.

___. *Remaking Society*. Montréal-New York: Black Rose Books, 1990.

___. *Social Anarchism or Lifestyle Anarchism: An Unbridgeable Chasm*. San Francisco: A.K. Press, 1995.

___. *The Ecology of Freedom, The Emergence and Dissolution of Hierarchy*. Montreal-New York: Black Rose Books, 1991.

___. *The Limits of the City*. Montréal-New York: Black Rose Books, 1986.

___. *The Next Revolution, Popular Assemblies and the Promise of Direct Democracy*. London-New York: Verso, 2015.

___. *The Philosophy of Social Ecology, Essays on Dialectic Naturalism*. Montréal-New York: Black Rose Books, 1996.

___. *Towards a Liberatory Technology*. Athens: Diethnis Vivliothiki, 1979. (in Greek).

___. *Urbanization Without Cities: The Rise and Decline of Citizenship*. Montréal: Black Rose Books, 1992.

Chodorkoff, Dan. "Interview to Michalis Tremopoulos," in *Αρνούμαι* 7, May 1992: 39–41. (in Greek).

Thucydides, *History* [B, 65.9]. trans. Richard Crawley. London, J. M. Dent; New York, E. P. Dutton. 1910.

NOTES

1. During a personal meeting with Stavros Karageorgakis.

2. For the cancellation of the trip to Greece in 1992 see Biehl, Janet, *Ecology or Catastrophe, The Life of Murray Bookchin*, (Oxford-New York: Oxford University Press, 2015), 229.

3. Murray Bookchin, *The Next Revolution, Popular Assemblies and the Promise of Direct Democracy*, (London-New York: Verso, 2015), 17–38.

4. Murray Bookchin, *The Limits of the City*, (Montréal-New York: Black Rose Books, 1986), 51.

5. Thucydides, *History* [B, 65.9], trans. Richard Crawley (London, J. M. Dent; New York, E. P. Dutton. 1910).

6. Murray Bookchin, *The Ecology of Freedom, The Emergence and Dissolution of Hierarchy*, (Montréal-New York: Black Rose Books, 1991), 130–133.

7. Murray Bookchin, *Social Anarchism or Lifestyle Anarchism: An Unbridgeable Chasm*, (San Francisco: A.K. Press, 1995)· Murray Bookchin, *Re-enchanting Humanity, A Defense of the Human Spirit Against Antihumanism, Misanthropy, Mysticism and Primitivism*, (London: Casell, 1995).

8. Murray Bookchin, "Social Ecology versus "Deep Ecology: A Challenge for the Ecology Movement," in *Green Perspectives* no. 4 & 5, Summer 1987. Murray Bookchin, *Remaking Society*, (Montréal-New York: Black Rose Books, 1990), 21–24. Murray Bookchin, *The Philosophy of Social Ecology, Essays on Dialectic Naturalism*, (Montréal-New York: Black Rose Books, 1996), 100–101, 115–119.

9. Murray Bookchin, *Remaking Society*, (Montréal-New York: Black Rose Books, 1990), 108.

10. Murray Bookchin, "What is Communalism? The Democratic Dimension of Anarchism," In *Left Green Perspectives* 31, October 1994.

11. Murray Bookchin, *The Limits of the City*, (Montréal-New York: Black Rose Books, 1986),121.

12. Aristotle, *Politics*, Book I, 1253a, trans. H. Rackham (Cambridge, MA, Harvard University Press; London, William Heinemann Ltd. 1944).

13. Aristotle, *Politics*, Book VII, 1324a, trans. H. Rackham.

14. Murray Bookchin, *Urbanization Without Cities, The Rise and Decline of Citizenship*, (Montréal-New York: Black Rose Books, 1992), xvii.

15. Bookchin, *Urbanization*, 52. See also, Bookchin, *The Next Revolution*, 29.

16. Bookchin, *Urbanization*, xviii, 59. See also Bookchin, *The Next Revolution*, 72.

17. Bookchin, *Urbanization*, 59.

18. Bookchin, *Urbanization*, 64. Bookchin, *Ecology*, 131.

19. Bookchin, *Urbanization*, 65.

20. Bookchin, *Urbanization*, 27.

21. Murray Bookchin, "What is Communalism? The Democratic Dimension of Anarchism;" Murray Bookchin, *The Ecology of Freedom*, 119–120, 293; Murray Bookchin, *The Next Revolution*, 37; Murray Bookchin, *The Limits of the City*, (Montréal-New York: Black Rose Books, 1986), 51.

22. Janet Biehl, *Ecology or Catastrophe*, (Oxford-New York: Oxford University Press, 2015), 194.

23. Murray Bookchin, *Hierarchy and Domination*, (Athens: Eleftheros Typos, 1977) (in Greek); Murray Bookchin, *Ecology and Revolutionary Thought*, (Athens: Eleftheros Typos, 1978) (in Greek); Murray Bookchin, *Towards a Liberatory Technology*, (Athens: DiethnisVivliothiki, 1979) (in Greek).

24. Murray Bookchin, "Interview to Michalis Tremopoulos," in *Αρνούμαι* 8, December 1992, 28–31. (in Greek).

25. Dan Chodorkoff, "Interview to Michalis Tremopoulos," in *Αρνούμαι* 7, May 1992, 39–41. (in Greek).

26. "Bookchin in Greece!" in *Αρνούμαι* 7, May 1992, 42. (in Greek).

27. Murray Bookchin, *Anarchism and Social Ecology*, (Thessaloniki: Ecological Movement of Thessaloniki, 1986) (in Greek).

28. http://eutopia.gr/

Murray Bookchin in Greece: The Publication of His Works and the Impact of His Ideas

Costas Despiniadis

Translated by Eleni Dimitriadou

THE EMERGENCE OF anarchist ideas in Greece has a long history. Already in the nineteenth century emerged the influence of the early socialist ideas of Saint-Simonism. The first explicitly anarchist newspapers and groups made their appearance at the end of the nineteenth century, in Patras, Pyrgos of Ilia, Volos, and elsewhere.

However, this first appearance of anarchist ideas was interrupted not long after World War I, followed by a period when anarchist ideas were essentially non-existent in Greek society, except, perhaps, in individual cases of intellectuals without any social impact. This situation continued throughout the interwar period and even beyond, as the Greek Communist Party (*Κομμουνιστικό Κόμμα Ελλάδας*, KKE) constituted the only powerful pole of the Left in Greece, reaching its culmination in the period of resistance to the German occupation and, shortly after, that of the Greek Civil War. To the left of the KKE were only a few small Trotskyist groups, encountering brutal suppression both by the representatives of the Greek state who collaborated with the Germans and by the Stalinists of the KKE.

It would take a few decades for the severed thread of anarchist ideas in Greece to reconnect. The fall of the military dictatorship in 1974 brought about a boom of leftist, radical, and antiauthoritarian publishing.

Already in 1973, one year before the fall of the dictatorship, the relative slackening of censorship resulted in the emergence of the first leftist publishing houses, which were no longer compelled to submit books for censorship and approval before they were published. At the same time, the first anarchist publishing houses emerged. These included the International Library (Diethnís Vivliothíki), founded by Christos Konstantinidis along with a small group of anarchist activists, and the Free Press of George Garbis, who had then returned from England, where he as a university student he had been exposed to anarchist ideas.

With rudimentary financial means, but abundant solicitude and fighting spirit, these publishers began to connect with those who were oppressed by the dictatorship and thirsty for radical ideas. This took place at a time when there were not only difficulties with the flow of information, but also with the level of knowledge of foreign languages.

At that time, the youth were ready to express their political radicalism. During the 1973 uprisings against the junta in the Athens Law School and the Polytechnic, the first, small in terms of membership, anarchist groups appeared. These were essentially formed by the core group of individuals who gathered around the aforementioned anarchist publishing house, Diethnís Vivliothíki.

Our first acquaintance with Murray Bookchin's work was from three editions of *Listen Marxist!* (1978); *Desire and Need in the Revolutionary Movement* (1978); and *Towards a Liberatory Technology* (1979), published in Greek by Diethnís Vivliothíki in the late 1970s. These three publications bear translators' names as imaginative pseudonymous groups, such as "Vandals' Association of Thessaloniki," "Association of Good Striplings and Damsels, Split Faction of the Vandals' Association of Thessaloniki," and "Office of Public Secrets and Collaborative Expropriation in Thessaloniki." There was still a fear of a new coup in the first few years following the fall of the dictatorship, which is why many of the translators of early versions of anarchist books in Greece used pseudonyms. Today, we are at liberty to say that these three works of Bookchin were translated by Athanasios Babadjimas, who had a good knowledge of English and had come in contact with Bookchin's work when he studied in the US.

Around the same period (in the late 1970s and early 1980s), we saw the publication of a few more of Bookchin's books (some without an exact publication date), this time by the second historical anarchist publishing house of Greece, Eleftheros Typos. In all, Eleftheros Typos, which continued its project of publishing Bookchin's work during the 90s, released eight short books: *The Limits of the City* (1979); *Hierarchy and Domination* (N.p.d.); *Ecology and Revolutionary Thought* (1980); *Spontaneity and Organization* (N.p.d); *The Radicalization of Nature* (1985); *Marxism as a Bourgeois Philosophy* (1987); *The Spanish Revolution of 1936: A Critical Account* (1995); and *The Overpopulation Myth* (1997).

At this point, it should be emphasized that these first editions were essentially selections of Bookchin's essays, either from *Post-Scarcity Anarchism* or from other works, and not his entire books, a choice that was justified by publishers' limited resources at that time. Also, some translated titles may not accurately reflect the original titles, and some translations may have omissions, as they were created at a time when Greek-language translations of certain terms and political concepts were not yet standardized.

Despite such shortcomings, the seeds were sown and Greek readers were exposed to Bookchin's thought. On the one hand, the anarchists in Greece found in Bookchin's critique of Marxist political philosophy a valuable theoretical ally in their own dispute with the powerful Stalinist KKE and its offshoots. On the other hand, in a country that was in a process of "development" following the Western capitalist example—with all what this implies for the destruction of nature and the environment—nascent ecologists could read Bookchin's prolific analyses on these issues.

This "ecological dimension" (after the purely "anarchist") was the second area where the Greek activists encountered Bookchin's thought. The ecological movement first made its appearance in the 1980s. During this period, some of the people who turned towards the ecological movement came either from the antimilitarist movement of conscientious objectors or from that of the anarchists. They constituted the most radical parts of the ecological movement that were in search of a revolutionary, and not reformist, ecological perspective. Thus, what these people found in Bookchin's work, primarily in his theory on political ecology, was a fruitful source of theoretical feedback for their activism. An illustration of this meeting with Bookchin's thought is a typewritten brochure of an interview with Bookchin, titled *Anarchism and Social Ecology*, issued in 1986 by the Ecological Group of Thessaloniki.

In the early 1990s, the anarchist publisher Michalis Protopsaltis, who in the meantime was actively involved in the ecological movement, published two books: Bookchin's essay, *What is Social Ecology?* (1992) and his book *The Modern Crisis* (1993), the Greek edition of which bears the title *The Modern Ecological Crisis*. In the same period, Exandas Publications released the Greek edition of the book *Remaking Society* (1993), which was the first of Bookchin's works released by a mainstream commercial publishing house, probably indicating that at this point his thought was reaching a wider audience and not only some "initiate" activists.

Shortly afterwards, thanks to people who had significant involvement in the movement of conscientious objectors, such as Yiannis Glarnetatzis, we had the release of two more of Bookchin's works, *Towards an Ecological Society* (1994) and *The Limits of the City* (1996). Both of these books were translated by Glarnetatzis and, once again, were published by a mainstream publishing house, Paratiritis. Characteristic of the appeal that Bookchin's thought had already begun to have on Greek readers was the publication, in 1996, by the same publishing house, of the book, *Political Ecology*, written by Dimitrios Roussopoulos, a close collaborator and publisher of Bookchin, and, in a sense, a successor of the latter regarding his own writings.

The Eutopia journal and its eponymous publishing house, with the participation of people with libertarian views, appeared in 1999. Central elements of the founders' action included the ecological issue and the issue of libertarian communalism. The original subtitle of the journal was "for direct and economic democracy, for libertarian-confederate communalism," while the current subtitle is "periodical edition for libertarian communalism." Both subtitles reveal how Bookchin's ideas inspired Eutopia's founders.

This is the first political and publishing group in Greece that explicitly referenced Bookchin (it would not be an exaggeration to say that it is the first "Bookchinist" group in Greece), and it frequently includes essays of the American philosopher in the issues of its journal, which remains in circulation. Eutopia Publications recently released two additional books by Bookchin: *FAI: The Organization of the Anarchist Spanish Movement in the Pre-civil War Years* (1927–1936) (2014), and *The Next Revolution* (2017).

In addition to the members of Eutopia, other Greeks were very clearly influenced by Bookchin's work and referenced it explicitly in their writing and talks in the early 2000s. Through Bookchin's thought (and this developed in the last years of his life), these people disassociated their political position (sometimes under conditions of intense polemic) from both the traditional anarchist movement and the respective ecological one. Thus, in the 2000s, and for the first time in Greece, we had activists, albeit few in number, who identified themselves as communalists, maintaining a clear distance from the anarchist and libertarian traditions. Moreover, we also had a number of books published (mainly, but not exclusively) by individuals who seceded from the Greek edition of the journal, *Inclusive Democracy*, created by Takis Fotopoulos (a thinker who had also been influenced by Bookchin in formulating his own theories). These books include: *Social or Lifestyle Anarchism* (Isnafi, 2005); *History, Civilization, and Progress: Outline of a Critique of Modern Relativism* (Isnafi, 2005); *The Communalist Project* (Alexandria, 2006); *Reflections on Marxism and Anarchism* (Isnafi, 2010).

This evolution in Bookchin's thought has displeased some members of the Greek anarchist movement in Greece, as they realized that this important thinker was now including them in his criticisms and sometimes his polemics.

In the last decade, the publication of Bookchin's works steadily continues, and due to the increased economic position of Greek publishers—even of small and alternative ones— we are seeing the publication of his larger, more extensive efforts, and not just the selections of short essays as before.

Thus, Vivliopelagos Publications released the important historical book, *The Spanish Anarchists. The Heroic Years of 1868–1936* (2011), Alexandria Publications released the four-volume work on the history of revolutionary movements, *The Third Revolution* (2009–2017), and Antigoni Publications released one of the basic theoretical books, *The Ecology of Freedom* (2016). The publishing group Ekdoseis ton Synadelfon released an extended selection of essays under the title, *Libertarian Routes*, with a preface by Dimitrios Roussopoulos and an introduction by

Bookchin's companion, Janet Biehl. We ought to note here, as it is denotative of the wider presence in Greece of ideas inspired by Bookchin, that Janet Biehl's essay, *Ecofascism,* was also released by Isnafi Publications in 2003, while Debbie Bookchin's essay *How My Father's Ideas Helped the Kurds Create a New Democracy* was published recently (Ekdoseis ton Synadelfon, 2019). Alongside the publications of Bookchin's major works, the interest in his ideas has been reinforced by the "Kurdish issue."

Since the 1980s, the "Kurdish issue" has preoccupied public opinion quite intensely in Greece, mostly from a patriotic and nationalistic perspective. In fact, the traditional political hostility between Greece and Turkey (steadily stirred up and reinforced by official state policies and the nationalists in both countries) led parts of the Greek political establishment to see an ally in the face of the Kurdish fighters. This attitude, however, is certainly not induced by some kind of pure internationalist solidarity towards a repressed people, but instead by an ulterior motive, a logic which in Greek is summed up with the saying "the enemy of my enemy is my friend.[1]" Moreover, it is an open secret that in the 1980s and 1990s, the "Kurdish issue" in Greece was a prime field of action for the Greek secret services.

How superficial and utilitarian this interest was on the part of the Greek politicians was made clear in 1999, when the Greek government caved into pressure from western allies and handed over the Kurdish leader, Abdullah Öcalan, to the Turkish authorities. The full meaning of this event goes beyond the scope of this text. In the context of assessing the impact of Bookchin's ideas in Greece, the important aspect is that the development of the Kurdish movement in Rojava, as well as the salient influence of Bookchin's thought on Kurdish fighters, have all made—for the very first time—the Kurdish issue in Greece a matter of international solidarity. In this context, it is worth noting that as soon as the Rojava movement took its current form, the hypocritical interest of Greek nationalists for the Kurds appears to have ceased forever!

This renewed, solidarity-driven interest has also been reflected in the release of relevant books by noncommercial publishers who are part of the respective solidarity movement. Thus, Eutopia Publications recently released *Make Rojava Green Again* (2019), a book that has been circulating in many countries, while it has recently been banned in Germany where its copies were confiscated.[2] As a demonstration of the new Greek solidarity with the Kurds is the publishing of four books by Abdullah Öcalan, in Greek, in which the later effect of Bookchin's thought on the Kurdish leader is quite evident: *Liberating Life: Woman's Revolution* (2017); *Democratic Nation* (2017); *Democratic Confederalism* (2017). These were all published by the anarchist publishing house, Publications Stasei Ekpiptontes.

Conclusions

Completing this short essay, we can succinctly draw several conclusions. The interest in Greece for publishing Bookchin's works over the past 40 years has been stable, and it was not a response to the many short-lived theoretical fashions that suddenly appear in the Greek publishing field, only to disappear just as suddenly. The publication of approximately 30 volumes of Bookchin's works by ten different publishers, as well as essays in various journals, demonstrate this lasting interest.

In various ways, Bookchin's thought affected Greek anarchist, libertarian, ecological and communalist movements, and although it never became dominant in these movements (with the exception of the very limited communalist one), it has always been distinct. Bookchin provided these movements with tools for the critique of Marxist ideology and of conventional ecology, while he had essentially been the theorist who introduced Greece to political ecology, communalism, and libertarian communitarianism. Undoubtedly, Bookchin's historical studies on preceding revolutionary movements were also important, as they offered a sense of historical continuity and genealogical ancestry that activists, usually focused on an often ephemeral empirical "practicism," often lack.

The attitude of the Greek anarchist movement—one of the largest and most powerful in Europe—had been rather ambivalent towards Bookchin, reflecting, perhaps, the shifts in Bookchin's thought during his theoretical journey. However, most of his Greek publishers and readers clearly come in one way or another from the wider anarchist-libertarian movement.

Despite the plethora of Bookchin's works published in Greek, particularly when considering that many were the work of small publishers with limited financial means, the truth is that some of his key works are still not translated in Greek (e.g. *Urbanization Without Cities*, Black Rose Books, 1992). Additionally, the uncoordinated publishing effort by diverse publishers with often disparate objectives has resulted in the lack of systematization that could permit the readers to follow the evolution of Bookchin's thought. Instead, it appears that publishers and translators preferred to selectively pick and choose whatever fitted their purposes. In fact, Bookchin himself pointed out this weakness in the preface to the Greek edition of his essay, "The Communalist Project."

In closing, allow me to make a personal comment, as I have tried to be as objective as I could throughout my brief report on the impact of Bookchin's ideas in Greece: I am a steady but critical reader of Bookchin, both agreeing and disagreeing with his views., I consider it to be the duty of any reader to read the political philosophers and writers critically and with vigilance, feeding and activating their own thought and not searching to find ready-made recipes and solutions. In my opinion, this benefits both reader and writer.

I have always appreciated the breadth of knowledge of this essentially self-educated man, the originality of many of his ideas, his insight regarding risks that he pointed out, and above all, his lifelong devotion to the cause of universal human emancipation, as well as to the liberation of nature from human domination.

A political philosopher who selflessly devoted all of his intellectual potential to such causes is worth reading.

BIBLIOGRAPHY

Biehl, Janet and Staudenmaier, Peter. *Οικοφασισμός*, [Ecofascism] (Ioannina: Ισνάφι, 2003).

Bookchin, Debbie. *Πώς οι ιδέες του πατέρα μου βοήθησαν τους Κούρδους να δημιουργήσουν μια καινούργια δημοκρατία*, [How My Father's Ideas Helped the Kurds Create a New Democracy] (Athens: Εκδόσεις των Συναδελφων, 2019).

Bookchin, Murray. *Άκου μαρξιστή*, [Listen Marxist!] (Athens: Διεθνής Βιβλιοθήκη, 1975).

____. *Η οικολογία της ελευθερίας, [The Ecology of Freedom] (Athens: Διεθνής Βιβλιοθήκη, 1978).*

____. *Προς μία απελευθερωτική τεχνολογία, [Towards a Liberatory Technology] (Athens: Διεθνής Βιβλιοθήκη, 1979).*

____. *Τα όρια της πόλης*, [The Limits of the City] (Athens: Ελεύθερος Τύπος, 1979).

____. *Η οικολογία και η επαναστατική σκέψη*, [Ecology and Revolutionary Thought] (Athens: Ελεύθερος Τύπος, 1980).

____. *Η ριζοσπαστικοποίηση της φύσης*, [The Radicalization of Nature] (Athens: Ελεύθερος Τύπος, 1985).

____. *Ο Μαρξισμός σαν αστική κοινωνιολογία*, [Marxism as a Bourgeois Philosophy] (Athens: Ελεύθερος Τύπος, 1987).

____. *Η ισπανική επανάσταση του 1936*, [The Spanish Revolution of 1936] (Athens: Ελεύθερος Τύπος, 1995).

____. *Ο μύθος του υπερπληθυσμού*, [The Overpopulation Myth] (Athens: Ελεύθερος Τύπος, 1997).

____. *Αναρχισμός και κοινωνική οικολογία*, [Anarchism and Social Ecology] (Thessaloniki: Οικολογική Κίνηση Θεσσαλονίκης, 1986).

____. *Τι είναι κοινωνική οικολογία*, [What is Social Ecology] (Athens: Βιβλιοπέλαγος, 1992).

____. *Η σύγχρονη οικολογική κρίση*, [The Modern Ecological Crisis] (Athens: Βιβλιοπέλαγος, 1993).

____. *Ξαναφτιάχνοντας την κοινωνία*, [Remaking Society] (Athens: Εξάντας, 1993).

____. *Προς μια οικολογική κοινωνία*, [Towards an Ecological Society] (Thessaloniki: Παρατηρητής, 1994).

____. *Τα όρια της πόλης*, [The Limits of the City] (Thessaloniki: Παρατηρητής, 1996).

____. *Η οργάνωση του αναρχικού ισπανικού κινήματος στα προεμφυλιακά χρόνια (1927–1936)*, [The organization of the anarchist Spanish movement in the pre-Civil War years (1927–1936)] (Athens: Ευτοπία, 2014).

____. *Η επομενη επαναστaση*, [The Next Revolution] (Athens: Ευτοπία, 2017).

____. *Κοινωνικός αναρχισμός η Lifestyle αναρχισμός*, [Social or Lifestyle Anarchism: An Unbridgeable Chasm] (Ioannina: Ισνάφι, 2005).

____. *Ιστορία, πολιτισμός και πρόοδος: Περίγραμμα μιας κριτικής του σύγχρονου σχετικισμού*, [History, Civilization, and Progress: Outline of a Critique of Modern Relativism] (Ioannina: Ισνάφι, 2005).

____. *Το πρόσταγμα του Κομουναλισμού*, [The Communalist Project] (Athens: Αλεξάνδρεια, 2006).

___. *Μαρξισμός και αναρχισμός,* [Marxism and Anarchism] (Ioannina: Ισνάφι, 2010).

___. *Οι ισπανοί αναρχικοί: τα ηρωικά χρονια 1868–1936,* [The Spanish Anarchists: The Heroic Years of 1868–1936] (Athens: Βιβλιοπέλαγος, 2011).

___. *Η τρίτη επανάσταση* Vol 1–4, [The Third Revolution Vol 1–4] (Athens: Αλεξάνδρεια, 2009–2017).

___. *Η Οικολογία της Ελευθερίας, Η Ανάδυση και η Διάλυση της Ιεραρχίας,* [The Ecology of Freedom: The Emergence and Dissolution of Hierarchy] (Thessaloniki: Αντιγόνη, 2016).

___. *Ελευθεριακές διαδρομές,* [Libertarian Routs] (Athens: Εκδοσεις των Συναδελφων, 2017).

Internationalist Commune of Rojava. *Να ξανακάνουμε πράσινη τη Ροζάβα,* [Make Rojava Green Again] (Athens: Ευτοπία, 2019).

Öcalan, Abdullah. *Απελευθερώνοντας τη ζωή: Η γυναικεία επανάσταση,* [Liberating Life: Woman's Revolution] (Athens: Στάσει Εκπίπτοντες, 2017).

___. *Δημοκρατικός συνομοσπονδισμός,* [Democratic Confederalism] (Athens: Στάσει Εκπίπτοντες, 2017).

Roussopoulos, Dimitrios. *Πολιτική Οικολογία,* [Political Ecology] (Thessaloniki: Παρατηρητής, 1996).

NOTES

1. "Ο εχθρός του εχθρού μου είναι φίλος μου."

2. The German authorities declared on February 12, 2018, a ban on the German-based Kurdish publishing house Mezopotamya. The ban led to the confiscation of at least 200 copies of the book *Make Rojava Green Again*.

Murray Bookchin and Contemporary Greek Social Movements: The Influence of Social Ecology on Democratic Political Discourse

Alexandros Schismenos

> *Terms that are related to individuals like Marxist, or Hegelian, or Bakuninist, or Kropotkinist, are completely outside my intellectual and emotional horizon. I'm a follower of no one; I'm a Bookchinite, and nobody has a right to claim that but me. When I die, Bookchinism comes to an end, and all the allusions to it both among Marxists and anarchists.*
> — MURRAY BOOKCHIN, 1981

IT CAN BE ARGUED that there is no objective measurement of the influence of an individual's thought upon collective social movements, especially in the case of direct democratic social movements for human emancipation from authority. This is certainly the case with Murray Bookchin, a revolutionary thinker who renounced Marxism to re-imagine anarchism and renounced anarchism to form his own political proposition of communalism and democratic confederalism.

While it is impossible to measure the influence of Bookchin's thought and action on the current social-historical global timescape, it is also impossible to ignore it, visible as it is in the revolutionary democratic institution of Kurdish Rojava, and within contemporary ecological and social movements. When I embarked on an inquiry into the importance of Bookchin for Greek social movements, I understood that it was a task never to be completed. The libertarian, anarchist editor Michalis Protopsaltis used to say, "It's not the naked truth coming out of the well, it is just my opinion."

Subsequently, this article is not intended to be conclusive, but rather indicative. It can be considered as a brief historical and philosophical outline of a history still in the making.

It will be helpful to begin by delimiting the historical and social framework of this narrative, which will be concerned with modern Greek history in general and the history of democratic social movements beyond Marxism in particular. The first section of this essay is an outline of this history. Then some of the main philosophical and political questions that arise will be considered. The second section, will address three overlapping, converging, but also schematically distinct political traditions: namely anarchism, ecology, and democracy which provide different focal points for Greek social movements within a common political horizon: the emancipation of humanity from authority and the liberation of nature from exploitation. Particular instances of Bookchin's involvement with Greek radical democratic political discourse will be considered, and the third section briefly addresses Bookchin's participation in the international committee of the Greek-edited journals *Society and Nature,* (*Κοινωνία και Φύση*), and *Democracy and Nature* (*Δημοκρατία και Φύση*), his resignation, and his disagreement with Castoriadis, who is also an important figure for modern Greek social movements. The fourth and final section, will discuss the correspondence of Bookchin and the imprisoned Kurdish leader Abdullah Öcalan, which resulted in the political turn of the Kurdish movement toward the implementation of democratic confederalism in Rojava. This section will focus on contemporary Greek movements and the influence of Bookchin's ideas on present political praxis.

The word "democratic" is here used with the exclusive meaning of direct democracy, which defines a political institution of society without State authority, without mechanisms of political repression, and capitalist exploitation. As Bookchin described it, democracy is:

> The idea of a people that exercises a great deal of federalist or confederalist control, the ideal of a grassroots type of democracy, the idea of the freedom of the individual which is not to get lost in the mazes of anarcho-egotism à la Stirner, or for that matter right-wing libertarianism.[1]

This idea has inspired social movements in Greece since the late 1970s and the explosion of a colorful, heterogeneous, and radical counterculture with anarchist tendencies after the fall of the seven-year military dictatorship, the Junta of the Colonels (1967–1974). During this dark period of military fascism in Greece which followed decades of right-wing nationalist governments established with the help of the US after the communist defeat in the Civil War of 1946-1949, new underground ideas and revolutionary trends made their appearance among young people and university students. The echo of 1968, the participation of Greek students in the French May of 1968, and the existence of a wide anti-Junta sentiment in Europe, had started to penetrate the iron curtain of censorship, as did the voice of the tortured from the jails and the exiled from the desolate islands. Anarchism, which had vanished from the Greek political landscape after the rise of the Communist Party in 1918 (founded by the name SEKE, later KKE) re-emerged alongside forbidden music like rock and forbidden social practices like freedom of speech, freedom of sexuality, and freedom of art.

Greece: The Re-Emergence of Anarchism and Democratic Politics

The first anarchist ideas and collectivities in Greece emerged in the late nineteenth century in the port city of Patras, where the first political collective self-defined as anarchist was founded under the name Anarchist Association of Patras, *Αναρχικός Όμιλος Πατρών*. The Greek State responded with repression and violence, and by 1897, the year the Greek Kingdom met humiliating defeat in a war against the Ottoman Empire, most of its members were imprisoned. However, Greek anarchist collectives were spreading across Greece, as the country was expanding and social injustice flourished alongside poverty and oppression. Anarchism was overshadowed by Leninism after 1917, and during the Second World War, the Stalinist KKE faction of Greek resistance to German occupation eliminated all Trotskyist and anarchist groups.

On November 17, 1973, Polytechneio, the Polytechnic University in the center of Athens was occupied by students protesting against the military Junta. The occupation ended when tanks invaded the building. The outlawed KKE had condemned the occupation. Among the rebelling students, a new generation of anarchists emerged, one of which wrote on the wall of the occupied building "*ΚΑΤΩ Η ΕΞΟΥΣΙΑ*," or "DOWN WITH AUTHORITY." Doctor of political philosophy and participant in the events Giorgos N. Oikonomou has described Polytechneio as the first direct democratic uprising in Modern Greek history.

This social-historical phenomenon, the reappearance of anarchist and direct democratic ideas beneath the conservative surface of Greek society is better described by the words of Protopsaltis, who was part of that movement:

A powerful and imaginative libertarian movement, beyond the Left, an independent course of action with zero roots in Greek society, with a complete lack of not only historical experience but also life experience, since the older anarchists did not exceed 23–25 years old. They rely on instinct and voluntarism, believe in their spontaneity, and improvise while opening the way. The two factors that favor them are, first, the echo of the subversive and creative spirit of the 1960s, which swept the planet, socially and culturally, while having in Greece as its ally the favorite wind of Metapolitefsi. And secondly, the magical interaction between Stinas and Castoriadis, Stinas being a symbol of people's struggles for emancipation, and Castoriadis being a symbol of human thinking, have come together as action and theory come together in historical praxis in a reciprocal interaction. And it is their influence that has shaped, in the years of the Junta, the first groups and gatherings, the first cells for the dissemination of antiauthoritarian ideas.

Bookchin's name and writings first appear in Greece within this social-historical context, as one of the radical thinkers of the 1960s that Greek revolutionary youth engaged with in order to escape the Marxist-Leninist bondage imposed on the Left by the hegemony of KKE. This quest for a revolutionary theoretical and practical experimentation beyond Marxism was led by two figures: first, there was Agis Stinas, the pseudonym of Spyros Priftis (1900–1987), a Trotskyist and one of the most important revolutionaries of the Greek workers' movement; second, there was Cornelius Castoriadis, who had since the mid-1960s criticized Marx from a revolutionary perspective inspired first by workers' councils socialism and then by direct democracy. It was thanks to these two revolutionaries that the Greek public came in contact with the ideas of Murray Bookchin. Bookchin, who had criticized Marxism and moved on to anarchism provided the theoretical tools for a powerful critique of Marxist materialism and a synthesis of ecology, anarchism, and democracy. In 1981, he had reached the same conclusion that Greek anarchists had learned by bitter experience: "Marx's theory of historical materialism [...] is virtually a debris of despotism."

In the first years of Metapolitefsi (the transition from military dictatorship to a parliamentary oligarchy), anarchist publishers published Greek translations of Bookchin's work. This included Christos Konstantinidis (*Χρήστος Κωνσταντινίδης*) of *Diethnis Vivliothiki* (*Διεθνής Βιβλιοθήκη*) who published *Listen, Marxist!* in 1975, or Georgios Garbis (*Γιώργος Γαρμπής*) of *Eleftheros Typos* (*Ελεύθερος Τύπος*) who published *The Limits of the City* in 1979, *Ecology in Revolutionary Thought* in 1980, and *Marxism as Bourgeois Ideology* in 1987, etc. Articles by and on Bookchin appeared in anarchist magazines like *O Kokkoras pou lalei sto skotadi* (*Ο Κόκκορας που λαλεί στο σκοτάδι*), *Anarchos* (*Άναρχος*), *Ta anthi tou kakou* (*Τα άνθη του κακού*), *Eleftheriaki Kinisi* (*Ελευθεριακή Κίνηση*), *Eftopia* (*Ευτοπία*), and *ContAct*, to name a few.

Bookchin's influence helped libertarians and antiauthoritarians move toward ecology, which in Greece had not inspired social movements like it had in Western Europe and the US. During the 1980s, anarchist trends in Greece were more inspired by the workers' movement, and Italian Autonomia. In the 1990s, more individualistic, nihilistic, and anticonsumerist trends of anarchism appeared via the US, the cultural influence of which dominated the new mass media. Since most of these trends, associated with a late blooming of punk-rock music in Greece, originated in the US, Murray Bookchin's critique of their original form proved a powerful antidote to the desocialization of the movement. Bookchin's confrontation with deep ecology, as well as with State Green and NGO Ecology provided Greek democratic discourse with the analyses needed to plant the seeds that would result in the emergence of direct democratic social ecological movements in Greece during the first decades of the twenty-first century.

Bookchin even became personally involved in this discourse, participating in the international advisory board of *Society and Nature* and *Democracy and Nature* journals.

Anarchism, Ecology, and Democracy:
Distinct and Interconnected Fields of Political Theory

There are three distinct, but overlapping and interconnected, fields of political thought which correspond to three interconnected areas of social and political struggle. Bookchin's influence has been important to all three, but most important is his attempt to integrate their focal points within the horizon of direct democracy and social ecology.

Anarchists in Greece were deeply impressed by the small brochure *Listen Marxist!*, which seemed to correspond to Marx's critique by Castoriadis. Bookchin expressed the sentiment of many when he proclaimed that:

> The problem is not that Marxism is a "method" which must be reapplied to "new situations" or that "neo-Marxism" has to be developed to overcome the limitations of "classical Marxism." The attempt to rescue the Marxism pedigree by emphasizing the method over the system or by adding "neo" to a sacred word is sheer mystification if all the practical conclusions of the system flatly contradict these efforts."[2]

Castoriadis, from the other side of the Atlantic, had also condemned the attempts to rescue Marxism by reducing it to a method: "[…] method cannot be separated from content in this way, especially not when it is a question of historical and social theory. Method, in the philosophical sense, is simply the operating set of categories."[3]

The newly formed anarchist-libertarian movement read works by both thinkers, and these works were used against communist orthodoxy, which continued to be hegemonic until the collapse of the USSR. Bookchin presented a new anarchist thinking that was not contemplative but practical, that took on the central question of authority and power and proposed an alternative social institution.

It would not be an exaggeration to say that antiauthoritarian movements in Greece discovered ecology by reading Bookchin and Castoriadis. When, in 1987, clashes erupted at the mountainous village of Mesochora between police forces and local residents who were protesting the construction of the highest dam in Europe for the diversion of the second longest river in Greece, Acheloos, the members of the Anarchist Union, (Ένωση Αναρχικών), failed to appreciate the importance of the struggle.

Individual anarchists, influenced by readings of Bookchin, participated in the first ecological groups that resulted mostly in the formation of the *Ecologoi-Enallaktikoi (Οικολόγοι-Εναλλακτικοί)* political party which participated in the November 1989 Parliamentary Elections, electing one representative. Slowly, elements of the Greek political party system started moving toward a "green" state policy agenda, which did not seem to be of much interest to their electorate, certainly not so much as that of the green parties emerging in Western Europe.

Social ecology provided an alternative to the machinations of State policies and representative politics. Murray Bookchin touched on deeper issues, connecting the ecological crisis to capitalist domination, social injustice and the dominant capitalist worldview of mastery over nature: a worldview that promotes the exploitation of nature, originating from a system based on the exploitation of humanity. Bookchin's synthesis evoked a different perspective and a different ethical set of values:

> I believe that there has to be an ideal and I favour an ethical anarchism which can be cohered into an ideal. I believe that it's terribly important to have a movement that is spiritual, not in the supernatural sense, but in the sense of German Geist, spirit, which combines the idea of mind together with feeling, together with intuition. I'm sorry that some self-styled anarchists have picked up on the word spirit and have turned me into a theological ecologist, a notion which I think is crude beyond all belief. There has to be a body of values. I would prefer to call them ecological because my image of ecology goes beyond nature and extends into society as a whole—not to be confused in any way with sociobiology, which I think is an extremely regressive, reactionary tendency.[4]

Bookchin raised some difficult questions for the anarchist movement at the time. In Greece, the punk, Nietzschean, and Foucaultian trends promoted a similar "self-styled" anarcho-individualism which, however, formed a large part of the heterogeneous counter-culture. It seemed difficult to accept the need for a core of values. The word "ethical" seemed scandalous to some, who had experienced anarchism as a form of self-rebellion against a society with highly conservative "ethics" continually imposed by the State, the Church, and the family. In these times of political immaturity and the retreat into individualism or State-funded party "socialism," the social-historical reality itself posed those same questions that Bookchin had iterated.

On the other hand, anarchists oriented toward society found it difficult to escape from the myth of the proletariat. Having confronted Marxism, their analysis of traditional political narratives was still focused on the proletariat as the messianic class of world-history. The scarcity of available translated works blended thinkers such as Benjamin, Nietzsche, Foucault, and Stirner with Castoriadis and Bookchin, along with the re-discovery of historical revolutionary figures like Nechayev, Durruti, Bakunin, and Kropotkin.

The question of the ethical and political content of anarchism was raised by Bookchin and has remained unresolved. Nevertheless, Bookchin's attempt to answer it helped him move toward the issue of democracy and the project of democratic federalism, criticizing anarchism from a revolutionary and practical standpoint, as he had previously done with Marxism. In 1981, before his breach with anarchism, he had tried to define his own view as eco-anarchism and anarcho-communalism:

> We have to clarify the meaning of the word. We have to give it a rich content. And that content has to stand apart from a critique of other ideologies, because the way you sharpen a knife is, frankly, on a grindstone. And the grindstone for me is Marxism. I've developed my anarchism, my critique of Marxism, which has been the most advanced bourgeois ideology I know of, into a community of ideas and ultimately a common sense of responsibilities and commitments. I don't think anarchism consists of sitting down and saying let's form a collective. I don't think it consists of saying we're all anarchists: you're an anarcho-syndicalist; you're an anarcho-communist; you're an anarcho-individualist. I believe that anarchists should agree to disagree but not to fight with each other. We don't have to go around as the Protestant reformation did, or as the socialist revolution did, and execute each other as soon as we are successful—assuming we'll ever be successful. But I believe that if we do have a commonality of beliefs we should clarify them, we should strengthen their coherence and we should also develop common projects that produce a lived community of relationships. And also, we should try to become better people, ethically speaking, reflect upon ourselves and our very limited existences and develop a sense of tolerance for each other, as well as for other anarchist groups with which we may disagree. But we're not committed to toeing a line called anarchism; there are many different anarchisms. My anarchism is frankly anarcho-communalism, and it's eco-anarchism as well. And it's not oriented toward the proletariat. I would like to see a critical mass of very gifted anarchists come together in an appropriate place in order to do highly productive work. That's it. I don't know why that can't be done except for the fact that I think that people mistrust their own ideals today. I don't think

that they don't believe in them; I think they mistrust the viability of them. They're afraid to commit themselves to their ideals.[5]

Bookchin's insistence on nature, equality, community and ethical content bridged social anarchism with the politics of direct democracy, already highlighted in the works of Castoriadis, but also in the works of the classics like Rousseau and Bakunin. The collapse of the Soviet Union after 1989 seemed to historically confirm his criticisms, both against historical materialism, since the regime that was supposed to bring forth socialism proved to be totalitarian, and against the myth of the proletariat, which had already been consumed by the expansion and saturation of the dominant capitalist ideals.

However, an ethical content and a political commonality among anarchists proved impossible, since major anarcho-individualistic trends were reinforced and supplemented by capitalist lifestyles. Bookchin's critique of lifestyle anarchists and his attempt to disassociate social anarchism from those trends was well received in Greece among anarchists that had re-engaged in politics on both a local and global scale through the anti-globalization movement.

Prague 2000, Genoa 2001, and Thessaloniki 2003 were major historical events for Greek social movements, which discovered another perspective and a broader dimension of social solidarity that transcended borders and also ideologies. The Zapatista uprising in 1994 had given new impetus to questions of community, networking, horizontal democratic institutions and global solidarity, alongside the example of a victorious movement without leaders and the attempt to build an autonomous community. The anti-globalization movement helped Greek activists question traditional forms of ideology, turn to society and start experimenting with democratic communities, collectivities and networks beyond classic anarchism. Networks of direct democratic assemblies with different references but a common project, like the Anti-Authoritarian Movement (Αντιεξουσιαστική Κίνηση—AK) were formed, based on a set of values as their common ground where a multitude of different standpoints could converge.

But the most important feature of the past decades was the emergence of grassroots social ecological movements. When the State's project of the diversion of Acheloos was brought up again in 2007, a movement from all across the country joined the struggle of the locals and managed to halt the project and continues to fight for the destruction of the damn today. In Chalkidiki, local communities came together with ecological and antiauthoritarian collectivities to fight against the gold mining project of the Canadian company Eldorado Gold. Having been confronted with fierce State oppression, the struggle continues. More recently, in Epirus and Western Greece a direct democratic ecological grassroots movement has emerged against oil and gas extractions by powerful oil trusts like Exxon-Mobile, Repsol, Total etc. These movements, converging in assemblies and forming networks of solidarity, represent a new social ecological consciousness, a new radical imaginary oriented toward autonomy and democracy.

The influence of Bookchin is also prominent in urban ecological movements, in the cities of Athens, Thessaloniki, Ioannina, and Volos, where desolation creates urban deserts, in movements for the liberation and re-creation of free public space, and more recently in movements against gentrification and construction. Urban ecological movements in Greece have discussed Bookchin's proposal of a democratic municipalism in several instances, with diverging conclusions. However, this writer's personal opinion is that while his proposed strategy is of great interest and importance, it remains on a theoretical level as regards to Greece, which is a highly centralized State, with municipal authorities directly dependent on the government and the main political parties. Although Bookchin acknowledged that his politics belonged and referred to the American tradition, his ideals far exceeded its borders:

> My concern is to develop a North American type of anarchism that comes out of the American tradition, or that at least can be communicated to Americans and that takes into consideration that Americans are not any longer people of European background. Another consideration is to find out what is the real locus of libertarian activity. Is it the factory? Is it the youth? Is it the schools? Is it the community? The only conclusion I could arrive at with the death of the workers' movement as a revolutionary force—you know the imagery of the proletarian vanguard, or proletarian hegemony— has been the community.[6]

In part, his adherence to the American communal tradition, very different from the European centralized nation-state tradition, has led to a misunderstanding of the European political experience, which in this writer's opinion is implicitly manifested in his involvement with the *Society and Nature* and *Democracy and Nature* journals and his subsequent disagreement with Castoriadis. On the other hand, Bookchin's criticism reveals a deeper philosophical disagreement.

Society and Nature: The Conflict with Castoriadis

Society and Nature[7] first appeared in Greek on May 1992, published by an editorial collective, which, among others, included Nikos Iliopoulos (Νίκος Ηλιόπουλος) and professor Takis Fotopoulos, *Τάκης Φωτόπουλος*, assisted by an international advisory board including Bookchin and Castoriadis. Seven issues were published until 1994, when the journal was renamed *Democracy and Nature* for three more issues, until publication stopped in 1997. Bookchin contributed with articles titled *Earth and the City: Libertarian Local Self-Administration* (issue 1), *Philosophical*

Naturalism, Social and Deep Ecology, Marxism and Bourgeois Sociology (issue 2), *The Importance of Confederalism* (issue 3, interview), *Nationalism and the 'National' Issue* (issue 5), and *Ecological Crisis and Capitalism* (issue 6). Finally, *Democracy and Communalism* appeared in the first issue of *Democracy and Nature*, which included an article by Castoriadis titled *Democracy as a Procedure and Democracy as Regime* and another one by Fotopoulos titled *A New Concept of Democracy*. After that, Bookchin resigned, protesting that these two articles undercut his own message and were proof that "the magazine has been overwhelmingly given over to the expression of the ideas of Castoriadis and Fotopoulos." Nevertheless, the magazine produced two more issues before folding.

This article will not be concerned with the events that led to this conflict, but rather on the philosophical differences between Castoriadis and Bookchin, as mentioned in Bookchin's letter. It is my opinion that it reveals a philosophical disagreement, as well as a discordance of life experience between the two thinkers, which provides a social-historical ground to their philosophical dissent. Bookchin presents his disagreement with Castoriadis in short:

> To Castoriadis' article alone, my reply could easily run longer than Takis', critiquing his subjectivism, his replacement of historical development with an archipelago of "imaginaries," his concept of autonomy, his evocation of workers' control, and his embarrassing idealization of the Athenian *polis* (particularly on the issue of slavery) to a point of vitiating what we can learn from the *polis* in discussions of direct democracy.

It would require another treatise to answer Bookchin's accusations thoroughly. To my knowledge, Castoriadis did not respond. There is one issue to be clarified, the issue of slavery and ancient Athenian democracy which, as far as we know, Castoriadis never idealized, nor ignored. He did point out that slavery was a common practice worldwide in antiquity so it could not be a constitutive element of ancient democracy, whose limitations he never failed to highlight:

> Nevertheless, explicit self-institution never became for them the principle of political activity encompassing the social institution in its totality. Property was never really challenged, any more than was the status of women, not to mention slavery. Ancient democracy aimed at achieving, and it did achieve, the effective self-government of the community of free adult males, and it touched to the least extent possible the received social and economic structures. Only the philosophers (a few Sophists in the fifth century, Plato in the fourth) went any further.[8]

Yavor Tarinski chooses to emphasize the two thinkers' common ground in his article *Reflections on Castoriadis and Bookchin*:

> Despite the differences and disagreements between them, Castoriadis and Bookchin shared a lot in common—especially the way they viewed direct democracy and ecology. Their contributions in these fields provided very fertile soil for further theoretical and practical advance. It is not by chance that in a period in which the questions of democracy and ecology are attracting growing attention, we listen ever more often about the two of them.

There are of course philosophical differences that lead to distinct political approaches on the issues of democratic institution and organization. One of the main philosophical differences we can locate between Castoriadis and Bookchin is their attitude toward Hegel.

Bookchin admired Hegel and recognized the roots of his own dialectical naturalism in Hegelian philosophy, without however, being Hegelian.[9] His dialectical naturalism is not oriented toward the spirit which negates nature but toward nature, whose dialectic is a manifold of phenomena articulated as a unity of difference or diversities, a non-hierarchical unity. The dialectics of nature are used against social hierarchies, in a very successful effort to refute the stereotype of natural hierarchies while establishing the concept of organic societies:

> In organic societies the differences between individuals, age groups, sexes— and between humanity and the natural manifold of living and nonliving phenomena—were seen (to use Hegel's superb phrase) as a "unity of differences" or "unity of diversity," not as hierarchies. Their outlook was distinctly ecological, and from this outlook they almost unconsciously derived a body of values that influenced their behavior toward individuals in their own communities and the world of life. As I contend in the following pages, ecology knows no "king of beasts" and no "lowly creatures" (such terms come from our own hierarchical mentality).[10]

Bookchin utilizes Hegelian philosophical concepts, like the dialectical principle of the negation of negation in a naturalistic framework. John Clark, in his critique of Bookchin's dialectical naturalism, accuses Bookchin of reducing Hegelian negation to "something as mundane as the process of a tree growing to maturity and producing fruit, after which the process begins again." Clark's description of Bookchin's dialectical naturalism is poor, however, one could also argue that the dialectical process of life is not mundane at all, especially compared to the original

Hegelian dialectical process of the Idea. Bookchin shares Hegel's respect for the *Geist*, the spirit, not in a theological manner, but in a similar metaphysical manner. Bookchin's ontology is an ontology of unity, that respects diversity within unity, a unity of human communities and ecosystems that is conceived as the "wholeness" of a manifold and not as a monolithic "oneness":

> But social ecology provides more than a critique of the split between humanity and nature; it also poses the need to heal them. Indeed, it poses the need to radically transcend them. As EA Gutkind pointed out, "the goal of social ecology is wholeness, and not mere adding together of innumerable details collected at random and interpreted subjectively and insufficiently." The science deals with social and natural relationships in communities or "ecosystems." In conceiving them holistically, that is to say, in terms of their mutual interdependence, social ecology seeks to unravel the forms and patterns of interrelationships that give intelligibility to a community, be it natural or social. Holism, here, is the result of a conscious effort to discern how the particulars of a community are arranged, how its "geometry" (as the Greeks might have put it) makes the whole more than the sum of its parts. Hence, the "wholeness" to which Gutkind refers is not to be mistaken for a spectral "oneness" that yields cosmic dissolution in a structureless nirvana; it is a richly articulated structure with a history and internal logic of its own.[11]

Articulated structure and internal logic are, for Bookchin, the foundations of ontological intelligibility, which give history a progressive rationality toward human emancipation. His dialectical naturalism bears the influence of both Aristotle and Hegel, without however, nature being reduced to spirit, nor spirit being reduced to nature. Despite the historical rationality of natural and social communities, Bookchin refuses to reduce human being to logic. He acknowledges poetry and imagination as constitutive elements of the human experience and asks for a holistic approach to both. "Poetry and imagination must be integrated with science and technology, for we have evolved beyond an innocence that can be nourished exclusively by myths and dreams."

The importance of imagination is central to Castoriadis and his conception of the historical self-creation of society. Castoriadis posits imagination in the origin of individual and social perception and attributes social institution to the social dimension of human imagination, the anonymous social imaginary:

> History is impossible and inconceivable outside of the productive or creative imagination, outside of what we have called the radical imaginary as this is

manifested indissolubly in both historical doing and in the constitution, before any explicit rationality, of a universe of significations [...] that are neither the reflection of what is perceived, nor the mere extension and sublimation of animal tendencies, nor the strictly rational development of what is given. The social world is, in every instance, constituted and articulated as a function of such a system of significations, and these significations exist, once they have been constituted, in the mode of what we called the actual imaginary (or the imagined).[12]

For Castoriadis, history is a creation of the collective social imaginary, hence it has no internal rationality, nor inherent progressiveness. Castoriadis takes a stance against Hegelian dialectics or any dialectics of objective rationality, proclaiming that any rationalist dialectics is necessarily closed, since it "at once presupposes and 'demonstrates' that the whole of experience is exhaustively reducible to rational determinations."

This idea is in itself a negation of human creativity and historically responsible, he claims, for the subjugation of the traditional revolutionary movement to Marxist dogmatism. Castoriadis' ontology constitutes a different image of Being-as-Becoming, which is magmatic, meaning stratified or layered in distinct ontological layers, each of which has its proper categories, where the continuum and the discrete are reciprocal and whence rational structures arise temporally within a vastness of indeterminacy. History does not have a rational guiding principle, but is the result of an impetus of social imaginary to create beings that have no analogues in the natural world: namely meanings and institutions.

My opinion is that Bookchin and Castoriadis' antithetical stance toward Hegel is the divergent point of their philosophical approaches. However, their philosophies have more points of convergence than imagined. As we saw above, Bookchin does not ignore the importance of human imagination. Castoriadis on the other hand, recognizes that there is an intelligible aspect of Being, offered to scientific measurement and rational exegesis, which however, does not cover the whole of being, nor the whole of history.

Another point of convergence is that both thinkers argue that ecology is a political matter and ask for a direct democratic resolution through a radical social transformation from below. Both stand against hierarchy, exclusions and inequality. Both have condemned capitalist growth and the dominant capitalist ideal or signification of unlimited exploitation of community and nature. And both have influenced Greek social movements toward autonomy and social ecology, toward developing new forms of organization, based on the acknowledgment of the reciprocal mutuality of the ecological and the political problem.

For Humanity's Future: Direct Democracy and Social Ecology

Abdullah Öcalan, leader of the left-wing Kurdistan's Workers' Party (PKK) was captured by Turkish secret services in Kenya on 15 February 1999, while being transferred from the local Greek embassy. The Greek public, sympathizing with the Kurdish struggle for independence blamed the Greek government and the incident was portrayed as an embarrassment.

Five years later, on April 2004, Murray Bookchin received a letter from the imprisoned politician through an intermediary. The letter revealed an unexpected political turn of the world-known Marxist leader, who confessed to Bookchin that he had "rebuilt his political strategy around the vision of a 'democratic-ecological-society." Öcalan rejected Marxism, renounced the nation-state model for his people and advocated in favor of a democratic confederation, similar to Bookchin's vision.

The rapid developments of the Arab Spring in 2008 and the brutal Syrian civil war that followed, presented the Kurdish people with the chance to implement that vision in the regions that they liberated from both the ISIS Islamists and Syrian government forces, mainly in Rojava.

The revolution of Rojava was received both as a surprise and an affirmation of hopes and dreams by Greek social movements. Public discourse on social ecology and practical forms of direct democracy flourished after the December 2008 nationwide riots and the 2011 worldwide Occupy movement. Educational and cultural campaigns by groups advocating social ecology, like Eftopia magazine, multiplied.

The antiauthoritarian newspaper and journal Babylonia, $Βαβυλωνία$, began organizing the International Antiauthoritarian B-fest in Athens from 2007–2017. During the festival, a vast array of different approaches to ecological and political issues were presented and discussed by thinkers like Howard Zinn, Naomi Klein, Jacques Rancière, Kristin Ross, Debbie Bookchin, and activists from social movements around Greece and the world, from the ZAD movement in France to the Standing Rock movement in the US. In Thessaloniki, from 2010 the Direct Democracy Fest has brought together people from Rojava to Bulgaria. In 2017, the Transnational Institute of Social Ecology (TRISE) Conference was also held there.

There is a global common ideal, a global radical imaginary, scattered and dispersed, but interlinked among communities of struggle, a set of values like equality, freedom, solidarity, and democracy that emerges alongside a different worldview of nature and society.

It is a flickering network of collectivities against neoliberalist expansion and capitalist growth, which comes about at a most decisive moment of human history. A moment where a combination of crises—ecological, social, anthropological, and global—presents humanity with an existential threat. A threat to humanity's existence, that is neither cosmic nor theological, but social and political. A threat that feeds on political indifference, individualism, consumerism, and the most advanced mechanisms of control. However, social resistance is also a multifarious and the future is still open.

The influence of Murray Bookchin is immeasurable, since it is constantly expanding; it does not inspire any form of Bookchinism, but rather a theoretical and practical legacy that continues to live on in humanity's social struggles.

BIBLIOGHRAPHY

Bookchin, Murray. *Listen, Marxist!* (New York: Time Change Press, 1971).

___. *The Open Road Interview,* (1981). https://robertgraham.wordpress.com/murray-bookchin-the-open-road-interview-1981 last visited August 17, 2019, 14.10.

___. *The Ecology of Freedom: The Emergence and Dissolution of Hierarchies* (Buckley: Chesire Books, 1982).

___. *The Philosophy of Social Ecology: Essays on Dialectical Naturalism* (Montreal: Black Rose Books, 1996).

Castoriadis, Cornelius. *The Imaginary Institution of Society* (Cambridge: Polity Press, 1987).

___. "The Idea of the Revolution," interview, *Thesis Eleven, 26* (1990).

G. Fountas. *Anarchist Lexicon (Αναρχικό Λεξικό)* (Athens: Εκδόσεις των Συναδέλφων, ekdoseis ton synadelfon, 2014).

Oikonomou, Giorgos. *Polytechneio 1973 (Πολυτεχνείο 1973, Η απαρχή του αυτόνομου κινήματος),* (Athens: Nisides, Νησίδες, 2013).

Protopsaltis, Michalis. *Otan o kokkoras lalouse sto skotadi* (Athens: Όταν ο κόκκορας λαλούσε στο σκοτάδι, Βιβλιοπελαγος Vivliopelagos, 2018).

Tarinski, Yavor. "Reflections on Bookchin and Castoriadis," *Babylonia journal* (2016). https://www.babylonia.gr/2016/06/10/reflections-on-castoriadis-and-bookchin/ last visited August 17, 2019, 19.31.

NOTES

1. Bookchin, 1981.

2. Bookchin, 1971.

3. Castoriadis, 1987.

4. Bookchin, 1981.

5. Bookchin, 1981.

6. Bookchin, 1981.

7. All the issues of *Democracy and Nature* (originally named *Society and Nature*) be found in PDF format here: www.democracynature.org/, last visited August 17, 2019.

8. Castoriadis, 1990.

9. Bookchin, 1996.

10. Bookchin, 1982.

11. Bookchin, 1982.

12. Castoriadis, 1987.

Bookchin's Influence on Öcalan and the PKK's Evolution

Hawzhin Azeez

FROM THE WRITINGS of a brilliant but obscure scholar in Burlington, Vermont, to the lonely jail cell of a revolutionary struggling to reconcile years of failed efforts, emerged a revolution unlike anything previously seen. Through a synthesis of the work of Murray Bookchin and Öcalan, the Kurdish liberation movement dismantled its modus operandi, moved away from Marxist-Leninist and pro-statist aspirations, and adopted a radical new paradigm resulting in one of the most remarkable revolutions of the last century. Through Bookchin, Öcalan produced the theory of democratic confederalism, and came to the conclusion that the Kurds' efforts to acquire a state of their own would not be the ultimate solution to their liberation. As a mark of deep respect for Bookchin's work, Öcalan called himself a "student" of the philosopher. No western political thinker, therefore, has been as influential on the Kurdish liberation movement than Bookchin.

Yet, the association between Bookchin and Öcalan is more than just a story of two revolutionaries committed to the liberation of the oppressed. It also involves a profound reinvention on the personal and the political level; an unlearning, a willingness to change and evolve, discarding dogmatism and ideological purity—it is this openness which demonstrates deep commonalities between two thinkers who struggled with their separate senses of disillusionment, conflicted with the burden of finding a path towards freedom.

The combined legacy of Bookchin and Öcalan encourages us to dismantle internalized and institutionalized hierarchical oppressions including colonization, patriarchy, racism, and ecological destruction. However, the prevailing analysis of the two by leftist scholars and activists has been tainted by Orientalist biases. The Left has seen the relationship between the two as one in which the influencer, the teacher, the knower, is a Western thinker from the dominant colonizing culture and the influenced, the student, the receiver, is from the colonized culture. The flow has been interpreted to be only one way: top-down.

As a result, Kurds have had to witness the appropriation of the revolution in Rojava, essentially reducing our collective agency and reflective capacity. For many post-colonial scholars and Third World thinkers, it is impossible to read the Left's interpretation of the relationship between Bookchin and Öcalan without being made acutely aware of historical power dynamics and the structured flow of knowledge, ideas, and ways of knowing which trickle down from the developed, Western world towards the oppressed and the wretched of the earth in the global South. It is important to approach the connection between Bookchin and Öcalan on this basis, to note that long before he discovered the works of Bookchin, Öcalan came to the table with a wealth of experience in leading a revolutionary movement; he was already engaged in the difficult task of searching for an alternative paradigm for Kurdish freedom. Bookchin's work helped to solidify Öcalan's emerging ideas into a more coherent whole.

It is paramount to note influences where they occur, along with commonalities between Bookchin's social ecology and Öcalan's democratic confederalism; it is just as paramount that we note the divergences, developments, and innovations the Kurdish liberation movement has implemented as a result of geopolitical, historical, and cultural realities. How deeply Öcalan was influenced, and how much he innovated the theories proposed by Bookchin to fit the Kurds' aspirations of freedom, is the central focus of this chapter.

This essay will start with an overview of Bookchin's theory of social ecology. The second part of the essay will look at who Öcalan is, his history within the Kurdish liberation movement and his establishment of democratic confederalism based on the adoption of social ecology as a founding pillar of this paradigm. The essay will then conclude by looking at the emerging women's liberationist efforts as an indication of Öcalan's having already started the seeds of democratic confederalism.

Murray Bookchin and Social Ecology

Like many organic intellectuals, Murray Bookchin's ideology was defined by his praxis—a wealth of activism and involvement in a range of movements and organizations that continuously challenged him to evolve ideologically. As a result of his participation in the streets, unionism in factories, membership in left-oriented organizations, antiwar protests, and the crucial Institute for Social Ecology, Bookchin produced one of the most revolutionary theories of the last century. Having never attended college, Bookchin was a prolific writer and published many books and essays on the concept of social ecology over the years, fine-tuning and expanding on his theory.[1] He wrote a number of important texts including *Our Synthetic Environment* (1962), *Post Scarcity Anarchism* (1971), *The Ecology of Freedom* (1982), widely cited as his magnum opus, and *Urbanization Without Cities* (1992).

Bookchin perceptively assessed modern society in the Western world, and theorized a shift away from Marx's vision of worker-led liberation, and instead towards a liberation based on ecology. Marxism, for Bookchin, had essentially failed to address the inherent, cyclical, and growing range of oppressive hierarchies that capitalism is so proficient at producing. Bookchin did not believe that the working class would rise up, because Marxist revolution does not result in the withering away of the State, but the "very consciousness of domination." Likewise, in *Post Scarcity Capitalism,* Bookchin condemns socialism because "hierarchy, sexism and renunciation do not disappear with 'democratic centralism,' 'a revolutionary leadership,' a 'worker's state,' and a 'planned economy.'" In his essay *The Communist Project*, Bookchin argues that older ideologies such as Marxism and anarchism are "no longer capable of addressing the new and highly generalized problems posed by the modern world, from global warming to post-industrialization."

Industrial capitalism has contributed to a system of hyper individualism, desolation, privatization, and greed, resulting in a distinct lack of community and mutual cooperation. Science and technology have increasingly been used to justify subordinating nature, causing a range of disconnections and disruptions within society. The idea that science and technology would end human suffering and usher in a new era of peace, health, and stability has largely failed as evidenced by the proliferation of nuclear weapons, mass hunger in the Third World, and widespread poverty in the developed world. Instead, we must turn towards a science of ecology, which, according to Bookchin, is essentially about "the balance of nature." Moreover, "inasmuch as nature includes man, the science basically deals with the harmonization of nature and men." Bookchin upholds the importance of this science of ecology because it is a "critical science" in its own right; but just as importantly, it is unlike any system or theory of political economy as it is an "integrative and reconstructive science." For this reason, "it is impossible to achieve a harmonization of man and nature without creating a human community that lives in a lasting balance with its natural environment."[2]

Even before industrial capitalism began to oppress the workers, it established hierarchies of oppression through its domination of the environment and ecological destruction. If the masses are made numb from the processed food they consume and disconnected from the natural rhythms of the earth in large, over-populated, concrete metropolises, they will witness the mass destruction of the environment. If the natural environment is also our social environment, then the destruction of the planet causes a reverberating devastation in society and the unfettered continuation of environmental violence will be catastrophic. Bookchin was deeply concerned with the tensions between actuality and potentiality, between present and future, which can attain "apocalyptic proportions in the ecological crises of our time." The resulting theory produced in response to this imminent catastrophe drew on the best of existing theories such as Marxism and anarchism, but also developed beyond them, forming a unique synthesis and a new political philosophy of freedom and cooperation.

The driving idea behind Bookchin's theory of social ecology is the necessity of the elimination of all forms of hierarchies. According to Bookchin, hierarchies tend to stunt and limit the body-politic, depoliticizing and depersonalizing the political process under the authoritarian grasp of the State, which is not only inorganic but at the same time is a monstrous over-growth of a system that has no real roots, no grounding, and no connection. The hierarchies of power and oppression caused by the coercive capacity of the State result in an unnatural system of coexistence exacerbated by technology, pesticides, "resources of abundance," oppression, violence, sexism, and capitalism. These tools serve as the weaponry of the State, allowing it to recreate and systematically entrench its monopolistic, centralistic, and bureaucratic tendencies. The three pronged, mutually reinforcing systems of hierarchy, class, and state power combine to diminish the creative capacity of humanity; as a result, human creative energy is misdirected from serving life towards servicing systems and institutions of power and privilege resulting in systems of sexism, racism, ecological destruction, and worse. The solution is bottom-up forms of activism, participation, resistance, and democracy.

This new philosophy of freedom is seen in communalism, which combines the best of these political theories, while addressing and expanding on their limitations. Communalism conceives of a new type of community which would be deliberately decentralized so as to reduce its ecological impact. Moreover, communalism attempts to "recapture the meaning of politics in its broadest, most emancipatory sense"—more importantly, it seeks to "fulfill the historic potential of the municipality as the developmental arena of mind and discourse." The municipality then becomes a profound site of transformative development, the reclamation of the power of the individual within the community, and the reclamation of the political process away from the State.

Bookchin's approach is also heavily opposed to representative democracy because the capitalist system's establishment of neoliberalism ensures the hierarchy of privatization and market ethics. Parties, across the political spectrum, adopt "unquestioning obeisance to global market capitalism." This set of ethics ensures "policies as products, voters as passive consumers, politicians as producers, elections as markets." Bookchin argues that, as opposed to the homogenizing, atomizing, privatizing urbanism, there is still a powerful tendency towards "community" which needs to be fostered and nurtured. Liberation under social ecology can only evolve out of the deeply personal and local sites of the village, in the neighborhoods of cities and towns. In his revision of the history of the City,

Bookchin advocates for the essentiality of some form of a "Hellenic model" which can be implemented through municipal assemblies, thereby circumventing the need for the State to provide basic rights. Municipalities of course are the fundamental sites of community, gathering, politics, progress, and democracy. As a result, "social ecology brings all of these threads together in its opposition to hierarchy and domination as a critical theory and its emphasis on participation and differentiation as a reconstructive theory." Bookchin then seeks to bring these various modes of representation together in what he calls "a community of communities" or a confederation.

As he neared the end of his life, Bookchin grew bitter at the lack of profound and lasting change based on his ideas, largely because of his disenchantment with the international Left. Bookchin had seen many movements come and go, initially retaining their revolutionary, radical momentum, but soon losing it amongst the complexities of leftist contradistinctions and dogmatism. Some of his essays, such as the now famous *Listen, Marxist!* and *Social Anarchism or Lifestyle Anarchism* dismayed many traditional leftists. He criticized the Left for tendencies ranging from primitivism to lifestyle politics, from an aversion to organization to elitist affinities.[3] Bookchin disliked ossification of any form. This explains why he moved his ideological position from Stalinism to Trotskyism in the 1930s, to anarchism in the 1950s until the late 1990s, and then finally produced his notion of communalism or libertarian socialism which crystallized close to a century's worth of his experiences and views. Such shifts were essential in developing a comprehensive theory and allowed Bookchin to experience and reflect on the potentials and limitations of each theoretical framework. Yet, they also, according to Bookchin himself, led to a paucity of followers, relegating him to disillusionment and obscurity.

Öcalan and Democratic Confederalism

Born in the 1940s in a small village in Eastern Turkey, Abdullah Öcalan's identity and political orientation was shaped in the formative periods of the Turkish state. The new Turkish political leadership, under its first leader, Mustafa Kamal, emerged on the backs of mass expulsions, ethnic cleansing, and genocide of minorities such as the Armenians, Christians, Greeks, and Kurds. The initial democratic and pluralistic promises of the Republic soon gave way to oppressive and authoritarian policies in the name of national unity, progress, and modernization. These mass oppressions and expulsions resulted in the deaths of 1.5 million Armenians and the expulsion of over 1 million Greeks. The oppression of Kurds likewise escalated due to the rise of Kurdish nationalism and the fateful outcome of the Sykes-Picot Agreement. By the time Öcalan arrived in Ankara

University in the 1960s, he had been deeply politicized against this backdrop of violence, ethnic cleaning, displacement, and the denial of Kurdish identity.

By the early 1970s, as a result of membership in various political groups, Öcalan's activism resulted in his imprisonment. There, he became progressively disillusioned with the Turkish Left's failure to address inherent racism, which hampered their capacity to formulate a response to the oppression experienced by ethno-religious minorities such as the Kurds. He became increasingly convinced that the plight of the Kurds needed its own path. By 1978, Öcalan founded the PKK, combining Kurdish nationalism and Marxist-Leninism, and which soon after launched an armed insurgency against the Turkish state with the hope of acquiring Kurdish independence and statehood. At this stage, the very words "Kurds," "Kurdistan," and all representations of Kurdish culture were made illegal in a systematic policy of linguicide and cultural genocide. Öcalan was to spend the next twenty years in Syria promoting and directing the liberationist efforts of the PKK. When the tide of politics shifted, the Syrian government expelled Öcalan, leading to his eventual capture and incarceration in 1999 on the island of İmralı.

While in prison, faced with the failure to liberate the long-oppressed Kurds, Öcalan began a close reading of Marx, Freud, Foucault, Bookchin, Wallerstein, Braudel, and Nietzsche, among others. However, it is important to note that Öcalan was already familiar with many such works and had questioned the failures and limitations of real socialism well before his incarceration. This period was marked by Öcalan's attempt to systematically formulate and pen his thoughts. In his words, he was "someone searching for practical ways out of the crisis the Middle East and the Kurds are in" when he came across the work of Bookchin.[4]

Öcalan devoted much time to re-analyzing the mis-steps of the PKK in its attempts at liberation. The PKK had not only reformulated itself repeatedly as a result of internal strife and ongoing external pressures, but it had also confronted its own authoritarian tendencies. Öcalan's reading of Bookchin's *The Ecology of Freedom* helped to crystalize the inherent inconsistencies and contradictions that the PKK, as a revolutionary liberationist movement, had repeatedly encouraged. The response was, as argued in *The Ecology of Freedom*, the elimination of hierarchies starting from within that is so central to a truly liberationist ideology.[5]

Bookchin's *Urbanization Without Cities* also had a deep impact on Öcalan's revisionist attempt as it outlined a new social contract in which the State was decentralized, and in which society reasserted itself over the organizational and institutional capacities and structures of governance. The Hellenic model, free from its exclusionary, elitist, patriarchal, and class propensities, was seen as the ideal format of face-to-face democracy and governance by Bookchin. This approach fit the nature of Kurdish culture and existence in the four parts of Kurdistan.

Bookchin's solution to the hierarchical, capitalist, and ecological problem within society was the elimination of the State or at least heavily decentralizing it.[6] Öcalan consequently transformed the existing paradigm of liberation being tied to Kurdish statehood; rather, he considered the State as the antithesis of the true, lasting, organic type of liberation required for the oppressed and the dispossessed. Öcalan firmly stated that "fascist exercise of power is the nature of the nation-state. Fascism is the purest form of the nation-state." Öcalan built on Bookchin's theory and merged it with the liberationist needs of the Kurds and other oppressed and stateless communities in the region.

Öcalan's shift away from a nationalist position marked a radical shift in the revolutionary trajectory of the Kurdish movement. If hierarchies are oppressive and an integral part of the nation-state model, if they breed racism and fascist tendencies like the mass incarceration of minorities and the oppressed, then surely nationalism, with its unwavering focus on uniformity of identity, should be critiqued. Nationalism tends to reinforce and reproduce the same hierarchies of power, often to the detriment of minority groups. Öcalan stated that bourgeois nationalism had bred "mass destruction and genocide," and had only served as a tool of oppression for elites and a colonial instrument of "divide-and-rule strategy." This approach could no longer be the way to Kurdish liberation.

Likewise, armed conflict was no longer the solution to the liberation of the oppressed and dispossessed communities.[7] An alternative solution had to be envisioned in which a democratic society is actively, consciously created from the ashes of history's fascism and violence. For the Kurds, divided between four oppressive states, the solution was no longer the removal of the colonial borders in order to unify. Rather, the alternative was to completely abandon the need to remove the borders, and to move towards a stateless ideology in which physical borders are transcended by a collective democratic attitude of mutual coexistence and respect.

In 2005, Öcalan released the manifesto *The Declaration of Democratic Confederalism in Kurdistan*, calling for a significant change in approach and policy. Democratic confederalism is founded on three key concepts: grassroots democracy, gender liberation, and ecological sustainability. The Kurdistan Communities Union (KCK) was established in 2007 and spearheaded the implementation of the social blueprint that Öcalan was producing. This new blueprint was characterized by an anti-statist perspective which promoted an anti-hierarchical, multiculturalist, and consensus-orientated praxis. In line with this ideology, the KCK announced a general commitment to a stateless democratic confederal system to unite the Kurds. Rojava, in 2012, became the laboratory that started to implement this model on a wide scale across its cantons. This process involved the establishment of, among others: communes, cooperatives, assemblies, and civil society groups that would eradicate traditional exercises of power along ethno-religious schisms.[8] Academies were set up across Kurdistan to promote civic education, or *perwarda*. This process required a committed rejection of fossilized thinking and behaviors by the people, and the liberation from thinking in terms of hierarchical structures.

Many scholars and experts have noted the commonalities and linkages between Bookchin's thoughts and that of Öcalan, particularly in the application of communalism, feminism, and ecology. This process has tended to erase the agency and subjectivity of the Kurdish movement as well as Öcalan's own efforts because it understands democratic confederalism to be synonymous, or at best to mirror, Bookchin's social ecology. Many scholars, for instance, have noted that Öcalan, upon encountering Bookchin's work, began a "profound process of ideological re-evaluation, transforming the PKK's agency and aims." This implies that Öcalan and the movement suddenly turned away from Marxist-Leninism and nationalism and towards social ecology, as if it had not already been influenced by decades of revolutionary struggle. Yet, the reality is that the Kurds' liberation efforts were always dialectical and in motion, containing synthesis, evolution, progress, and revision. The influence of Bookchin on Öcalan needs to be viewed in this light. In fact, Öcalan was beginning to question Leninism as early as 1994, but his critique lacked systemization and method. By the time he discovered Bookchin, Öcalan was already transcending orthodox Marxism and patriarchal nationalism. A better approach is to see the connection between Bookchin and Öcalan as reflecting a continuity of progress and innovative change from Marxism, to anarchism, to social ecology, to democratic confederalism. The final outcome is a combination of the best of the previous theories and frameworks, originating with Bookchin, and further developed by Öcalan.

For many experts, the emergence of democratic confederalism's central criticisms is often seen as a reflection of Bookchin's direct influence on Öcalan. After all, Öcalan discovered Bookchin while he was incarcerated from 1999 onwards. However, the trajectory of Öcalan's own ideological growth and evolution is often ignored in this analysis. Before discovering Bookchin, for instance, Öcalan's vision of Kurdish liberation had always contained a feminist framework of women's liberation. Kurdish women were involved from the very conception of the PKK.[9] Women such as Sakina Cansız were founding members, and were quintessential in formulating the party's view towards women's liberation. Her memoir *My Whole Life was a Struggle* outlines years of recruitment and education in which women were integrated into liberation efforts and the resistance of patriarchal nationalism. Cansız's renowned resistance against inhumane torture and gender based violence[10] she suffered during her twelve years of incarceration in the 1980s set a new precedent for women's resistance, capacity, and influence within the Kurdish movement. Waves of women joined the party, causing the patriarchal and traditional cultural values within the movement to be systematically challenged.

Through the leadership of Öcalan, and women like Cansız, women began to form their own separate and autonomous practices and tactics. The first women's congress in the PKK was held in 1995 promoting the idea of women's involvement but also ideological and military independence in the liberation movement. In 1998, Öcalan declared the party a feminist group, to the dismay of many male members. He had long noticed that women were subjected to patriarchal nationalism both within the nation-state model as well as the Kurdish liberation movement. This resulted in concrete steps being taken towards autonomous women's liberation efforts within the greater liberation struggle. One outcome of these efforts is Jineology,[11] which involves the subversion of hierarchies of power in the family, the tribe, the religious order, and the social honour-based system, as well as within capitalism, science, and history. When the Kurdish women formed the YPJ in Rojava, they had over three decades of women's struggles to draw on.[12] Öcalan and the Kurdish movement had understood the centrality and non-negotiability of women's liberation long before Öcalan's incarceration and his discovery of Bookchin's writings.

Philosophers and intellectuals have produced numerous iterations of the ideal utopian society. However, it took a visionary like Öcalan to transform that ideal into an organizational plan. His charisma and authority are often used against him as evidence of his dictatorial potential. Yet, his power to direct a radical social revolution while incarcerated on İmralı Island as its sole prisoner for well over a decade speaks, instead, for his profound political and cultural influence. The Kurds did not have to implement Öcalan's vision, nor the dream of a state-based liberation for the Kurds. His 21 year incarceration for the crime of demanding Kurdish cultural, political, and linguistic rights gave him the cultural authority to bring about one of the most profound revolutions of the twenty-first century. Had it not been for Öcalan's visionary status and cultural influence, it remains doubtful whether Bookchin's work would have been read as widely or received the level of recognition that it has.

Conclusion

The aim of this essay has been to note that the Kurdish movement already contained anti-statist, anticapitalist, and antipatriarchal sentiments to varying degrees throughout the party's history. Öcalan's incarceration allowed him the time to formulate his ideas, essentially creating a blueprint for creating a radically new society. Bookchin's writings around social ecology greatly helped to solidify, stimulate, and integrate many of the questions Öcalan had been grappling with for years. For decades, Bookchin struggled to convince leftists of the importance of social ecology and, for the most part, this process failed—until the Kurdish movement adopted this theory as its main approach.

Like Bookchin's many shifts in the trajectory of formulating his theory of social ecology, Öcalan too turned away from Marxist-Leninism and nationalism and aspired towards a different ideology that would address the complex nature of the Kurdish struggle. By the time Öcalan came across Bookchin's writings, he had already begun a revisionist process and had arrived at the realization that the PKK's revolutionary socialism and nationalist agenda was not adequate in formulating an effective liberation ideology. Being intensely aware of the failures of these fossilized approaches, Öcalan's views strongly resonated with Bookchin's dislike of ideological ossification and his drive to evolve and change. These parallel views demonstrate an affinity between two equals with comparable attitudes towards progress and change.

Thus far, the question has centered on how Bookchin has influenced and shaped Öcalan, and by extension the liberation struggles of the Kurds. This chapter attempted to address this question, but in the process, it also aimed to alert the international Left to its inherent orientalist and internalized hierarchies of thought concerning the flow of ideas, ways of knowing, knowledge, and theory. In contrast, a bottom-up perspective reveals how the Kurdish liberation movement—indeed how Öcalan—popularized the obscure work of the disillusioned philosopher, Bookchin. Decades of revolutionary struggle and activism, decades of torture and death in the jails of the oppressive states, years of self-reflection and revisions, and decades of learning and unlearning within the Kurdish liberation movement ensured that sufficient courage and dedication aligned to transform theory into reality—something which the international Left has so far failed to accomplish. The question we are left with now is: what lessons can the international left learn from the collective legacy of Murray Bookchin, from the charisma and innovations of Öcalan, and from the courage and determination of the Kurdish liberation movement?

BIBLIOGRAPHY

Akkaya, Ahmet, H., and J. Jongerden. "Reassembling the Political: The PKK and the Project of Radical Democracy." *European Journal of Turkish Studies* (2012): 14.

Bookchin, Murray. *Post-Scarcity Anarchism*. (Edingburgh: AK Press, 1971).

_____. *Urbanization Without Cities: The Rise and Decline of Citizenship* (Montreal: Black Rose Books, 1992).

_____. *The Modern Crises*. (Montreal: Black Rose Books, 1988).

_____.*Remaking Society*. (Montreal: Black Rose Books, 1989).

_____.*Social Anarchism or Lifestyle Anarchism: An Unbridgeable Chasm*. (San Francisco: AK Press, 1995).

_____. *The Ecology of Freedom: The Emergence and Dissolution of Hierarchy*. (Oakland: AK Press, 2005).

_____. *The Next Revolution: Popular assemblies and the Promise of Direct Democracy*. Edited by Debbie Bookchin, and Blair Taylor. (London: Verso, 2015).

Cansız, Sakine. *Sara: My Whole Life was a Struggle*. Translated by Janet Biehl. (London: Pluto Press, 2018).

Damon, Arwa. "Female Fighters: We Won't Stand for Male Dominance." *CNN*, 6th of October, 2008, https://edition.cnn.com/2008/WORLD/meast/10/06/iraq.pkk/index.html.

Duzgun, Arwa. "Jineology: The Kurdish Women's Movement." *Journal of Middle East Women's Studies* (2016), 12:2, 284–286.

Egret, Eliza and Tom Anderson. *Struggles for Autonomy in Kurdistan*. (London: Freedom Press, 2016).

Enlo, Cynthia. *Bananas, Beaches and Bases: Making Feminist Sense of International Politics*. (Berkeley: University of California Press, 2014).

_____. *Maneuvers: The International Politics of Militarizing Women's Lives*. (Los Angeles: University of California Press, 2000).

Enzinna, Wes. "Bizarre and Wonderful: Murray Bookchin, Eco-Anarchist." *London Review of Books*, 19th of July, 2017, https://pultizercenter.org/publications/london-review-books.

_____. "The Rojava Experiment." *International New York Times*, Paris. Nov. 28, 2018.

Ferreira, Bruna and Vinicius Santiago. "The Core of Resistance: Recognizing Intersectional Struggle in the Kurdish Women's Movement." *Contexto Internacional*, Vol 40:3, 2018), 479–500.

Gerber, Damian and Shannon Brincat. "When Öcalan Met Bookchin: The Kurdish Freedom Movement and the Political Theory of Democratic Confederalism." *Geopolitcs*, 2018.

Graeber, David. "Why is the world ignoring the revolutionary Kurds in Syria?." *The Guardian*, 8th of October, 2014, https://www.theguardian.com/commentisfree/2014/oct/08/why-world-ignoring-revolutionary-kurds-syria-isis.

Hassanpour, Amir. *Nationalism and language in Kurdistan, 1918–1985*. (San Francisco: Mellen Research University Press, 1992).

Leverink, Joris. "Murray Bookchin and the Kurdish Resistance." *Roar Magazine*, 9th of August, 2015, https://roarmag.org/essays/bookchin-kurdish-struggle-Öcalan-rojava/.

Muhammad, Umair. "An Unsuitable Theorist? Murray Bookchin and the PKK," *Turkish Studies* vol 19 no. 5 (2018): 799–817.

Öcalan, Abdullah. *Prison Writings, Vol I: The Roots of Civilization*. (London: Pluto Press, 2007).

_____. *Prison Writings, Vol II: The PKK and the Kurdish Question in the 21st Century*. (London: Pluto Press, 2011a).

_____. *Democratic Confederalism*. (Cologne: Transmedia Publishing, 2011b).

_____. *Prison Writings, Vol III: The Road Map to Negotiations*. (Cologne: International Initiative, 2012a).

_____. *War and Peace in Kurdistan: Perspectives for a Political Solution of the Kurdistan Question*. (Cologne: International Initiative, 2012b).

_____. *Liberating Life: Women's Revolution*. (Neuss: Mesopotamian Publishers, 2013).

_____. *Manifesto for a Democratic Civilization, Vol I*. (Porsgrunn: New Compass, 2015).

Ozcan, AK. *Turkey's Kurds: A Theoretical Analysis of the PKK and Abdullah Öcalan*. (London: Routledge, 2005).

Peters, Michael A. "Ecopolitical Philosophy, Education and Grassroots Democracy: The 'return' of Murray Bookchin (and John Dewey?)," *Geopolitics, History, and International Relations vol 9. no 2*, (2017): 7–14.

Stanchev, Peter. "The Kurds, Bookchin, and the Need to Reinvent Revolution," *New Politics*, 15:4, 2016, 77–82.

Wals, Arjen EJ and Michael A. Peters. "Flowers of Resistance: Citizen Science, Ecological democracy and the Transgressive Education Paradigm." *Sustainability Science: Key Issues*, edited by Ariane Konig. (New York: Routledge, 2018).

Žižek, Slavoj. "Kurds are the most progressive, democratic nation in the Middle East." *Kurdish Question*, 22nd of October, 2015.

NOTES

1. Criticism and concern over hierarchies and domination—not only theoretically, but also on the organizational level as well—are central concerns of Bookchin's work. Bookchin strongly believed that the streets, the local community and progressive groups were the pulse towards maintaining the necessary level of politicization that was essential for social change; an approach that led him to often be ahead of the curve in determining emerging social issues and future conflicts. For instance, according to his companion and biographer, Janet Biehl, as far back as the 1960s Bookchin was advocating for solar and wind power as alternative sources of energy, while also having the foresight to warn against the greenhouse effect at a time when no one else had caught on to its importance (Biehl 1999, 7). From his unionist work to joining the Socialist Workers Party in the 1930s, to working with a Trotskyist group called the Movement for a Democracy of Content in the 1940s, to being a member of the Congress or Racial Equality in the 1960s, to co-pioneering the Left Green Network in the 1980's, while publishing widely, supporting and editing a number of journals, Bookchin attempted to remain connected to progressive trends, organizations and ideas.

2. Bookchin is also very clear about the distinction between ecology and environmentalism, noting unequivocally that the former is the central focal point of his thesis. Environmentalism, for Bookchin, contains a superficial analysis and approach to the resolution of collective, intersecting social problems. Ecology, on the other hand, is by its very nature anti-hierarchical and democratic because each member of the ecosystem has a place and role to play (Bookchin 1971, 5, 60)

3. In his book, *The Next Revolution: Popular Assemblies and the Promise of Direct Democracy*, Bookchin argues that Marxists have a propensity to "overorganize people into parties, unions, and proletarian 'armies' guided by elitist leaders," while anarchists tend to shun "organization and leaders as 'vanguards' and celebrate revolutionism as an instinctive impulse unguided by reason or theory" (2015, 157).

4. Öcalan has also written more than 40 books, including *Prison Writings: The Roots of Civilization* (2007), *Prison Writings Volume II: The PKK and the Kurdish Question in the 21st Century* (2011), and *Prison Writings III: The Roadmap to Negotiations* (2012).

5. Capitalism, was therefore a secondary problem that could be addressed if the issue of hierarchies was addressed within societies. At the same time, by removing oppressive hierarchies, the ecology and the environment, the sacred land in which so much blood had been shed for its liberation, could be saved and liberated. Through this process, a new society would emerge which would be focused on collective liberation, co-existence, mutual aid and cooperation as opposed to the repetition of age-old, primordial fights and wars which had ravaged Syria.

6. Bookchin described the state as a "completely alien formation," and went so far as to call it a "thorn in the side of human development."

7. The roadmap for peace and democracy also involved the fundamental element of the "third way" approach in addressing the Kurds' legitimate aspirations for liberation. This solution explicitly rejected conflict and violence, and was against engaging in invasive, hegemonic regional aspirations. The armed forces must remain fundamentally and at its ideological core a mechanism of self-defense. This is an integral policy which the Rojava revolution has adhered to strongly, since to resort to these forms of violence is not only to uncritically repeat history, but to also contribute to the reproduction of hierarchies of power and violence. This policy would guide the relations of the Kurds regionally with their neighbors, allowing for a new era of peace, mutual cooperation and non-violence to emerge.

8. Now the question remained as to how to implement this new blueprint of a democratic, multicultural, ecological and feminist society in a nation that had been defined for decades as victims of intense state repression, displacement and ethnic cleansing policies. Civil society groups must become a foundational approach towards promoting a democratic civic attitude within citizens, and are "seen as central" to the formation of an organic democratic society (Öcalan, 2011a).

9. Öcalan notes that women's liberation was on the agenda from the very inception of the PKK (2011a). Despite this, the movement retained heavily patriarchal practices which has required decades of re-education and unlearning through comprehensive implementation of perwarda.

10. Sakina's breasts were cut off by her Turkish torturers while in jail. It is stated that she refused to utter a cry of pain as a form of resistance, and demonstration of women's strength and courage.

11. Öcalan on sexism: "Another ideological pillar of the nation-state is the sexism that pervades entire societies. Many civilized systems have employed sexism in order to preserve their own power. They enforced women's exploitation and used them as a valuable reservoir of cheap labor. Women are also regarded as a valuable resource in so far as they produce offspring and allow the reproduction of men. A woman is both a sexual object and a commodity. She is a tool for the preservation of male power and can at best advance to become an accessory of the patriarchal male society." (Öcalan, 2011b).

12. The geopolitical conditions facing the Kurds ensured the necessity of armed self-defense being an integral part of this struggle. Women's armed groups YPJ (Rojava, Western Kurdistan), HPJ (Rojhilat, Eastern Kurdistan), YPS-Jin (Bakur, Northern Kurdistan) and YJS (Shengal). These women's groups as well as their political and civilian arms all work under the collective umbrella of YJA STAR (see Egret and Anderson 2016).

Bookchin and the Kurdish Movement in Turkey

Recep Akgün

Introduction

Beginning in the 1990s, Turkish revolutionaries began a search for fresh radical and libertarian ideas as opposed to the orthodox Marxist-Leninism dominating leftist politics in Turkey. Readers began to acquaint themselves with Murray Bookchin thanks to the work of leftist[1] publishing houses within the country, which generated increasing interest in his ideas in Turkey.[2] This interest was not limited to mere intellectual curiosity. New social and political movements became visible during these years, connected, ultimately, to the political developments and transformations of leftist politics brought about during the 1990s. A search for new ways of doing politics was triggered within Turkey, inspired by libertarian and antiauthoritarian political ideas.[3] Since then, the scope of politics within the country has widened from classic forms of struggle—labor movements, struggles for parliamentary democratization, revolutionary Marxism, social democracy—to environmental, feminist, and antiwar mass politics. Clusters of new groups emerged which were interested in these issues: environmentalists, the New Left, conscientious objectors, anarchists, and antiauthoritarians.

Most of these groups, particularly those composed of anarchists, libertarian leftists, and environmentalists, were not only interested in Bookchin's ideas intellectually but began to implement them within their organizations and political activities. But their initiatives were alien to Turkey's left. Though the experiences of certain sections of the Left had acquainted them with social ecology, Turkish society was, in large part, unfamiliar with the ideas elucidated by Bookchin. Some struggles around environmental issues did gain the attention of leftist organizations during these years. However, the groups concentrating their energy on the challenges raised by social ecology remained marginal and minor. It is in this sense that, although inspiring several organizations, Bookchin produced little effect on Turkey's leftist politics as a whole during the 1990s.

However, another event, far more extraordinary and interesting, took place in the early 2000s. Abdullah Öcalan, one of the founders of the Kurdistan Workers' Party (PKK),[4] arrested and imprisoned by the Turkish state in 1999, began to share an affinity for Bookchin's ideas.[5] Along with Öcalan, the PKK and other allied groups[6] declared that their new social, political, and cultural ideas were being formed under the influence of Bookchin.[7] An opening for this influence was provided by the PKK's reformulation of its ideological, political, and social perspectives. Starting in the mid 1990s, the party committed to solving the Kurdish problem through democratic struggles and began advocating for a peace agreement with the Turkish state. These demands took on a new form following Öcalan's arrest in 1999.[8] Ultimately Öcalan and the Kurdish movement made Bookchin's philosophy a component of their theory and practice.[9]

This essay deals with the influence of Bookchin's ideas on the new political outlook of the Kurdish movement in Turkey. In the case of Turkey, this renewal has not only been limited to the Kurdish movement but also extends into other leftist, libertarian, and antiauthoritarian social and political struggles. By constructing alliances, the Kurdish movement has had an increased influence on the political and social agenda of divergent political groups. In other words, through the application of the ideas developed by Bookchin as well as Fernand Braudel, Immanuel Wallerstein, and other leftist thinkers, the Kurdish movement and its allies have strived to spread libertarian practices and values among wide sections of the Turkish population. Aiming to transform society, these movements have impacted social and political structures as well as everyday life in Turkey. They also aimed to create alternatives within the social and political spaces in the country, even if they couldn't gain power in this way. In other respects, these practices produced new subjectivities and experiences that reformed leftist politics and its general social and political structures. Such an impact came in spite of their weakened effect and influence due to increased state repression. This brief essay explores how Bookchin has influenced the renewal of the Kurdish movement since the mid-2000s, what opportunities this renewal has offered, and whether they offer the foundations for political change within Turkish society.

A Short History of the Kurdish Movement in Turkey: From the PKK to Legal Kurdish Parties

In the late 1970s, Kurdish parties and organizations were established in Turkey, as well as in Iraq, Iran, and Syria. These groups sought the liberation of Kurds and the defence of Kurdish independence, either through greater autonomy or the establishment of a Kurdish state. Among these parties, the PKK became the strongest in Turkey following a military coup in 1980. Unlike some of the other Kurdish political organizations in Turkey, the PKK did not consider the Kurdish problem as exclusively an issue of inclusion. They aimed at a radical transformation of society, promoting Marxist ideals and claiming that their national liberation struggle was part of a worldwide revolution. Along these lines, the PKK tried to initiate an armed revolution, developing a grassroots armed force in the 1990s.

The PKK also initiated a new political strategy, pushing for a peace agreement with the Turkish state to solve the Kurdish problem. However, these attempts to arrive at some agreement all ended in failure. Instead, the process, from the beginning of the 1990s to Öcalan's arrest in 1999, coincided with a period of violent war between the PKK and the Turkish state. This war resulted in the mass migration of Kurds from Kurdish regions, as well as the death of Kurdish guerillas, Turkish soldiers, and Kurdish civilians. During the 1990s, other sections of the Kurdish political movement mostly remained within the boundaries of the law. This period saw the establishment of a succession of legal political parties, as well as social and cultural institutions. As a result, Kurdish political candidates began to enter into the Turkish parliament in alliance with social democrats.[10] These elections further marked the appearance of human rights and pro-democracy movements.

Through the new political front built up in the 90s, the Kurdish movement, although focusing on a solution to the Kurdish issue, went beyond it, joining with other social and political movements in Turkey. In particular, they sought to develop an alliance with the Marxist left in the country by involving themselves in the struggle to democratize Turkey. During this process, despite the Kurdish movement being faithful to Marxist-Leninist ideological orientations and political methods such as hierarchical organizational structures and state-centric revolution, the civic activism conducted by the Kurdish movement placed special emphasis on women's liberation and a critique of oppressive capitalist and traditionalist subjectivities.[11] Yet, a dramatic shift would emerge after Öcalan's arrest in 1999. In the early 2000s, Öcalan turned to more peaceful solutions to resolve the Kurdish problem, seeking to advance what was a stagnating project. The Kurdish movement consequently began to reorganize both its legal and illegal wings.

Accordingly, in 2005, the PKK increased the role of its organizations along with its armed forces. Thus, the party gained new political organs dealing with mass politics and conducting negotiations with the Turkish state. This was the rise of legal methods of engaging in politics. At the same time, Öcalan endeavored to reformulate the Kurdish movement's ideological orientations. Through his prison correspondence and writings, Öcalan began to allude to different libertarian and antiauthoritarian thinkers such as Bookchin, Wallerstein, Braudel, and Bakunin. The introduction of these intellectuals began to distinguish the Kurdish movement from orthodox Marxist-Leninist struggles. Bookchin was a primary source of inspiration during this shift. His views were used by both Öcalan and the Kurdish movement to shape their practical and theoretical perspectives. The next section will analyze this new solution and tendency, including Bookchin's ideas in the context of democratic autonomy/confederalism.[12]

Bookchin and the Project of Democratic Autonomy or Confederalism

After changes to the Kurdish movement's ideological make-up, its politics also began to shift. Organizational structures, political strategies, and a social philosophy emerged that gave it visibility within Turkey. The Kurdish movement proliferated into grassroots and mainstream politics in the country. The actions they inspired went beyond armed struggle. In the mid-2000s, they provoked mass demonstrations, popular uprisings, and massive civil disobedience in Kurdish urban regions and the western metropoles of Turkey, such as İstanbul, İzmir, Adana, and Mersin, areas where large Kurdish populations live. These actions increased the quantity and influence of grassroots and political organizations within the Kurdish movement. As semi-autonomous organizations such as youth and women's movements grew, they gained confidence in using horizontal mechanisms as well as vertical ones.

Along with its grassroots organizing, the Kurdish movement pursued an electoral strategy, entering into parliament and gaining control of municipalities, targeting the majority of the Kurdish population for their support. Although the principal activities of the Kurdish movement concentrated on solutions to the Kurdish problem during this process, they were nonetheless active and allied with the other Marxist and leftist groups in the country's cultural, social, and political struggles. This was the process in which the Kurdish movement renewed its internal structures and political and social perspectives. Ultimately, through this broad political strategy, the Kurdish movement began to become "Turkeyized."[13]

In the 2010s, these changes to the Kurdish movement began to be expressed under a set of ideas and projects framed through the terms of "democratic autonomy," "democratic confederalism," or "democratic modernity."[14] This project aimed to find a solution to the Kurdish problem that would not require the establishment of a Kurdish state. Öcalan defines the aim, directions, and foundations of the emerging ideal for a democratic confederalism as follows:

> This kind of rule or administration can be called a non-state political admin-istration, or democracy without a state. Democratic decision-making processes must not be confused with the processes known as public administration. States only administrate, while democracies govern. States are founded on power; democracies are based on collective consensus. Office in the state is determined by decree, even though it may in part be legitimized by elections. Democracies use direct elections. The state uses coercion as a legitimate means. Democracies rest on voluntary participation (ÖCALAN, 2015a: 25).

Within this framework, democratic autonomy is offered as a solution to the Kurdish problem. On the other hand, it is also framed as permitting the radical transformation of the entirety of the societies in which Kurds live. This project could not be exclusive to the Kurdish people, but demanded the inclusion of all other ethnic and cultural groups in Turkey. Hence, democratic autonomy presents a novel concept of citizenship in Turkey. This citizenship is designed to challenge the official legal framework of citizenship in the Republic of Turkish. Citizenship, as it is currently formulated, is based on Turkish identity, which homogenizes multiple social, ethnic, and cultural groups of the population through different mechanisms and discourses that range from exclusion to assimilation. Thus, democratic autonomy shaped the forms of new social and political subjectivities beyond the assimilative practices and discourses of the Turkish state. The Kurdish movement aims for equal citizenship for all of the country's ethnic groups, and the transformation of Turkey's political regime. A new constitution is demanded along these lines to strengthen the power of local governments and municipalities. However, democratic autonomy is neither identity politics, a liberal democratic ideal, nor simply a legal challenge. It is the creation of a new social and political order. Under this banner, the project offers a radical social, cultural, and political transformation of Turkey.

Bookchin is the main source of inspiration for this radical project.[15] The Kurdish movement, including Öcalan, the PKK, as well as its other member parts, used Bookchin's ideas to shape their politics. Democratic autonomy aims at producing a social and political agent that can be reproduced through the constitution of a new society. It also aims to create political structure built on ecological, democratic, and feminist principles. Just as Bookchin presents a new social and political subjectivity against capitalism and patriarchy,[16] democratic confederalism seeks to produce a new citizenship as part of a social and political system that goes beyond a capitalist modernity typified by nationalism and patriarchal oppression. The democratic confederalist project seeks a different kind of modernity, one that does not assimilate and divide through nationalism nor produces inequality. Although it seeks an alternative modernity, like Bookchin,[17] democratic confederalism does not reject rationality and science.[18] In its radical social and political project to transform the countries in which it exists, the Kurdish movement has emerged as a new libertarian revolutionary current attempting to transcend economistic political ideologies. To expand their reach, members of the Kurdish movement suggest a decentralized and direct democratic method of self-governance at the most local level. Such a politics is, by its nature, radically inclusive. As Öcalan notes, "democratic confederalism is open towards other political groups and factions. It is flexible, multicultural, antimonopolistic, and consensus-oriented."

Thus, the Kurdish movement has transformed its politics from the mere national liberation of Kurds and aspires, more broadly, to a radical transformation of society. In this respect, the Kurdish movement's project is for all of society. In order to do this, it has developed new strategies and broader more inclusive alliances, while taking an active role in existing social and political movements, including feminism, environmentalism, human rights and antiwar struggles, and labour and pro-democracy movements.[19]

Öcalan and the Kurdish movement are dealing with the practical application of Bookchin's libertarian ideas. While Bookchin's theory mostly focused on issues of subjectivity, the ontology of politics, the philosophy of nature, ontology, and epistemological metaphysics, the Kurdish movement developed the application of Bookchin's thought. In other words, it has developed a toolbox theory, seeking to localize it within historical and contextual theoretical discussions. The Kurdish movement extracted the essence of the ideas developed by Bookchin in order to solve problems within Middle Eastern societies. Bookchin's thinking on libertarian municipalism, confederalism, citizenship, and ecology form the foundations of their struggle for democratic autonomy. By implementing these ideas, the Kurdish movement has had a great influence on Turkish society and its politics.

The Forms of Politics and the Subject of Democratic Autonomy

As the Kurdish movement cultivated a new politics, it began to produce collective social political subjectivities as well. Having abandoned the construction of a Kurdish state as a means to resolve the Kurdish problem, the Kurdish movement started constructing social, cultural, and political environments where autonomous experiences and practices became reality.[19] Organizational structures emerged from economic cooperatives for institutions capable of satisfying basic daily needs to social structures ordering interpersonal and communal relations. In addition, the Kurdish movement expanded its influence by winning control of municipalities. In trying to actualize direct democratic means and mechanisms for popular decision-making, the Kurdish movement became popularized. During this period, the movement tried to bring together different ethnic groups in Kurdish regions. At the same time, it tried to organize democratic autonomy through popular organizational structures in western Turkey.

Since its inception, the Kurdish movement has been interested in the radical transformation of the Middle East and the rest of the world. Yet, before the 2000s, their primary political project had been the development of an independent Kurdish state. With its new orientation, the Kurdish movement aimed to effect change within their host countries rather than seek their separation from them.

Thus, the construction of social and political subjectivities through institutions of democratic autonomy became more critical. The Kurdish movement developed a series of projects, forming alliances with Turkey's left in order to gain the support of broad cross-sections of Turkish society, resulting in the formation of the Peoples' Democratic Party (HDP).

These developments contributed to the emergence of a brand of politics that could build the direct democratic mechanisms required for a mass collectivist experience. This praxis was designed as an alternative to already existing politics in Turkey. Though they have so far failed to wrestle power across the country from the Turkish state, the Kurdish movement, nonetheless, has contributed to the strengthening of libertarian politics in Turkey. It should be noted that the Kurdish movement continued to use alternative politics, with its vertically structured parties, and through the radical democratic and populist practices of the HDP.[20] The HDP's left-populist strategies and tactics were especially capable of winning municipalities. Turkey's 2014 general elections and the entrance of the HDP into parliament was also helpful, giving the Kurdish movement increased legitimacy in the face of state repression.

By putting itself in the same league as other radical social and political projects, the Kurdish movement has strived for the liberation of the Kurdish people as well as for the population of the Middle East in general. In other words, in the minds of its participants, the liberation of the Kurds is considered as being related to and dependent upon the radical transformation of the societies and countries in which they reside. Thus, the Kurdish movement uses different means, ranging from self-governance mechanisms to popular mass politics, targeting both Kurds as well as other social, political, cultural, and ethnic groups in the country. Through these efforts, the Kurdish movement gained a base of support for both the Kurdish people and most of the leftist and libertarian groups under the HDP that were entering into the political scene. The increasingly anti-AKP stance of the Turkish population —in reaction to the excessive antagonistic and authoritarian politics of Erdoğan— meant that the Kurdish movement, particularly the HDP, continued to gain popular sympathy.[21]

Then came 2015, when everything changed. The peace process began to unravel after the June 7 elections, in which the HDP exceeded the 10% threshold to enter parliament as a third party, thereby preventing the AKP from taking power alone. Erdogan was furious.

Subsequently, conflict between the PKK and Turkish state reignited after the tragic Suruç bombing. Hundreds of socialist, leftist, and anarchist youths were gathering at a youth center in Suruç, a Kurdish town in Turkey, before a humanitarian trip to deliver aid to Kobane, a city of Rojava. The Islamic State (who typically received covert Turkish military support) bombed the youth center. Thirty-three were killed. The PKK retaliated with bombings and attacks on local police forces, and the state responded in kind, with a vicious cycle of attacks over several months. Thus, all of a sudden, the peace process, which had been patiently working away since 2009, ended.

The downward spiral worsened with the Hendek Events, when the Patriotic Revolutionary Youth Movement (YDG-H—a semi-autonomous urban youth organization affiliated with the PKK) declared democratic autonomy and started a popular mass uprising. Their street barricades in Kurdish cities in eastern Turkey were met by a very violent response by the Turkish military which imposed curfews. There were many deaths of civilians and activists. These events caused a massive migration of the Kurds from the region.

Turkey's left and the Kurdish movement were exposed to increasingly violent opposition. State-imposed pressure began to limit the activities of a broad cross-section of the political left. This included legal sections of the Kurdish movement and the HDP party members elected to represent municipalities. State repression escalated with the mass banning of Kurdish political organizations, publishing houses, and other institutions, as well as the arrest of activists, journalists, and even members of parliament, including the co-chairs of the HDP, Selahattin Demirtaş and Figen Yüksekdağ.

Further limits were imposed on the Kurdish institutions after the state of emergency declared after the failed military coup of July 16, 2016. Prior to these developments, the Kurdish movement, especially the HDP, had been making headway in gaining the sympathy of Turkey's population. However, these conflicts saw the Turkish state push the Kurdish movement from a broader approach of "Turkeyization" to be wedged in a narrower focus on the Kurdish question all over again. On the other hand, despite the Kurdish movement's realm of activities becoming strictly limited by increasing pressure, the HDP continued to be a center for resistance and opposition to Turkey's dominant political system and the AKP.

As a parliamentary party, the HDP limits its activities to representative politics. However, the people and groups that make up the party interest themselves with much broader practical political, social, and cultural experiences. Consequently, the HDP is interested in building democratic autonomy. After realizing their capabilities, some sections of Turkish society, particularly the nationalist and conservative wings, have attempted to prevent leftists and the Kurdish movement from reaching wider society. These barriers combine with the continued repression and control imposed by the Turkish state as well as the failure of peace agreements.[22] Together, these factors contribute to ongoing enmity, distance, and antipathy among many people living in Turkey. Despite these limitations, the democratic autonomy project has the potential to strengthen libertarian politics, support broader projects in the Middle East, and grow singular and collective subjectivities. Such a politics goes beyond the limits imposed by a nationalism constructed by Turkish republicanism, conservatism, and neo-liberalism because it attempts to construct a society based on radical pluralism, ecology, and communalist principles.

Conclusion

The Kurdish political movement has undergone a paradigm shift since the mid-2000s. One can easily make the claim that this change is a part of a renewal in leftist political theory and philosophy. Most of this renewal appeared as a transition from orthodox leftist thinking to more heterodox libertarian thinking. Even though most thinkers recognized as post-structuralist and postmodernist libertarians criticized previous leftists' paradigms—for their economism, authoritarian organizations, human centrism, and sexism—they were not interested in new methods of collective politics and macro-social transformations and revolutions.[23] Put differently, they ignored questions of how to change the world, how to make a revolution, and the strategies for the construction of a new social and political order. On the other hand, some recent theorists like Murray Bookchin, Negri and Hardt, Laclau and Mouffe,[24] contemporary anarchist thinkers and libertarians, deal with the problems of creating individuals who embrace communalist principles, political constitutions, and revolution. Bookchin is among those still inspired by classical anarchist and revolutionary libertarian ideas, emphasizing metaphysical and ontological discussions on politics and society. He draws attention to the universal problems of the ecological crisis, patriarchy, and hierarchy, differing, in these respects, from post-structuralist analysis by offering strategies for the reconstruction of society around the politics of municipalism, ecology, and communalism. Likewise, the paradigm shift within the Kurdish movement embodied in the projects and ideas of democratic autonomy parallels the progress being made in leftist thought. Even if its anti-authoritarian ideas go beyond orthodox Marxist views, it does not reject the social and political revolution. And yet, it goes beyond mere philosophical discussions by implementing practical solutions to social, economic, cultural, and political problems in the Middle East around libertarian ideas.

In these respects, the Kurdish movement takes the ideals embodied in direct democracy, self-governance, horizontally organized social forms, criticism of capitalism, sexism, and human centrism. Their inspiration ranges from political ideas like Bookchin's communalism to radical democracy and leftist populism.

They carry a solution to the Kurdish problem that goes beyond nationalism, situated within the general context of transformation in Middle Eastern societies and change around the world. Following this paradigm shift, the Kurdish movement began to put greater emphasis on the fact that the fate of the Kurdish people is inseparable from the future that awaits the people of the Middle East and the rest of the world. The Kurdish problem became considered a part of the universal issues posed by sexual discrimination, the ecological crisis, and capitalist modernity more generally.

BIBLIOGRAPHY

Akgün, R. *The Possibilities and Limitations of Articulations and Political Subjectification Mechanisms in Turkey* (PHD Dissertation, METU, 2018).

Bakar, C. *The Spatial Imaginary and Politics of Democratic Autonomy: A Neighborhood Assembly Experience in Beyoğlu* (Master Dissertation, Boğaziçi University), 2015.

Best. S and D Kellner. *Postmodern Theory*. (New York: The Guilford Press, 1991).

Biehl, Janet. "Bookchin, Öcalan, and Dialectics of Democracy," 2012. Retrieved 15.03.2020, from http://new-compass.net/articles/bookchin-öcalan-and-dialectics-democracy.

_____. *Ecology or Catastrophe: The Life of Murray Bookchin*. (New York: Oxford University Press, 2015).

Bookchin, Debbie. *How My Father's Ideas Help The Kurds Create a New Democracy*. Retrieved 18.03.2020 from how-my-fathers-ideas-helped-the-kurds-create-a-new-democracy.

Bookchin, Murray. *Remaking Society*. (Montreal: Black Rose Books, 1992).

_____. *Social Anarchism or Lifestyle Anarchism*. (Montreal: Black Rose Books, 1995).

_____. *The Philosophy of Social Ecology: Essays on Dialectical Naturalism*. (Montreal: Black Rose Books, 1996).

_____. *The Politics of Social Ecology: Libertarian Municipalism*. (Montreal: Black Rose Books, 1997).

_____. *The Ecology of Freedom: The Emergence and Dissolution of Hierarchy*. (Oakland, Edinburgh: AK Press, 2005).

_____. *Social Ecology and Communalism*. (Oakland, Edinburgh: AK Press, 2007).

_____. *The Next Revolution: Popular Assemblies and the Promise of Direct Democracy*. (London: Verso, 2015).

Demokrat Haber, 2016. Retrieved 02.04.2020 from https://www.demokrathaber.org/guncel/ocalan-ile-unlu-yazar-murray-bookchin-arasindaki-yazismalar-h62488.html

Duman, Y. *Rojava: Bir Demokratik Özerklik Deneyimi*. (İstanbul: İletişim Yayınları, 2016).

Gerber, D. and S Brincat. *When Öcalan met Bookchin: The Kurdish Freedom Movement and the Political Theory of Democratic Confederalism*. Geopolitics, 2018. Retrieved 05.04.2020 from, https://www.tandfonline.com/doi/pdf/10.1080/14650045.2018.1508016?needAccess=true

Güneş, C. *The Kurdish National Movement in Turkey: From Protest to Resistance*. (New York: Routledge, 2012).

_____. *The Kurdish Question in Turkey: New Perspectives on Violence, Representation and Reconciliation*. (New York: Routledge, 2013).

Gürer, C. *Demokratik Özerklik: Bir Yurttaşlık Heteropyası*. (İstanbul: Nota Bene Yayınları, 2015).

Knapp, M, A Flack, and E Ayboğa. *Revolution in Rojava: Democratic Autonomy and Women's Liberation in Syrian Revolution*. (London: Pluto Press, 2016).

Öcalan, Abdullah. *Interviews and Speeches*. (London: Kurdistan Solidarity Committee; Kurdistan Information Centre, 1991).

_____. *Seçme Yazılar, Cilt I*. (İstanbul: Melsa Yayınları, 1992).

_____. *Kürdistan Devriminin Yolu (Manifesto)*. (Köln: Weşanen Serxwebun Yayınları, 1993a).

_____. *Seçme Yazılar, Cilt II*. (İstanbul: Zagros Yayınları, 1993b).

_____. *Prison Writings: The Roots of Civilisation*. (London; Ann Arbor, MI: Pluto, 2007).

_____. *Prison Writings Volume II: The PKK and the Kurdish Question in the 21st Century*. (London, 2011).

_____. *Prison Writings III: The Road Map to Negotiations*. (Cologne: International Initiative, 2012).

_____. *Liberating life: Women's Revolution*. (Cologne: International Initiative Edition, 2013).

_____. *Democratic Confederalism*. (London: Transmedia Publishing, 2015a).

_____. *Manifesto for a Democratic Civilization, Volume 1*. (Porsgrunn: New Compass, 2015b).

_____. *Manifesto for a Democratic Civilization, Volume 2*. (Porsgrunn: New Compass, 2017).

_____. *Political Thought of Abdullah Öcalan*. (London: Pluto Press, 2017b).

Tatort Kurdistan. *Democratic Autonomy in North Kurdistan: A Reconnaissance into Southeastern Turkey: The Council Movement, Gender Liberation, and Ecology in Practice*. (Porsgrunn: New Compass, 2015).

Toplum ve Kuram. *Dağdan Taşmak: Kürt Hareketinin Dönüşüm Seyri. Vol. 5.*, 2011.

WEBSITES

https://www.hdp.org.tr/tr

https://www.hdp.org.tr/en

https://www.hdp.org.tr/tr/peoples-democratic-party/8760

https://www.hdp.org.tr/tr/parti-programi/8

https://halklarindemokratikkongresi.net

https://halklarindemokratikkongresi.net/hdk/program/50

NOTES

1. I use the term leftist to refer to political organizations of leftist social democrats, leftist liberals, and Marxists, as well as to libertarian and antiauthoritarian political currents such as feminists, anarchists, LBGTQia2+s, and ecologists.

2. Ayrinti Publishing House was one of them, focusing on the publication of books by libertarian and antiauthoritarian authors.

3. In the mid-1990s the student movement in the universities was the primary wing of Turkey's left New social and political organizations and movements, such as feminist, LGBTQia2+, and environmental struggles, also started to come onto the scene. Outside these political and social experiences, some Marxist organizations tried to develop new types of political experiences from radical democracy to autonomism.

4. An armed organization established by Öcalan and other Marxists, mostly Kurdish, to establish an independent state. In the 2000s, the political activities of the PKK went beyond mere armed struggle as mentioned later. It then developed a new praxis to solve the Kurdish problem and established new organizations. Thereby, the PKK became a part of a general organization, the KCK, which consists of different organizations and institutions in Turkey and all over the world. The PKK led to the establishment of a general Kurdish organization that aims to be a roof organization for all of the Kurdish people in the country including even the Kurds who are not

affiliated and sympathized with PKK. Named the Democratic Society Congress, DTK also supports KCK's projects such as democratic confederalism.

5. One of Öcalan's translators, Reimar Heider, carried out a correspondence with Bookchin in 2004. Öcalan was aware of this correspondence and had instructed his lawyers to help inform Bookchin that the American thinker, along with Immanuel Wallerstein were the writers he was currently most engaged with.

6. As it is known there have been Kurdish political organizations in Turkey and other countries where the Kurds live, such as Iraq, Iran, and Syria. However, Hereafter I will use the term the Kurdish movement and Kurdish political movement in reference to the organizations that are directly part of, sympathizers of, close to, and, acting in tandem with the PKK.

7. There are some studies highlighting the influence of Bookchin on the Kurdish movement's ideas and practices. For example see, Biehl, 2012; Gerber & Brincat, 2018.

8. There is a huge literature about this change. For some of the studies within this literature see, Toplum ve Kuram, 2011; Güneş, 2012; 2013; Gürer, 2015. Öcalan's books are also useful to understand this shift. For writings that are typical to his thinking and perspective before the 2000s see Öacalan,1992; 1993a; 1993b. In his writings after the 2000s he focuses on the world capitalist system and modernity rather than solely on the Kurdish problem. for example see, (Öcalan, 2007; 2011; 2012; 2015a; 2015b; 2017a; 2017b).

9. The following captures some key aspects of Bookchin's influence on the Kurdish movement: "Öcalan, especially after his imprisonment in 1999, has adopted key aspects of Bookchin's thought within his own political model of 'democratic confederalism'. Öcalan stated that his 'world view' stands close to Bookchin's, especially in regard to the theory and practice of municipalities. The Declaration of 2005 marked the formal and practical shift from Marxist-Leninism towards the implementation of Bookchin's social ecology." (Gerber; Brincat, 2018: 3)

10. In 1991, the members of the Kurdish Party, People's Labor Party (HEP), entered into the parliament in alliance with the Social Democratic Populist Party (SHP). HEP was active in the peace agreements between the PKK and the Turkish State started by Özal, former prime minister and the president of Turkey. However, some of the MPs of the party were arrested in 1994 and the party was banned. Since the 1990s, the PKK's members and other Kurdish activists established a lot of parties, most of which were banned (Gürer, 2015: 147).

11. It must be noted that these criticisms by Öcalan focus on the liberation of Kurdish people which was under the domination of the Turkish republic colonialist policies, the traditional Kurdish culture, and the compradors in Kurdish society constructing an inauthentic Kurdishness. In parallel with Franz Fanon's ideas, Öcalan advocated the Kurdish people's liberation becoming an authentic subject beyond the colonialist forms of the social and political subjectivities. Therefore, the women's liberation in this process was still seen as a part of the national liberation. For these points, see Öcalan, 1993.

12. As it is explained in detail later, the democratic autonomy or democratic confederalism is a project to solve the Kurdish problem with the radical transformation of the Middle Eastmiddle east societies. The two concepts might be considered as different because a democratic autonomy refers to the autonomy of Kurds in Turkey, the democratic confederalism is a political system including different political and social groups in a confederalist political system like in Rojava. However, democratic autonomy is the solution to the Kurdish problem in Turkey as a practical implementation of democratic confederalism. As it is explained through democratic confederalism and democratic autonomy the Kurdish movement goes beyond the Kurdish problem and two-term designates a social and political system besides the principles of communalism. Thus, it is wrong to consider these concepts separately. Öcalan also sometimes uses the term of a democratic republic. Therefore, the concepts can be used interchangeably and I will use them so. Öcalan has a brochure explaining the project and the idea of democratic confederalism. (Öcalan, 2015a).

13. This term was foundational for the development of the HDP (Peoples' Democratic Party) (a party

established by the initiative Kurdish movement in 2012, and including other leftist forces in the country) political perspectives claiming itself as not only Kurds but Turkey's party. As mentioned, before HDP a number of Kurdish parties were established and these parties developed several different strategies to participate in the elections including an alliance with the leftists in the country to pass the election threshold of 10 % and entering into the elections with independent candidates. These alliances became institutionalized around HDK (Peoples' Democratic Congress) in 2011. Some components of HDK founded HDP which brought together different political and social groups and passed the threshold in the 7th June 2014 elections. Each organization is supportive of the solutions offered by the Kurdish movement, but aims at a politics going beyond Kurdish problem. For HDK's program see, https://www.halklarin demokratikkongresi.net/hdk/program/50. For HDP's program see, https://www.hdp.org.tr/tr/ parti-programi/8 and also see, https://www.hdp.org.tr/en/who-we-are/peoples-democratic-party/8760

14. Democratic autonomy and democratic confederalism are two terms that designate a social and political system founded upon communalist principles. It is possible to use these two terms interchangeably. To understand the theoretical sources of this project and its implementations in different cases, some studies are useful. For example see, Bakar; 2015; Gürer, 2015; Tatort Kurdistan, 2015; Knapp & Flach & Ayboğa, 2015; Duman, 2016.

15. The study by Gerber and Brincat is useful in concentrating upon the relationship between Bookchin and this project. See: Gerber and Brincat, 2018.

16. You can see Bookchin's influence on the Kurdish movement's new ideas in many aspects, some of his books are enough to remark the similarities between him and the Kurdish movement. Thus, see: Bookchin, 1992; 1997; 2005; 2007).

17. Bookchin criticizes the mystical understanding of the world and praise of irrationality against scientific thought, instead presenting a scientific epistemology related to social ecology. See Bookchin, 1996.

18. Even though Öcalan rejects positivist scientific perspectives, he doesn't reject science entirely. (Öcalan, 2015)

19. The Kurdish movement has always been active in these fields of social and political movements and struggles. But in the new era, the movement became more interested in strengthening these fields although they aren't relevant to the Kurdish problem.

20. HDP considers itself as one of the forces to put into practice the democratic autonomy project in Turkey. It is evident in HDP's program see, https://www.hdp.org.tr/tr/parti-programi/

21. Since AKP came into power 2002, opposition accumulated into different blocs and alliances of groups from the nationalists to the leftists. After the Gezi events, different social and political groups came together temporarily, and when HDP came onto the scene, the opposition of leftist, social democrats, libertarians, Marxist groups, and some social groups gathered around HDP, at least during the elections in 2015. In that sense, HDP became one of the centers for the political stances of anti-AKP. Moreover, some of the leftist and Marxist groups also took an active role in HDP being organized by joining into organizational structures, directly supporting it and leading their supporters to vote for HDP in elections, or developing election alliances. Some parts of my PhD thesis analyzes the means and experiences of HDP strategies, mechanisms for the construction of the political articulations and subjectivities. See Akgün: 2017.

22. In the peace process, the Kurdish movement—especially HDP—attracted the sympathy of different social and political groups before having negative attitudes, feelings, and perceptions. Even some of the ultranationalists expressed positive feelings. Thus, it became evident that under some conditions, the structured dispositions and habits of the agents may change leading them to have different political positions. Therefore it is plausible to infer that if Kurdish problem is solved in peaceful means and agreements, the Kurdish movement may have the possibility to spread into the different sections of society gaining a political force in the country.

23. Even though these thinkers have very different views and some rejected postmodernist and poststructuralist views, they have common in the emphasis on the plurality, differences and the heterogeneity on the construction of human life. The other common point for the thinkers such as Foucault, Deleuze, Baudrillard, and Lyotard is that they aren't interested in and presented no idea about the collective emancipatory politics as Best and Kellner pointed out. (1991)

24. It is true that Bookchin is very different from these thinkers, but similarly wrote on the radical collective politics going beyond mere economism delving into the problems of collective political subjectification and social and political common.

Spreading Murray Bookchin's Ideas in Germany

Wolfgang Haug

IN SEPTEMBER 1978 I, along with other anarchists in southern Germany, founded the publishing group, Trotzdem Verlag. At that time, many activists had ceased their political activities due to increased repression following the deadly attacks by the Marxist-Leninist Red Army Faction, and the lethal response by German police. In 1979, I first encountered Murray Bookchin and his ideas when he participated in the *Autogestione* congress in Venice, Italy. Two years later, we translated and published his contribution, together with those of others from the congress, in the book *Selbstverwaltung*.[1] This was the beginning of an ongoing involvement with his work which lead to a lifelong personal friendship until his death. In the 1970s and early 1980s, we were deeply interested in the concept of self-management. Many self-organized printing shops, housing projects, alternative community centres, bookshops, magazines, bicycle shops, publishing groups, and theatre initiatives were founded throughout Germany. However, we lacked a theory in which to ground these projects, and the subculture in general, and to counter the prevailing capitalist narrative.

Cognizant of the value of a personal relationship for organizing political projects, I met with Murray Bookchin, his daughter Debbie, and Dimitrios Roussopoulos at the international anarchist meeting in Venice, Italy, in 1984. Our group, the Forum for Libertarian Information (FLI), presented a seminar on labour at the congress. It was agreed that the working class was no longer an agent for revolutionary change. At that time, we theorized that robots would take over the workplace which would no longer be the centre from which a social revolutionary future could develop. Murray agreed with this assessment; likewise, we appreciated his thoughts on the rise of urbanization and the decline of citizenship. We decided to collaborate further.

The FLI began to translate and publish important articles by Murray in our quarterly anarchist magazine, *Schwarzer Faden* (The Black Thread through History). The first article, on his approach to the ethics of nature, appeared in April 1985.[2] In September 1985, we published his thesis on libertarian communalism[3] and discussed these ideas in meetings of the FLI as well as in our magazine's May and August 1986 issues.[3] His concept of libertarian communalism was important to us because it corresponded with our approach to community organizing as a counter to the parliamentarism of the Green Party.

When the German edition of Murray's work, *The Ecology of Freedom,* was published in 1985, he attended the Frankfurt Book Fair and attended our FLI meeting to discuss his work.[4] In support of his efforts to reconceptualize anarchism, *Schwarzer Faden* published an interview with Murray conducted by Peter Einarssen in November 1987 and February 1988[5]; in May 1989, it presented the US-based Left Green Network, which Murray co-founded.[6] The issues in December, 1989, and April, 1990, included Janet Biehl's article "Social Ecofeminism" (*Sozialer Anarchafeminismus*).[7] Trotzdem Verlag later published these articles in a small book in 1991. Biehl's work, influenced by Bookchin, connected feminism to the social question and simultaneously argued against esoteric tendencies in feminist discussions.

In Frankfurt, we hosted Dimitrios Roussopoulos from Black Rose Books when he attended the Frankfurt Book Fair. In August 1991, we published Murray's article about the Enlightenment to launch the German edition of *Remaking Society,* which would be published in 1992. Our goal was to revisit the great questions of the Enlightenment: the commitment to reason, a quality education for all, the use of technology and science, human coexistence in an ecological society, and the role of anarchism in demanding freedom, revealing hierarchies, and creating a culture of mutual aid.

In September 1992, *Schwarzer Faden* reprinted Murray's October 1991 article on libertarian municipalism.[8] And in the December 1992 issue, we gave him an opportunity to respond to Ulrike Heider's critique.[9]

In 1993, Andi Ries and I contributed to a workshop on Murray's libertarian municipalism at an anarchist event in Frankfurt. The workshop was packed, which led us to realize that, sometimes, an overcrowded room can prevent an audience from truly understanding new political ideas.

In summer, 1994, I travelled to Canada and the US, visited Dimitrios and his partner, Lucia Kowaluk, in Montreal, and Murray and Janet in Burlington, as well as social ecologists Chaia Heller, Cindy Milstein, and others. In Murray and Janet's flat, we discussed social ecology, the different attitudes of Europeans and Americans to guns, the overuse of medication, and the importance of the Civil War for Americans.

In August, 1994, we published both Murray's article about the future of cities[10] and, following his advice, a translation of L. Susan Brown's anarchafeminist answer to power-feminism. In January, 1995, *Schwarzer Faden* published an interview with him about his critique of "lifestyle anarchism," as he called it.[11] His claim was that anarchism must speak to the people again, and not only to anarchist circles. In June, 1995, *Schwarzer Faden* published Janet's article on ecofeminism and deep ecology.[12] We shared the view that there was a tendency towards anarchism becoming part of a chic bourgeois lifestyle, but we also saw that Murray's view could lead him to condemn young people who were still searching for their identity as "self-styled individualistic anarchists" and who hadn't yet learned the real purpose of anarchism: i.e. the social revolution.

Meanwhile, thanks to our close working relationship with Dimitrios, we published the German edition of *The Rise of Urbanization and the Decline of Citizenship* in 1996. Bookchin pointed to the origins of real, face-to-face democracy in the Athenian *polis*. Of course he didn't overlook the failures of this first democracy, such as the existence of slavery, patriarchy, warfare, and class antagonisms, but he did hope for a free and egalitarian future for all citizens. When the book fair was over, Dimitrios visited me in Grafenau near Stuttgart where we conducted an interview regarding his work with *Our Generation* and Black Rose Books, published in January 1996.[13]

In 1997, we organized a debate between Murray and Noam Chomsky in the pages of our magazine. Murray had critiqued Chomsky's book, *Powers and Prospects*, so we began issue 60 with a chapter of that book: "Goals and Visions."[14] Our aim was to discuss different ways of bringing anarchism back into the political sphere. Murray's response to Chomsky in issue 61 states that "ideas and practical action" must be united.[15] In issue 63, in 1998, we published Chomsky's "Consent Without Consent" and an article by David Morris about free cities, which examined Murray's concept of municipalism.[16]

In issue 64, we advertised the first congress of libertarian municipalism, being held in Lisbon in August, 1998. For this event, the starting point of a new international anarchist movement, we worked closely with Dimitrios to publish the German edition of Janet's book, *The Politics of Social Ecology: Libertarian Municipalism*,[17] to coincide with the English original put out by Black Rose in 1998. It was published in time for the beginning of the congress. People who couldn't afford to buy the book could read the chapters on citizenship and dual power in the following issues of *Schwarzer Faden*. Anarchist comrades who produced the Portuguese magazine, *A Batalha,* had organized the conference at the Faculty of Architecture, University of Lisbon, and the lectures and workshops were promising. I was confident that the conference had been productive and that it would subsequently create a new network of activists. Online tools for discussion had been established and were used before and after the congress. Murray himself could not come to Lisbon because of his health so he was videoconferenced into the sessions. A larger delegation from the Spanish CGT (Confederación General del

Trabajo) plus attendees from other countries contributed to the impression that there was enough of a critical mass to create a new transnational network of activists. We examined the international attendance very carefully, and the political conditions in each country, to gauge the organizational potential for future coordination. In the next issue, J. Frank Harrison from Nova Scotia, whom I had met in Lisbon, wrote an article for our magazine about Bookchin and Peter Kropotkin, demonstrating their common attitudes and theories.

However, when the next congress was organized in Plainfield, Vermont, I was unable to travel there because of a lack of money and time, so a comrade of mine travelled to Vermont instead. Unfortunately, the conference's screening process came as a surprise to the European anarchists, and my comrade was rejected because he had proposed a contribution on Gandhi. Murray told him that a pacifist would be not welcome. I was offended and disappointed for my friend who, in 2019, is still active as a nonviolent, antimilitaristic anarchist. But more importantly, I felt that the momentum created in Lisbon had been checked due to a fear that participants who did not believe in social ecology would infiltrate the movement. Of course, fear is detrimental to the creation of all social and cultural movements. The crisis was evident and, unsurprisingly, after the Plainfield meeting, the new movement generated in Europe fell silent. By 2004, when *Schwarzer Faden* closed, there was not a single article on social ecology being published in the magazine.

When Murray died, I wrote an obituary in the nonviolent anarchist paper, *Graswurzelrevolution* published in October, 2006.[18] The piece was also published on the internet by Anarchopedia and received a few thousand views. The second obituary in German was written by members of the Kurdish PKK. Here, for the first time, I encountered the fact that the Kurds had read and discussed Murray's work, including his books that I have published in German. It also turned out that Abdullah Öcalan read Bookchin in prison in İmralı, Turkey, and had organized a paradigm shift within the PKK, leaving behind national liberation politics and engaging in an open-minded political movement called "democratic confederalism."

After Murray's death, Dimitrios and Lucia visited me in 2012 and we conducted a long interview regarding participatory democracy, the antiglobalization movement, the World Social Forum, and the efforts of citizens to take an active part in controlling their cities. This interview was published in two series in April and May, 2012 in *Graswurzelrevolution*. We also discussed, for the first time, Dimitrios' plans to establish a social ecology centre in Europe, based in Greece, in order to renew the movement. In 2013, we were reunited on the island of Crete with younger comrades from Greece, Norway, Sweden, France, and Italy, organized with the help of Brain Tokar of Vermont. At this point, the Transnational Institute of Social Ecology (TRISE) was born. In 2019, TRISE established an office in Athens and was incorporated as a legal nonprofit association in Finland. The aim of TRISE is to be a pan-European resource for all those concerned with the democratization of democracy and interested in social ecology.

In January 2016, *Graswurzelrevolution* published a piece I wrote on Murray's changing views on anarchism. In the meantime, the war against ISIS in Syria and Iraq was being fought by Kurdish troops and their allies. After receiving military air support from international forces, they created a decentralized society in the multiethnic region of Rojava in northern Syria based on community assemblies, local organizations, equal rights for men and women, dual power, self-organization, and active citizenship. Janet was invited to visit Rojava and has been there several times, most recently to create an illustrated book of the people of the region. Also, one former member of our Trotzdem/*Schwarzer Faden* crew, Michael Wilk, a medical doctor, travels regularly to northern Syria to assist the wounded. Unfortunately, Murray did not live to see these elements of his thought put into practice. He would never have imagined that it would happen in Syria, and yet Rojava is a testament to the fact that his vision can be realized. Therefore, it is imperative that his ideas continue to be disseminated.

NOTES

1. Murray Bookchin, et al. *Selbstverwaltung. Die Basis einer befreiten Gesellschaft. 1. Auflage* (Reutlingen: Trotzdem-Verlag, 1981).

2. Murray Bookchin, "Die Radikalisierung der Natur—Zur Ethik eines radikalen Naturverständnisses" (in: *Schwarzer Faden* Nr.17, 1985: 22–34). Available at the Internet Archive: https://archive.org/ stream/SchwarzerFaden_lidiap/1985-17-Schwarzer%20Faden_f#page/n33/mode/2up. Accessed: August 20, 2019.

3. Murray Bookchin, "Thesen zum libertären Kommunalismus" (in: *Schwarzer Faden*, Nr.19, 1985: 14–25. Discussion in SF 21, 1986: 58–59; and 22, 1986: 61–62). Available at the Internet Archive: https://archive.org/stream/SchwarzerFaden_lidiap/1986-22-Schwarzer%20Faden_f#page/n61/ mode/2up. Accessed: August 20, 2019.

4. Murray Bookchin, *Die Ökologie der Freiheit. Wir brauchen keine Hierarchien.* (Weinheim: Beltz Verlag, 1985).

5. "Interview mit Murray Bookchin vom Oktober, 1984, 2 Teile," (in: *Schwarzer Faden* Nr. 26 and 27, 1987: 37–47; and 1988: 40–44). Available at the Internet Archive: https://archive.org/stream/ SchwarzerFaden_lidiap/1987-26-Schwarzer%20Faden_f#mode/2up. Accessed: August 20, 2019.

6. Friederike Kamann, "Left Green Network" (in: *Schwarzer Faden*, No. 31, 1989: 49–52). Available at the Internet Archive: https://archive.org/stream/SchwarzerFaden_lidiap/1989-31-Schwarzer% 20Faden_f#page/n51/mode/2up. Accessed: August 20, 2019.

7. Janet Biehl, "Der soziale Ökofeminismus" (in *Schwarzer Faden*, Nr. 33, 1989: 11-17). Available at the Internet Archive: https://archive.org/stream/SchwarzerFaden_lidiap/1989-33-Schwarzer% 20Faden_f#page/n15/mode/2up. Accessed: August 20, 2019.

8. Murray Bookchin, "Libertärer Kommunalismus—ein Konzept für eine konkrete Utopie" (in: *Schwarzer Faden*, Nr. 43, 1992: 20–25) Available at the Internet Archive: https://archive.org/ stream/SchwarzerFaden_lidiap/1992-43-Schwarzer%20Faden_f#page/n1/mode/2up Accessed: August 21, 2019; Murray Bookchin, "Libertarian Municipalism: An Overview" (in: *Green Perspectives* 24: A Social Ecology Publication, 1991).

9. Murray Bookchin, "Vonheinem: 'Narren der Frieheit'" (in: *Schwarzer Faden*, Nr. 44, 1992: 48–51) Available at the Internet Archive: https://archive.org/stream/SchwarzerFaden_lidiap/1992-43-Schwarzer%20Faden_f#page/n1/mode/2up Accessed: August 21, 2019.

10. Murray Bookchin, "Die Frage nach der Zukunft der Städte" (in: *Schwarzer Faden* No. 50, 1994: 28–35). Available at the Internet Archive: https://archive.org/stream/SchwarzerFaden_lidiap/1994-50-Schwarzer%20Faden_f#mode/2up Accessed: August 21, 2019.

11. Murray Bookchin, "Anarchismus is sehr shick geworden" (in: *Schwarzer Faden* No. 52, 1995: 4–10). Available at the Internet Archive: https://archive.org/stream/SchwarzerFaden_lidiap/1995-52-Schwarzer%20Faden_f#mode/2up Accessed: August 21, 2019.

12. Janet Biehl, "Ökofeminismus und deep ecology: Ein unlösbarer Konflikt?" (in: *Schwarzer Faden* No. 54, 1995: 16–23) Available at the Internet Archive: https://archive.org/stream/Schwarzer Faden_lidiap/1995-54-Schwarzer%20Faden_f#page/n15/mode/2up Accessed: August 21, 2019.

13. Wolfgang Haug, Andi Ries. "25 Jahr Black Rose Books: 'Prinzip 1: Du mußt die Selbastausbeutung alkzeptieren' Interview mit Dimitrios Roussoupoulos" (in: *Schwarzer Faden* No. 57, 1996: 47–54);

14. Noam Chomsky, *Power and Prospects: Reflections on Human Nature and the Social Order* (Boston: South End Press, 1991); Noam Chomksy, "Ziele und Visionen" (in: *Schwarzer Faden* No. 60, 1997: 34–47).

15. Murray Bookchin, "Die Einheit von Ideal und Praxis" (in: *Schwarzer Faden* No. 61, 1997: 21–29).

16. Noam Chomsky, "Consent Without Consent" (in: *Schwarzer Faden* No. 63, 1998: 17–26); David Morris, "Freie Städte an der Arbeit" (in: *Schwarzer Faden* No. 63, 1998: 28–29).

17. Janet Biehl, *Politics of Social Ecology: Libertarian Municipalism* (Montreal: Black Rose Books, 1997).

18. Wolfgang Haug, "Das Wichtigste in den USA heutzutage ist es, Bewusstsein zu schaffen" (in: *Graswurzelrevolution*, October, No. 312, 2006: https://www.graswurzel.net/gwr/category/ausgaben/312-oktober-2006/).

Montreal and Murray Bookchin

Dimitrios Roussopoulos

FEW CITIES, if any, can claim to be a laboratory of social ecology like Montreal. To be sure, various aspects of social ecology are being applied in northeastern parts of Syria, namely Rojava. Even so, major components of social ecology, as pioneered and advanced by Murray Bookchin, have been put into practice in Montreal. Whether consciously or unconsciously, this has happened rather consistently over five decades since the 1960s, and in both French- and English-speaking milieus.

The planting of the seeds of social ecology dates back to the 1960s, before Murray Bookchin came to Montreal. This included the printing and distribution of pamphlets and newspapers, public talks, study groups, and affinity groups (many of these activities organized through the longest-functioning anarchist bookstore in North America, Alternatives, now named L'Insoumise).

The second part of the 1960s in Quebec, and Montreal in particular, included an intensive series of community organizing efforts (*animation sociale* in French) in both English-speaking and French-speaking neighbourhoods. Much of the territorial mapping of Montreal—demographically, sociologically, and of the built environment—reflected the Quebec countryside, as thousands in the preceding years had flocked to the city for better employment. What emerged were distinct neighbourhoods with pronounced characteristics, such as distinct linguistic, ethnic, and social features. This was also a period of linguistic and political nationalism alongside left-wing trade unionism. The response of the political elite at the provincial level was the liberalization of one government institution or agency after another. At the municipal level of the metropolis, City Hall was frozen in time, with an authoritarianism rigidly maintained through the office of the mayor.

In the sixties, we began our discussions around the question of where to seek the locus of fundamental social change in a highly urbanized, industrial society. The conclusion was that the City and its neighbours would be our point of departure. Where was the weight of alienation and exploitation felt, we asked? In addition to the workplace, we felt that this burden was experienced where people live most of their lives—in their neighbourhoods. Indeed, the reality of their daily problems make the home/street as oppressive as, and one with, the workplace. We began our reflection by studying the work of Henri Lefebvre, who made a major leap in Marxist theory by drawing from the experience of May–June 1968 in Paris, France. He raised the banner of "the Right to the City."

Because we live in a highly urbanized society with a massive centralization of economic and political power, the major cities have become the axles of our society. Therefore it falls upon us to develop community organizing strategies that accept the geopolitical significance cities play in the fundamental transformation of our society.

Enter Murray Bookchin

By 1968–69, Murray Bookchin ventured to Montreal. He visited the office of the New Left international quarterly journal, *Our Generation against Nuclear War*. This journal, the first issue of which featured an introduction by Bertrand Russell, was founded in 1961. It started out as a "peace research" journal and its contents evolved over time.

In 1969, I had just completed a manuscript on the New Left in Canada, commissioned by a major Canadian publisher; they were taking what we felt like was a long time to publish the book, while myself and other activists were impatient to publish it. During Bookchin's visit to the city, where he introduced himself under his pen name Lewis Herber, we had stimulating political and intellectual discussions. This exchange launched a series of follow-up events and, in order to publish the book ourselves, we founded a new radical press in late 1969. Indeed, the name of our new book publishing project was Murray Bookchin's brainchild— Black Rose Books, based on a medieval peasant myth that they who find the black rose find freedom. It was a poetic story that, we found out decades later, he had entirely made up. With a budget of only a few hundred dollars, we published my aforementioned book and sold over 5,000 copies, touring the country on a speaking tour. This set us on the road to book publishing. Later that same year, we built on our momentum and organized a huge public meeting at which Bookchin gave a ringing and brilliant talk entitled "Revolutionary Anarchism." Even though it was his first public talk in Montreal, the University Settlement on rue Saint-Urbain was packed—an indication of the times, and a reflection of the groundwork which we had already seeded.

Janet Biehl, in her magnificent biography of Murray Bookchin, recounts his entry into Montreal, our meetings together, and our interactions over many years.[1] I shall not repeat what she does so well in her book, except to highlight a few events and accomplishments we shared together.

Montreal has had, from the 1960s on, a wide range of citizen committees in predominantly poor and working class districts. Much of this social activism was the result of community organizing. Two driving ideas were promoted: helping to organize the underclass and unorganized, and building participatory democracy. Attempts were made to bring these popular groups together. In time, a large number of political action committees were formed in various neighbourhoods which grouped together the local popular groups. These political action committees became the basis of a new left-wing municipal party, the *Front d'action populaire* (FRAP).

In essence, the FRAP was a political party that was a federation of local political action committees. In 1970, Montrealers obtained the right to vote at the municipal level for the first time. Previously, only Montreal's property owners had the right to vote. Given that Montreal had a tenant-majority population, the preceding elections were hardly a celebration of representative democracy. This same period was a turbulent one of both linguistic and left-wing nationalism throughout Quebec. This movement which sought to separate Quebec from the rest of Canada and form a new nation-state also included a terrorist wing, the *Front de libération du Québec* (FLQ). In November 1970, the month in which Montreal's municipal elections were scheduled to take place, this terrorist wing played into the hands of the prevailing political class by provoking by a series of bombings, kidnappings, and assassinations. Such actions gave an ideal pretext for the Establishment to declare a state of emergency, handing sweeping powers to all police forces and the military. Montreal was put under martial law. More than 700 individual activists were arrested and jailed. Radios announced the arrest of prominent activists, including the author of this essay. In fact, a periodical that we were publishing in French called *Noir et Rouge* (modelled on the English-language quarterly *Our Generation*), had its offices twice raided by the police carrying machine guns. They seized the third issue and locked these copies until our newfound magazine in their warehouse for eight months until our newfound magazine went bankrupt. That it was devoted to *nonviolent* revolution the police didn't quite catch. Several FRAP candidates were also arrested. People were afraid to go to the polling stations, as street corners had armed troops and tanks stationed throughout. Needless to say, the authoritarian, incumbent mayor was re-elected and his party seized another majority. No candidates won from the FRAP.

For some time thereafter, many activists and other concerned citizens were too traumatized to get on with a renewed wave of community organizing. Still, many small meetings took place all over Montreal. One of the main targets of opposition that was discussed was Mayor Jean Drapeau and the dominance of his hand-picked political party on city council.

Nevertheless, by 1972, social and economic unrest was boiling to the breaking point again. The largest general strike in the history of labour struggles in North

America broke out. Some 300,000 unionists not only marched in defiance but also occupied radio stations and factories. The Paris 1968 slogan, "It's only the beginning, we continue the fight" rang through the streets during mass demonstrations. At the neighbourhood level, street committees were resurrected and were preparing to challenge municipal authoritarianism again. By early 1974, a left-of-center political opposition was ready to publicly surface.

Prior to these events, in 1968, a seminal battle was launched by activists in the Milton Parc Citizens' Committee to save their downtown neighbourhood from complete demolition. This struggle, spearheaded by community organizers from the University Settlement, was very much inspired by the ideals of the 1960s New Left. They wanted to not only prevent the wanton destruction of a heritage neighbourhood peopled by low-income residents, but also wanted to create a cooperative community with nonprofit cooperative housing at its core. Door-to-door mobilization and public assemblies laid the basis for a militant movement which gained support from across the city. The entire drama is analyzed in detail elsewhere.[2] Suffice to say, the marches and demonstrations, sit-ins, arrests, hunger strikes, and trial continued into the 1970s. In fact, the struggle continued into the 1980s, when its victory established the *Communauté Milton Parc* (CMP). This community is the largest nonprofit cooperative housing project on an urban land trust in North America, providing secure housing to 1500 citizens. At the core of this organizing in various chapters of its history were four anarchist affinity groups of social ecologists very much inspired by the writing and the visits of Murray Bookchin. The essence of the CMP was to abolish private property within the six-block downtown neighbourhood by establishing a community land trust; this land trust would federate 22 housing cooperatives and nonprofit housing associations. In the years that followed, this enormous sociopolitical and economic accomplishment was a step towards the municipalization of urban land as a whole, which in effect took this neighbourhood, its built environment, and its citizens off the terrain of market capitalism. Indeed, under the public surface, even immediately after 1970, neighbourhoods with previous records of social and political activism were buzzing. The roots of renewal were there.

By the spring of 1974, the newly cast urban political left-of-center brought together a mixture of left nationalists of the Parti Québecois, social democrats of the New Democratic Party, and members of the small Community Party. Adding to this political landscape, some neo-Marxist intellectuals rapidly formed the Montreal Citizens Movement (MCM). The fact that it named itself a "movement," rather than an outright political party, reflected the fact that the principal organizers recognized that the base of activism in Montreal had a left libertarian sensibility that had to be taken into account. However, from outset, the MCM chose to focus on individual membership, rather than rebuilding the model of the FRAP.

A few months after it was formed, the MCM faced an election. They went onto achieve a stunning victory, electing 18 MCM city councillors from electoral districts where community organizing was most deeply rooted. The mayor faced a real opposition within city council for the first time. Meanwhile, on the trade union side, the libertarian-leaning Confederation of National Trade Unions (CNTU) issued a sweeping manifesto which stated categorically that unionized workers were more than workers. They were citizens, and as is true of all citizen or popular neighbourhood organizations, common work had to be undertaken to address issues of housing, transportation, rent controls, and quality-of-life issues. The CNTU manifesto was called "The Second Front," which indicated a major shift from business unionism, and reflected a deep social and political shift in the union movement.[3] Such a shift, which also was reflected (in one form or another) in the other two major trade union federations of the day, is evidenced by the role unions played in organizing protests and mass petitions for causes like free public transportation. One emblematic demonstration, organized in collaboration with radical student unions, saw 10,000 people gather in front of city hall.[4]

In turn, the MCM began moving steadily to the left. Before 1975, the anarchists and social ecologists decided to join and become active at the grassroots of the MCM. By 1975, an openly socialist executive committee was elected, and that year's MCM congress consolidated nascent ideas germinating among the membership.

These ideas included the decentralization of significant powers from city hall and its municipal council to the neighbourhoods by establishing a series of decision-making neighbourhood councils. Indeed, the MCM challenged the definition of city councillors as they had been strictly mandated, and argued for revocable delegates.[5] They also adopted a major radical social housing program. These and other propositions were democratically debated at Congress, and eventually led to an emerging split between electorialists/pragmatists and the large left-wing within the MCM.

Burlington and Montreal

From the mid 1970s to the mid 1990s the telephone calls from Burlington rang almost every second day, during which Murray and I had heavy discussions on what was going on, what should go on, and how to go about applying the politics of social ecology. These long discussions continued for years and also included philosophical issues. Meanwhile, Black Rose Books and *Our Generation* continued to publish essays and articles by Bookchin and others. The interaction between Murray Bookchin and some of the key left-wingers in the MCM was very fruitful. In fact, Stephen Schechter, a member of the MCM executive committee, while he and I worked on his influential book, *The Politics of Urban Liberation,* became an avowed anarchist in the process, creating further waves of such anarchism.[6]

The mainstream media were panicking and eventually fanned the flames of an internal split, leading to the creation of a new splinter political party, the Municipal Action Group (MAG). The stage was set for the 1978 election. Just before the election, a number of street committees in downtown Montreal were preparing a civil disobedience action to block a major city street (*rue Jeanne-Mance*) to through-traffic, as part of a campaign to convert it back to a residential street. For the first time, the MCM was called upon to not only endorse the action, but also to have MCM city councillors and candidates officially participate in the blockade. That they did. The street was blocked during rush hour for several hours.

Again, the mainstream media (largely francophone) condemned this action and started a campaign of red baiting against the MCM for trying to create "neighbourhood soviets" dressed up as neighbourhood councils. The media attacks were almost daily. The results of the 1978 elections and the split on the left-of-center political spectrum resulted in the election of only one MCM and one MAG councillor in City Hall, and the remainder of the seats were taken back by the ruling mayor, Jean Drapeau. After this defeat, the youthful left-wingers decided to return to their neighbourhoods and rebuild again, resulting in a political vacuum in the MCM.

From 1978 to 1986, the MCM moved to the center. But the resentment against the ruling mayor was so deep that many community organizations still preferred the lesser of two evils. In the 1986 elections, the MCM won the elections with a sweeping majority at city hall (55 seats of 58); in the process it had shed much of its left-wing program. The exception was the desire for decentralization and the creation of neighbourhood councils. Just before the fall 1986 election, however, the MCM leadership decided to postpone this proposal under after its first term. The seeds of a new internal split were planted.

Around this new split, there was a convergence between a political left and a growing ecological left of social ecologists. In the meantime, many of the essays of Murray Bookchin were published in the journal *Our Generation* and also the out-of-print books were brought back into print by Black Rose Books, with Murray busy writing new introductions and acknowledgements. All of these publications were proposed by mutual and verbal agreements between us. The common objective was to maintain in circulation a body of social ecology, while at the same time, arranging public lectures in various cities like Halifax, Montreal, Toronto, and Vancouver. I, for one, was committed to the wide range of these ideas, as we planned various activities and book projects into the 1990s.[7] To this end I also helped found a French-language book publishing project, Les Éditions Écosocieté, also devoted to social ecology, which has published the works of Janet Biehl,

Murray Bookchin, Chaia Heller, and other social ecologists. This publishing program has also contributed to a growing interest in social ecology in France and other French-speaking regions in Europe. Black Rose Books and I, personally, did everything we could to assure that Murray Bookchin's books were translated and published in Turkish, Greek, Italian, and French among other languages, and specifically by radical publishers. All of this work was done without bourgeois agreements between author and publisher, as has been the common practice since the founding of Black Rose Books. Our common objective was to get the works out there by all means and as widely as possible.

The Politics of Social Ecology

During this period, innovative green parties began to emerge in Europe and elsewhere. Ecological consciousness was having a larger impact. By 1988–89, a number of MCM city councillors and members had had enough, and resigned from the political party. On the other hand, the social ecologists began forming the basis of a municipal ecology party seeking to put libertarian municipalism as such into practice. In December 1989, a well-attended congress took place, and Ecology Montreal was born. At a major public lecture at McGill University in February 1990, Murray Bookchin, in another brilliant presentation, gave an unqualified endorsement to Ecology Montreal before several hundred young enthusiasts. This was followed by various smaller meetings to develop a strategy. Both Bookchin and I continued to not only interact on a regular basis but continued to refine the politics of social ecology. The Montreal election was set for the fall, and we presented 21 candidates, ten women and eleven men, with no candidate for mayor. The social ecology-inspired programme of Ecology Montreal was well received, but the election results, given the first-past-the-post electoral system, gave three of our candidates second place in votes (I came in second with the highest percentage).[8] A further attempt took place in the elections of 1994, but this time, the MCM itself was defeated by a right-wing political party and what followed is a whole story in itself.

After 1994, the social ecologists decided to return to a program of political education, conferences, seminars, and workshops, having concluded that the groundwork for a successful electoral victory was unattainable in the foreseeable future. With the Milton-Parc community as a base, we founded the Urban Ecology Center of Montreal (UECM) in 1996. For the following ten years, we promoted social ecology in a variety of ways through on-the-ground education and projects. Slowly and patiently, we not only influenced the best of the environmentalists to consider a more radical ecological approach, but also with the basic idea that our society, and the social relations therein, had to be changed. A plethora of community organizations across the city began echoing ecological concerns in their thinking and actions. The slogan of the UECM was "Toward an ecological and democratic city," and included everything that that entailed. We also published *Place publique*, a biweekly, bilingual newspaper distributed in the central areas of Montreal with a circulation that eventually climbed to 30,000. At the UECM, Murray Bookchin's influence was felt throughout, and the several lectures that I arranged at the School of Community and Public Affairs of Concordia University, based on his books, *Urbanization Without Cities* and *The Limits of the City* were a resounding success.[9] The many participants were hungry for more and the various pamphlets and reprints helped, as well as numerous follow-up workshops that we organized at the UECM.

Bringing Citizens Together

In the early 2000s, the World Social Forum was born. Inspired by its process and practice, the UECM, with other community organizations and various university faculties, held a series of five citizen summits. The first was held in 2001, with some 240 participants, and the fifth, in 2009, had over one thousand Montreal citizens and activists coming together. Along the way, Montreal's City Council, led by the new mayor Gerald Tremblay, held their own citizens' summit. This included us and brought together several thousand people who discussed several major themes: democracy, the urban environment, housing, economic development, and urban planning. What resulted from this experience—which was clearly influenced by us—was a municipal taskforce, *le Chantier sur la démocratie* (2002–2014), headed by myself, which established a major independent municipal agency for public consultation (*l'Office de consultation publique de Montréal*); the adoption of a Montreal Charter of Rights and Responsibilities, the first of its kind in the world, and a UNESCO-recognized document. This charter protects all citizens, including the homeless and non-status people, and recognizes the right of citizen initiatives whereby Montrealers can initiate major public consultations on public policies, thereby shifting a consultative democratic system to a more participative one. It also established an ombudsman's office that arbitrates conflicts between citizens, politicians, and bureaucrats.

Montreal also became the most decentralized city in North America, fulfilling a goal cherished by the urban left for decades. Borough councils were established in all 19 Montreal boroughs, each consisting of a borough mayor and city and borough councillors. Elected every four years, each borough council has its own budget based on the borough's population. Every month, meetings of both City Council and borough councils are subject to a question period open to all citizens. All of these reforms, once considered by the media and the Establishment as fanciful dreams, are now continually nurturing the political culture of the city. It is now not uncommon to have Montrealers identify themselves as citizens of the city, first and foremost.

Assembly Democracy

Other sections of Quebec and Montreal society have also been deeply affected by our activities. Students, both at secondary and university levels, have an ongoing radical democratic sensibility. In 2012, students had a massive general strike organized on March 22nd (recalling the student-led *Mouvement du 22 mars* in Nanterre, France, 1968), advancing many of the same ideas. The demonstration grew to 200,000 students in Montreal alone. Neighbourhood solidarity committees quickly came into being, banging kettles and pans when demonstrations were taking place in the streets (*les "Casseroles"*). In 2018, and again in 2019, more student strikes were held, ranging from 40,000 to 50,000 participants (with one lasting for five-days). What is significant to note is that these student strikes were all organized through decentralized general assemblies throughout Quebec, making decisions collectively through a leaderless, directly-democratic, federal structure. The issues that preoccupy students have ranged from issues of social injustice, that affect them directly, to broader ecological issues. 2018 and 2019 saw more than 60,000 young people march through the streets of Montreal, demanding "system change not climate change."

Finally, at the level of community politics, the social housing movement has moved toward the perspective of a solidarity economy based on land trusts, raising the issue of the municipalization of urban land. This was reflected in the "Montreal Declaration" of a major international conference of 400 community activists organized in April 2019 by a collective we created, From the Ground Up // À nous les quartiers.

In Montreal, social ecology has made its mark and continues to do so. When Murray Bookchin died in 2006, *Le Devoir*, the leading French-language daily, published a major article dedicated to him. And each time a new book is published on social ecology, *Le Devoir* devotes major review space.

In Europe, it is not surprising that social ecology continues to have major success in Europe as the Transnational Institute of Social Ecology (TRISE) comes into its own, having been established in Greece and Finland in 2003, with much personal effort by myself and other devoted social ecologists. Time and circumstances will determine where this process will lead next. But, in the meantime, a new generation joining an older generation is pushing forward with much determination. Clearly the genius of Murray Bookchin is still present.

NOTES

1. Janet Biehl, *Ecology or Catastrophe—The Life of Murray Bookchin* (Oxford: Oxford University Press, 2015).

2. Josh Hawley and Dimitrios Roussopoulos, *Villages in Cities—Community Land Ownership, Cooperative Housing, and the Milton-Park Story* (Montreal: Black Rose Books, 2018).

3. Marcel Pepin, *Quebec Labour: The Confederation of National Trade Unions: Yesterday and Today* (Montreal: Black Rose Books, 1972).

4. Judith Dellhein and Jason Prince (eds), *Free Public Transport—And Why We Don't Pay to Ride Elevators* (Montreal: Black Rose Books, 2018).

5. Timothy Lloyd Thomas, *A City With a Difference—The Rise and Fall of the Montreal Citizen's Movement* (Montreal: Véhicule Press, 1997): 57.

6. Stephen Schecter, *Politics of Urban Liberation* (Montreal: Black Rose Books, 1978).

7. "District 25," (Demos Media, Montreal. National Film Board of Canada, Montreal, 1992). Available at: https://www.mcintyre.ca/titles/NFB521379. Accessed: September 5, 2019.

8. Karen Herland, *People, Potholes and City Politics* (Montreal: Black Rose Books, 1992): 209.

9. Murray Bookchin, *Urbanization Without Cities: The Rise and Decline of Citizenship*, (Montreal: Black Rose Books, 1992); Bookchin, *Limits of the City* (Montreal: Black Rose Books, 1986).

From Athens to Cork: Collective Design as a Social Ecological Praxis of Community Building

Eve Olney

Mapping the Emergence of Non Disciplinary Practice

This paper outlines how a radical pedagogy[1] of collective design is being developed through a direct democratic common assembly method. This consideration of collective design is driven by a non-expert ethos that enables self-organised, creative initiatives around social living, that work outside of conventional schemes of disciplinary learning and practice. This particular scheme emerged from an idiosyncratic interweaving of different projects and practice research I was involved in from 2014-2017. I began developing a new collaboration of anti-neoliberal praxis, named Art Architecture Activism, in tandem to working with an Athenian-based urban activist group called Urban React in 2017. The collective design scheme is currently being applied within Urban React's project in the suburb of Kaisariani, Athens, and a project in Ireland called The Living Commons; two very different projects with two very different socio-cultural contexts.

Collective design is critically framed here as both an emergent and continuous material and philosophical process of community building. The underlining organizational principles are drawn from the project of direct democracy as epitomized by Cornelius Castoriadis' project of autonomy[2] and Murray Bookchin's conception of communalism through libertarian municipalism.[3] This paper foregrounds how, Bookchin's work, in particular, critically validates how the project is being developed and its longer-term political ambitions of creating concrete social change in Ireland. A key influence in the formation and development of this process of collective design is Bookchin's hypothesis on the social ecological reordering of society through libertarian municipalism. The intention is to build upon the philosophical, ethical and material infrastructures of communities through a common assembly process of collective design. These self-governed, commoning communities can then, in the future perhaps, with the support of the broader populace, be regarded as burgeoning municipalities and feasible social alternatives to the current market-driven state policies around housing that is causing a deeper social crisis in Ireland by the day.

The story of this project initially began in Athens in 2017, and the context of this narrative thread—from Athens to Ireland—is central to how each critical reflection and different stages of advancement gradually shape the collective design scheme into a structured socio-political project. I first came across the philosophical and political writings of Bookchin and Castoriadis when commencing research relating to the housing project in Athens. In particular, Bookchin's critical framing of communalism, and "its concrete political dimension, libertarian municipalism,"[4] seemed to address and bridge the problematic blind spots of patriarchal revolutionary socialism as well as anarchism's lack of projecting a feasible alternative social imaginary.

My own subject position within this description is relevant in terms of how I amalgamate my accumulated experience as a researcher, precariat, mother, activist and social practitioner to further inform the project. I locate the key point of critically pursuing this endeavour when I left academia in 2017 due to increasing exploitative working conditions within the neoliberal gig economy. As teaching and learning are now economically calculated and seamlessly established within neoliberal Neo-Tech logic[5] it became increasingly difficult to pursue the kind of practice research I am interested in. I have always worked in between disciplines and practices; mainly across cultural studies, social theory, architecture, and art. I also apply an ethnographic approach to my work because engaging with a subject through other people's experience often challenges the ethnographer to seek alternative faculties of knowing such as embodied, tacit, and sensorial; categories that are often unacknowledged within disciplinary praxis. Validating them as knowledge systems involves not just applying value systems that are human based but also challenges the reasoning behind existing systems of value that are institutionally and economically driven and applied to the general populace in terms of how people are currently valued as citizens.

Bookchin's concept of communalism carries an understanding of equality amongst people in terms of their capacity to be active citizens within the shaping and running of their own communities, through a direct democratic form of organization. Within this paradigm of governance, individuals are valued on their own human experience and how this helps them address their common needs. He argues that, within a libertarian municipalist economy, for example:

> We would expect that the special interests that divide people today into workers, professionals, managers, and the like would be melded into a general interest in which people see themselves as citizens guided strictly by the needs of their community and region rather than by personal proclivities and vocational concerns. Here, citizenship would come into its own, and rational as well as ecological interpretations of the public good would supplant class and hierarchical interests.[6]

Within this pursuit of a public good also consists a challenge to existing propagation of human subjectivity. Bookchin's description of subjectivity moves beyond popular Marxist concepts of citizens as proletariats or workers in terms of social actors needing to assume the control of production and, in turn, the economy. It also addresses the problematic lack of social duty often embedded within anarchism. Bookchin's vision of libertarian municipalism, that is channelled through an ongoing collective assembly process, lays the foundations of "a moral economy for moral communities," where notions of "class, gender, ethnic[ity], and status" are overridden by a shared "social interest." [7]

I am compelled by Bookchin's argument, as the shaping of subjectivity through an ideological, social, material process is a preoccupation within my practice research. Dispelling the normalized competitive classification of people within the workforce is entirely conflictual with the current neoliberal subjectivity of competitive entrepreneurship where each citizen allegedly has the freedom to create her or his own wealth and well being at an, arguably, unethical competitive cost to others. The concept of Art Architecture Activism, as a scheme of collaborative practice and action, emerged from a strain of research I was conducting in Ireland, regarding the artist's and the architect's complicity within oppressive neoliberalist practices and ideologies. The research involved an ethnographic critical approach that considered architecture's role—as a discipline, practice, and culture—in, what architectural theorist Douglas Spencer refers to as "the spatial complement of contemporary processes of neoliberalization." [8] Architecture's role in the oppressive shaping of subjectivity became a primary concern within my work. What Bookchin's hypothesis offers, however, is a more holistic perspective of how citizens can potentially redefine themselves in relation to the kinds of "creative and useful work" that will need doing in order to "meet the interests of the community as a whole," should they choose to engage with municipal libertarianism. [9] Architectural work will of course be absorbed into this process, as communalism, "seeks to integrate the means of production into the existential life of the municipality such that every productive enterprise falls under the purview of the local assembly." [10] This then progresses the challenge to the neoliberal subject beyond professional practice alone, and situates roles such as "architect" as merely one of many parts of a holistic social process.

In 2017, Art Architecture Activism was developed in response to addressing how the role of the artist/architect might cultivate alternative, non-hierarchical methods of collaborative practice. It can be understood as a collective curatorial model that employs art, architecture, practice-research and exhibition as an interface for activism, a critique of state institutions, as well as targeting arts funding [11] to initiate long-term social projects challenging precarious social living

conditions. This includes moving beyond temporary community-based participatory art engagements and pursuing community building through commoning
projects that result in long-term, concrete social change. The project-exhibition
scheme is led by activists, artists, architects, and others based across Europe who
collaborate with different communities and individuals from the specific city that
the scheme is working within at any one time. It engages in the geopolitical and
social contexts of the city in a way that directly relates the local to the global. To
date, the scheme has produced an exhibition in Athens, named, *Inhabiting the
Bageion: architecture as critique*[12] in October 2017 (and featured Urban React's
Kaisariani housing project), and an exhibition in Cork in September 2019, called
Spare Room (Irish Arts Council funded). The latter was themed around the Irish
housing crisis and—in keeping with Bookchin's earlier argument regarding moving
beyond generic differences—presented this status of crisis as a commonality across
structures of culture, class, ethnicity and personal politics.

Urban React's Kaisariani Project as a Case Study for Collective Design

Since early 2017, I have been engaged in an ethnographic collaborative practice
with Urban React. Urban React is a collective of activists who share a common
interest in alternative modes of teaching and practicing architecture as an inclusive
collective social practice. We adopt architectural, economic, and socio-political
tools to bring people closer to an autonomous and equitable society in the context
of common space. Urban React is currently working with the inhabitants of an old
refugee housing block in the Athenian district of Kaisariani to renovate their
building.[13] Urban React's goals are to collectively fix the structure of the building,
renovate the inhabited apartments, reclaim the central courtyard for the
inhabitants' use and, most importantly, renovate unoccupied apartments for
homeless refugee and Greek families. Urban React is introducing a co-ownership
scheme to protect the housing block from future gentrification and co-option.
Additionally, the inhabitants will have a ground floor apartment for holding
collective assembly meetings to manage the day-to-day running of their living
environment. This is initiated through an emergent process of collective design
and is independently funded.

Early on in the project it was agreed that we should not approach the
inhabitants with any kind of political agenda but instead focus on the common
problems within the area and explore ways of inclusively working together. There
existed the idea of "making politics" as opposed to following any particular political
ideology. As people became involved in the collective design process, of improving
their own and other's welfare, a different type of political agency could possibly

emerge and be identified within the workings of the group. There is also the understanding that just because there will be space available to hold assembly meetings the people themselves—or maybe few of them—might not avail of the space for this purpose. This is something that cannot be coerced but must emerge within the process of collective design. As Bookchin argues, "a communalist society cannot be legislated into existence"[14] and must happen through a gradual social transformation. "What counts is that the doors of the assemblies remain open for all who wish to attend and participate, for therein lies the true democratic nature of neighbourhood assemblies."[15]

It is through this project that the concept of collective design began to take shape. The initial idea was to develop it outside the limitations of disciplinary architectural practice, but engage with architectural students and individual architects that shared our ethical and ecological concerns. It was understood that collective design needs to be an ongoing, long-term, social project that is never considered to be complete. As previously inferred, its underlining principles were initially drawn from a social condition of direct democracy, characterized by Castoriadis; as a mode of social organization that is self-instituting and self-limiting. The limitations and shaping of the institutional structures would be determined by immediate needs and actions throughout the process. However, Bookchin's holistic, social ecological framework of social development as a means of, "reorder[ing] social relations so that humanity can live in a protective balance with the natural world,"[16] has facilitated more long-term thinking and planning regarding sustaining the communities that may arise out of this process. This is currently more discernible in the Irish project.

Although we understand collective design to be an emergent, inclusive, collaborative, experimental, social-cultural process it yet needs a definable scheme, both philosophically and practically, without necessarily fixing it in a disciplinary manner. The intention is that those who engage with the project will gain experiences and skills where they might be able to identify, in themselves, a more significant social role in the community, through a collective assembly process. Although each collective design project will be different—hence the need for flexibility—"our basic principles in such cases must always be our guide."[17] As it is an alternative to conventional architectural practice, its underlining principles must be clear and not become confused with neoliberal practices that claim to be community-centred. Urban sociologist Karol Kurnicki outlines issues with conventional "architectural solutions" as being "always provisional and elaborated with unequal share from various social actors and institutions." He argues that as the architectural process normally "excludes everyone except experts," there is a natural "elimination of criteria not directly related to architectural discourse and practice."[18] This excludes and alienates those who do not share the language and specific experience of those leading the project. Architectural theorist, Daisy Froud, highlights a different kind of problem within current community-based projects. She argues that the input from local residents is often overridden by stakeholders who hold professional profiles of expertise. She points out that despite Britain claiming a long social history of "community architecture" implemented within government policy:

> The overall emphasis [in the] most recent government publication on the built environment, 2014's Farrell Review...seems to be that the purpose of "education and outreach" is to create better informed citizens, who can demand "good design," as opposed to articulate politicised citizens who might question the social, cultural and economic foundations from which design emerges.[19]

Her example demonstrates a cyclical transference of opinion regarding what is good design and what is right for a community that inevitably leads to generic repetitions of what already exists. This contrasts sharply with Urban React's intended strategy of gaining informed input from communities expressing their specific needs, desires and experiential contexts of their living environment. Our interest in developing a new concept of collective design is in enabling community members recognise their own political agency through determining what kind of community and environment they want to be part of. We recognise this as a mutual learning process that every participant, regardless of their life experience, could undergo.

An expert-led approach is entirely incompatible with this and we therefore understand collective design as new kind of radical pedagogy[20] that is based upon the premise of equality. It is about the inhabitants of the housing block, as well as the members of Urban React, critically exploring how to be a community and the individual's role within that process. Scholar of social learning and identity development, Joe Curnow, argues the need for radical theor[ies] of learning:

> In order to truly theorize an approach to enabling radical praxis, we have to start with an understanding of how people learn... [We need to centre] pedagogical approaches in a theory of learning that explains how people become able to participate well in the work of building radical alternatives.

Within the concept of collective design, each particular place is an educational space; a site of learning. Therefore, as the core group driving this project, we need to consider what kind of social engagements might lead individuals to re-evaluate their own subject positions for the common good of their community. Curnow argues that "more often than not, people become politicized through engagement in communities where particular political analysis and actions are valued and performed collectively."[21] Bookchin, also projects that, "no one who participates in a struggle for social restructuring emerges from that struggle with the prejudices, habits, and sensibilities with which he or she entered it."[22] It is therefore vital that these collective design projects extend themselves, socially, beyond the actual sites that are being reconfigured, in order to avoid community groups becoming insular or parochial. In 2016, the Kaisariani Summer School was organised between Bern School of Architecture and members of Urban React. Architectural students spent a few weeks making studies of the housing block and talking to the inhabitants by way of engaging them in imagining future designs for the courtyard as a commoning space. This opens up the student's experience to a new field of social practice. The main intention of the exercise lies in attempting to shift people's perspective as they witness the gradual improvement of their living environment. Therefore a "subjective and material transformation" occurs simultaneously, through the collective design process. Educational theorist, Etienne Wenger discusses how the social and material work together:

> Engagement in social contexts involves a dual process of meaning making. On the one hand, we engage directly in activities, conversations, reflections, and other forms of personal *participation* in social life. On the other hand, we produce physical and conceptual artifacts—words, tools, concepts, methods...and other forms of *reification*—that reflect our shared experience and around which we organize our participation.[23]

Geographer Melissa García-Lamarca argues that a vital component of the process is that the inhabitants arrive at a point where they begin to "[generate] their own learned political practices" and control and direct "the way knowledge is created and transmitted for [their own] community development."[24] It must be the people themselves that lead decision-making and implement the changes on their own terms. Bookchin points to the transformative effects that "deal[ing] with community affairs on a fact-to-face basis," can have on those participating in "popular assemblies." Citizens become familiar with "making policy decisions in a direct democracy and giving reality to the ideal of a humanistic, rational society"[25] on their own terms.

Critical Reflections on the Development of Collective Design

Working within a people-led framework of collective design has proven difficult in the Kaisariani project due to social issues that are historically and culturally ingrained within this fractured community. Building up an inclusive set of relations with the inhabitants is a challenging and slow process. In 2017 Urban React used a converted van parked in the courtyard of the housing block, as an information centre to encourage participation in the project. This created visibility for the project and opportunities to build up trust and knowledge of each other. Although laborious and time-consuming this proved to be beneficial and a significant number of people signed up for the project. However, this kind of continuous engagement is not sustainable due to the personal situations of Urban React and, since then, contact remains quite sporadic. Some inhabitants have been interviewed on video for an ethnographic arts project as part of Art Architecture Activism. Recent contact with the residents has included filming an on-site video clip for an upcoming Fund It scheme.

Urban React also held communal eating events and social get-togethers in the courtyard to inspire a different perception of it as a social space. The Kaisariani Summer School architectural posters were used at commoning events to demonstrate future possibilities of the space. García-Lamarca discusses the creation of political subjects through collective knowledge and action. For example, during the communal eating event, people who had never met could identify themselves as being part of a group of neighbours. García-Lamarca stresses the importance of this concrete realization "that you are not alone," seeking solutions to everyday, practical issues through collective design can enable a process of re-evaluation that directly challenges everyday attitudes of disinterest, apathy, disillusionment, and, "people [can] become re-energized and injected with hope, and move through a process of re-belonging."[26] Bookchin further argues that, within this ongoing shift of perspective, "Hopefully, such prejudices, like parochialism, will increasingly be replaced by a generous sense of cooperation and a caring sense of interdependence."[27] Arguably, this aligns with Wenger's view that a "community of practice" can be considered "as a social learning system." According to Wenger a community of practice occurs when a group of people collectively accumulate knowledge and practices and "become informally bound by the value they find in learning together."[28] Curnow applies Wenger's theory to social movements and the kind of "tacit learning [that occurs] rather than explicit training on the ground."[29] Within collective design, "the community itself is the curriculum [as] members are learning, reproducing, and innovating through their work together."[30]

However, people-led collective design is always shaped through the specific social context and it takes time and consistency to build up trust and a shared sense of community. Following a number of instances where some inhabitants displayed racist attitudes towards others at social gatherings, it was understood that there needs to be a more informed and structured approach towards dealing with conflict. For example, as opposed to responding to conflictual situations as they occur, it was agreed that there should be an inbuilt systemic way of dealing with contestation within the collective design process. However, due to the ongoing difficulties and delays experienced by Urban React, collective design as a concept has largely remained analytical up until now. When discussing the pursuit of libertarian municipality, Bookchin points out that it "must be conceived as a process, a patient practice that will have only limited success at [times], and even then only in select areas that can at best provide examples of the possibilities it could hold if and when adopted on large a scale."[31] Urban React is committed to continuing this project despite the obstacles. Recent meetings with the inhabitants have needed to be either one on one or more loosely generated but there are plans to begin to formulate more structured gatherings according to the principles of collective design, before any construction begins.

The Living Commons—An Irish Context

It was during this experience with Urban React that I also began collaborating with individuals in Ireland who were interested in the idea of community building through a people-led collective design process. In response to the ongoing precarity in Ireland that we and others (in worse situations) are living within, we began developing the idea of creating a holistic, social ecological, commoning living, and working environment in Ireland—called the Living Commons—as an alternative living model to what is being churned out by the Irish government in response to the housing crisis.[32] The Living Commons is implemented through collectively-led, social ecological cultural programmes that enable those in precarious living situations equal participation in social, cultural, economic, and political life through the initiation of autonomously-run collective design programmes. Similar to the Urban React model, the Living Commons is researched and developed through cultural co-operative programmes channelled through a common assembly mode of governance. The objective of building a direct democratic living and working environment draws significantly from Bookchin's emphasis on the question of power within the idea of libertarian municipalism. He talks about "the tangible power embodied in organized forms of freedom that are rationally conceived and democratically constituted."[33] When partaking in public discussions around current sets of conditions in Ireland, I have noticed a tendency to categorise the social into different kinds of crisis. People talk about the banking crisis, and the housing crisis, or the crisis in healthcare as an attempt at coordinating a counter argument amidst a collective sense of powerlessness. People situate individual problems within a global scale of crisis that they believe they have no control over.

As in the rest of Europe, a crisis in governance has drastically reduced the standard of living in Ireland, in the last decade, while the price of properties and rental accommodation continues to soar. The number of homeless families has increased by 348% since 2014. There are currently over 10,400 homeless adults and almost 4,000 children in emergency accommodation (in a population of 4.88 million). Yet, the idea of cohousing, much less commoning living, is quite an alien concept in Ireland. This can be attributed to the absence of legal structures that can accommodate this scheme of living in tandem with the Irish Central Bank's prevention of community banks and cohousing Trusts to operate in Ireland. Home ownership is historically ingrained into Irish culture and until recently renting was only seen as a stepping stone to owning your own home. Despite the same two parties (Fine Gael and Fine Fail) historically leading the populace into further crisis people yet look to the State for solutions. Bookchin argues that this can also be regarded as an opportunity for activists who are attempting to implement radical difference. He believes that people in crisis, "can be mobilized to support our anarchist communist ideals because they feel their power to control their own lives is diminishing in the face of centralized state and corporate power."[34] García-Lamarca further contends that, "Collective advising assemblies are spaces where people...begin to disidentify with their position in the dominant economic and political configuration and begin to shed their guilt, shame and fear... and materialize new ways of acting and being." [35]

There is currently a promising attempt to bring cohousing into Ireland, led by SOA[36] (Self Organised Architecture). The emerging models within this, work within a capitalist system and are dependent upon initial economic investment to set up a cohousing system. Alternatively, the Living Commons has a specific focus on those who are currently living precariously, including homeless, people in emergency accommodation, direct provision[37] and/or in an insecure rental situation. The objective is to begin with a systemic structure that can coordinate social projects as self-governed political projects. Non-expert does not assume that participants have equal knowledge as people have variable social advantages and disadvantages. A people-led process does assume an equal capacity to contribute and learn and become an active, self-empowered member of a community. A number of social enterprises will be initiated by engaging with existing projects, in perma-farming, people's kitchen and bakery, near zero energy initiatives, food and craft markets. We are working towards a self-sustainable living model within three to five years.

Reflecting upon the logistics of the Urban React project, we concluded that the Living Commons requires full-time active members that can steer the project through the process of collective design towards a more holistic political project of direct democracy. A marked difference to the Kaisariani project is that we are initiating a commoning community as part of the collective design process, whereas at Urban React, are working with an existing (and segregated) group of inhabitants. Unlike Greece, we have the advantage in Ireland of an arts council funding stream that grants sufficient autonomy to the projects and artists it funds. We secured arts funding in 2018–2019 through the Art Architecture Activism scheme with a proposal of producing long-term projects that addressed the Irish housing crisis. The projects—that included the Living Commons—were given a public platform through an exhibition, titled, Spare Room,[38] in Cork city, September 2019. Spare Room became a vehicle from which to begin mapping and engaging with existing social projects in Ireland, and beyond, that (whether subconsciously or deliberately) work on principles of commoning and/or self-organization in Ireland. Over the two weeks of the exhibition we held twenty-three workshops and discussions of commoning practices around eating, making, seed banking, self-building, printing, reinstituting, mapping networks of existing commons and digital commoning. Additionally, we began an ongoing collaboration with art and sustainability practitioner, Spyros Tsiknas[39] and are integrating his practice research on "role play for non violent action" within our concept of collective design. Spare Room also functioned as an inclusive social space and we connected with numerous schemes and organizations who are interested in becoming involved in the Living Commons. Finally, through this initiative we have also secured an autonomous space with some land to begin the entire process.

Conclusion: The Next Steps

The next steps include creating a visible online mapping of projects and individuals that are already involved in self-organization in Ireland and begin interconnecting these groups through collective design programmes in the Spare Room space. As each programme develops—whether it is the people's kitchen, perma-farming, non-violent action, self-building, or others—they are interlinked with other programmes both within Spare Room and other locales. For example, the farming is interlinked with the people's kitchen and approaches to dealing with mental health which is itself interlinked with other programmes and so on. The objective is to build up a broad networked social framework where people are democratically responding to their own and others" needs. The existing programmes have been set up by those who have specific needs and have acted upon those needs; "a communal society orientated toward meeting human needs, responding to ecological imperatives, and developing a new ethics based on sharing and cooperation."[40] In Ireland the biggest challenge to creating an alternative social imaginary is the neoliberal normalization of crisis and poverty and the dominant national narrative that we are all complicit within our own crisis. There is widespread apathy, as well as the aforementioned reliance on party politics to resolve people's problems. This aligns with Bookchin's argument that, "the State justifies its existence in great part not only on the indifference of its constituents to public affairs but also—and significantly—on the alleged inability of its constituents to manage public affairs."[41] Working through a radically different system of human-led values and needs can create an inclusive educational space of political and social praxis.

As aforementioned, an acknowledgement of different modes of "knowing" can contribute to shifting normalized assumptions about seemingly concrete sets of socio-political conditions. For example, there is currently no value given to the kind of knowledge that comes from the experience of surviving poverty. Cultures of resistance must begin with a shared value system that is informed by people's needs and not economics. As Irit Rogoff argues, this entails placing value on:

> Knowledge that would [...] be presented in relation to an urgent issue, and not an issue as defined by knowledge conventions, but by the pressures and struggles of contemporaneity ...in the sense that ambition knows and curiosity knows and poverty knows.[42]

It is by working across different "faculties of knowing" that collective design functions as an emergent 'social theory of learning." It opens up a critical space where people can situate their own subject position in terms of how to be part of a sustainable and equal community. Within the praxis of learning through collective design the philosophical is always integrated within the doing/practice. This rejects the notion of a separation between intellectual knowing and embodied knowing. Such a social nexus of community learning and doing can build a culture of resistance counter to the current oppressive dominant order. As Bookchin argues,

> The citizens must be capable intellectually as well as physically of performing all the necessary functions in their community that today are undertaken by the State... ...Once citizens are capable of self-management, however, the State can be liquidated both institutionally and subjectively, replaced by free and educated citizens in popular assemblies.[43]

NOTES

1. The term "radical" is in reference to creating alternative teaching and learning methods that can rupture the current conventional "fixed" disciplinary methods. *The Radicalization of Pedagogy: Anarchism, Geography, and the Spirit of Revolt.* (Ed.s) Simon Springer, Marcelo Lopes de Souza, and Richard J. White, Rowman & Littlefield (London: New York, 2016).

2. Cornelius Castoriadis. *The Imaginary Institution of Society.* (Cambridge: Polity Press, 2005).

3. Murray Bookchin. *The Murray Bookchin Reader*, ed. Janet Biehl. (Montreal: Black Rose Books, 1999).

4. Murray Bookchin. *The Next Revolution, Popular Assemblies and the promise of Direct Democracy*. (London: Verso, 2015), xvii.

5. In his paper, "The Neoliberal Academy of the Anthropocene and the Retaliation of the Lazy Academic," Ryan Evely Gildersleeve uses the term "Neo-Tech" to describe the "the faculty performance review system" that channels, "the reconfiguration of knowledge through neoliberalism's biopolitical technologies, to quantify [his] scholarly contributions from the previous year." *Cultural Studies ↔ Critical Methodologies*, DOI: 10.1177/1532708616669522. Downloaded from csc.sagepub.com at University College Cork on November 27, 2016

6. Murray Bookchin. *The Next Revolution, Popular Assemblies and the promise of Direct Democracy*. (London: Verso, 2015), 91.

7. Bookchin, *The Next Revolution*, 91.

8. Spencer Douglas. *The Architecture of Neoliberalism*, (New York: Bloomsbury Academic, 2016) 1–2.

9. Bookchin. *The Next Revolution*. 19.

10. Bookchin. *The Next Revolution*. 19.

11. Within an Irish context, despite the arts council being publicly funded it is perhaps the last sphere in public life that offers autonomy to those who secure funding.

12. https://www.facebook.com/inhabitingthebageion.

13. https://urbanreact.wordpress.com/ https://www.spareroomproject.ie/urban-react

14. Bookchin. *The Next Revolution*, 29.

15. Bookchin. *The Next Revolution*, 53–54.

16. Bookchin. *The Next Revolution*, 14.

17. Bookchin. *The Next Revolution*, 60–61.

18. Karol Kurnicki. "Towards a spatial critique of ideology: architecture as a test," *Journal of Architecture and Urbanism*, 38:1, (2014), 80–89, DOI: 10.3846/20297955.2014.893642, 2014. P86. (Accessed 08 September 2016).

19. D Froud. "Normal People" and the Politics of Urban Space, in Froud and Harriss (ed.s) *Radical Pedagogies: Architectural Education and the British Tradition*, RIBA Publishing, (2015), 51.

20. See endnote No. 1.

21. J Curnow, "Towards a Radical Theory of Learning: Prefiguration as Legitimate Peripheral Participation," In (eds) Springer, Lopes de Souza and J. White, *The Radicalization of Pedagogy: Anarchism, Geography and the Spirit of Revolt,* (New York: Rowman & Littlefield, 2016), 27.

22. Bookchin. *The Next Revolution*, 89–90.

23. Etienne Wenger. Communities of Practice and Social Learning Systems: The Career of a Concept, 10.1007/978-1-84996-133-2_11, (2010). https://wenger-trayner.com/wp-content/uploads/ 2012/01/09-10-27-CoPs-and-systems-v2.01.pdf (Accessed 12 September 2018).

24. M. García-Lamarca, "Creating Political Subjects: collective knowledge and action to enact housing rights in Spain," In *Community Development Journal*, Vol 52 No 3 July 2017, (Oxford: Oxford University Press, 2017), p433.

25. Bookchin. *The Next Revolution*, 17–18.

26. M. García-Lamarca, "Creating Political Subjects: collective knowledge and action to enact housing rights in Spain," In *Community Development Journal*, Vol 52. No 3 July 2017, (Oxford: Oxford University Press, 2017), 427.

27. Bookchin. *The Next Revolution*, 89–90.

28. E. Wenger, R. McDermott, W. Snyder, *A guide to managing knowledge: Cultivating Communities of Practice,* (Boston, Massachusetts: Harvard Business School Press, 2002), 4.

29. J. Curnow, "Towards a Radical Theory of Learning: Prefiguration as Legitimate Peripheral Participation," In (ed.s) Springer, Lopes de Souza and J. White, *The Radicalization of Pedagogy: Anarchism, Geography and the Spirit of Revolt,* (New York: Rowman & Littlefield, 2016), 32.

30. Wenger (1998) cited in Curnow (2016), 33.

31. Bookchin. *The Next Revolution,* 60.

32. Irish housing minister Eoghan Murphy, received public backlash this year when he announced the development of a new co-living model where dozens of people would be required to share a kitchen. He likened it to living in a "boutique hotel."

33. Murray Bookchin. "Thoughts on Libertarian Municipalism," This article was presented as the keynote speech to the conference "The Politics of Social Ecology: Libertarian Municipalism" held in Plainfield, Vermont, USA, on August 26–29, 1999. The speech has been revised for publication. This article originally appeared in Left Green Perspectives (Number 41, January 2000). http://social-ecology.org/wp/1999/08/thoughts-on-libertarian-municipalism/

34. Bookchin. *The Next Revolution,* 56.

35. M. García-Lamarca, "Creating Political Subjects: collective knowledge and action to enact housing rights in Spain," In *Community Development Journal,* Vol 52 No 3 July 2017, (Oxford: Oxford University Press, 2017), 421.

36. https://soa.ie/

37. Direct Provision is the Irish government's accommodation scheme for people seeking asylum. There is widespread condemnation and activism regarding having these for-profit centres shut down due to the inhumane conditions that people are forced to live under. See, https://www.masi.ie/

38. SPARE ROOM is both the title of the exhibition coproduced by myself and artist/publisher Kate O'shea as well as the ongoing programme that the Living Commons is being developed within.

39. https://spytsiknas.wixsite.com/sustainable-art/blog—-projects/author/Spyros-Tsiknas

40. Bookchin. *The Next Revolution,* 85.

41. Murray Bookchin. *The Murray Bookchin Reader,* ed. Janet Biehl. (Montreal: Black Rose Books, 1999), 3.

42. I. Rogoff. "Free," e-flux journal #14 March 2010, p10. https://www.e-flux.com/journal/14/61311/free/

43. Bookchin. *The Murray Bookchin Reader,* 3.

Murray Bookchin in Flanders Fields, Belgium

Roger Jacobs

I CAN'T QUITE TRACE back to when and how I was introduced to the writings of Murray Bookchin. At some point in the 1980s, I picked up a Dutch reader with four of his most important essays.[1] Perhaps I was motivated by this book to procure more of his writings: I possess older editions of *Post-Scarcity Anarchism* and *Toward an Ecological Society*.[2] Underlines and margin notes in the handwriting of my younger years indicate which themes resonated with me: ecology and revolutionary thought; self-management and new technology; his essay *Listen, Marxist!*; spontaneity and organization; and two critical appendices on Herbert Marcuse and André Gorz. I remember that I obtained, by chance, *The Ecology of Freedom* via a work colleague.[3] This book impressed me so much that, in 1989, I started a more or less intense correspondence with Murray via Janet Biehl. Thanks to his writings, I developed a lifelong political compass by which to understand and change our society.

From Catholicism to a Wavering Anarchism

Like so many youngsters of my generation, I became a leftist in the years that followed the events of May '68. As the son of a working-class family with good school results, I won a public scholarship in 1972 to attend university. Originally Catholic, I studied philosophy at the Katholieke Universiteit Leuven (KUL), one of the largest universities in Belgium. There, I ended up in one of the most conservative departments of the university. But the walls of the Institut Supérieure de Philosophie could not fully quell the uproar of the bubbling student rebellion of that time. Supervised by a young Spinoza—a specialist who later on became a well-known conservative philosopher—I was introduced to the writings of Karl Marx. Outside the university, I attended lectures of both the Trotskyist intellectual and politician, Ernest Mandel (1923-1995), one of the leaders of the Fourth International, and of the somewhat grim Maoist ideologue Ludo Martens (1946-2011), who later wrote an apologetic book on Joseph Stalin, *Another View of Stalin* (1994).[4] They both criticized each other and the diluted version of "beefsteak socialism" of the social democrats and the Eurocommunists. They persuaded us of the lasting value of historical and dialectical materialism and Marx's economic analyses, and they emphasized the revolutionary potential of the working class and the necessity of democratic centralism. Their disciplined dwarf parties would assail all progressive movements for the next three decades with their dogmas.

For a year and a half, I was engaged in the midst of these Marxist-Leninists. That was long enough to realize that my Russian and Chinese "language" was not appreciated by the Flemish public. I interrupted my studies for awhile and returned home. My family lived on a connecting road between a big coal mine and the workers' village. I became acquainted with the members of a neighbourhood committee established by activists of an organization called World Schools (*Wereldscholen*). The leader of the organization was a Catholic priest, Jef Ulburghs (1922-2010), who had a lot of experience in pastoral work with working class people, including many immigrants of Italian, Spanish, and other origins. He described himself as a follower of grassroots socialism (*basissocialisme* in Dutch) and he was inspired by the political pedagogy of the Brazilian educational theorist, Paulo Freire (1921–1997), and the American community organizer, Myles Horton (1905-1990), of the Highlander Folk School. The "grassroots" in grassroots socialism has a special significance. Not everyone in the lower social levels belongs to the grassroots. The concept refers to a mosaic of locally scattered individuals and groups who react to oppression. It refers to people who are motivated by the desire to empower themselves and their communities. At the centre of this theory of grassroots socialism is not only the contradiction between capital and labour, but the contradiction between the powerful and the powerless which exists in many domains of society, and not only economically.

How was this grassroots socialism put into practice? Members of World Schools were active in neighbourhood committees, medical collectives in poor and working-class neighbourhoods, legal aid centres, all kinds of ecological action groups, education (through the People's University), and bible study groups. The workplace, and the struggle for better working conditions and, eventually, workers control, was only one domain of organizing among many others. The long term aim of such initiatives and projects was to develop an alternative to the existing institutions. In an article I co-wrote titled, "Toward a New Social Movement," (1978) we can read, "These projects should be effective in impacting the existing institutions and change them in a positive direction." (Pay attention to the vague terms in the statement.)[5] At the same time, these initiatives would benefit the participants' creativity and political "conscientization" (to use a term of Freire).

In the same text, there is talk of a certain aversion of the grassroots movement toward political parties—all parties in fact, progressive ones included. "The most important task of the grassroots movement is to start social experiments. Those who are involved must confront the oppressive situation and replace it with an alternative. When the political parties appropriate criticism [of the system], by channeling it via the existing institutions, this will result in shallow reforms." This statement boils down to a phobia for "politics." Tolerance toward progressive parties was acceptable, "but it is a bridge too far to support a local or a national government, let alone participate in such a government. This would run counter the essence of the grassroots movement and boil down to a betrayal of the people who can never 'win' or 'conquer power' because state power never equals people's power." A mutual friend, a priest and professor, referred in another article to the close relationship between direct democracy *(basisdemocratie)* and anarchism, suggesting that all top-down power is perverse because it no longer represents the people but only itself. Top-down power is, thus, ultimately anti-democratic.

Bookchin's Compass: A Light in the Darkness

In a clumsy way, grassroots socialism contained several inspirational ideas but it also ran with the hare and hunted with the hounds (both working class and new social movements, both Marxism and anarchism); it suffered from term confusion (politics, state, power, government); and it didn't set clear aims (e.g. "emancipatory influences on existing institutions"—how can you measure that?).

Bookchin's social ecology, on the contrary, presents a clear diagnosis and remedy for the problems of our time. He makes his point without ambiguities. On the one hand, he stated that the working class doesn't necessarily play a revolutionary role in a capitalistic system. As a young communist militant and union organizer, he witnessed how the organized working class could reconcile itself with capitalists in exchange for a more comfortable place under the capitalist sun. With the institutionalization of social consultation, first in the US and later in Europe, capitalists and capitalism was allowed to exist. Exit the "gravedigger of capital" as Marx described the working class.

Instead of that internal gravedigger capitalism, Bookchin claimed to have discovered the external one. The Achilles' tendon of the system is no longer the contradiction between capital and labour but that between capital and nature: capitalism does serious damage to the health of all people and nature. In his later writings, Murray elaborated that basic idea. He then states that the idea of human domination was the result of the gradual hierarchization of human differences and the more recent element of class exploitation in capitalism. Therefore, the solution of the ecological problems involves the typically anarchistic striving toward the abolition of all unequal power relations and capitalism. This entanglement of the ecological and anarchistic concerns he called "social ecology."

He didn't give up his appreciation of Marxism as the most coherent attempt to develop a socialist alternative. But he regretted the stagnation of Marxist theory since the 1960s, a stagnation which was camouflaged by the somewhat artificial addition of feminism and ecology to its basically workerist framework. He also rejected Marx's identification of politics with the State, focusing more on the concept of the "the administration of things." He appreciated anarchism because of its antistatism and the alternative of decentralized and confederated communities. But in the last stage of his life, he considered anarchism as the expression of a liberal ideology of unhindered autonomy. This was sometimes attended with antirationalism, individualism, and voluntarism, and the admiration for mediagenic actions against the State.

Bookchin thought that Marxism, anarchism, and revolutionary syndicalism shared an unjust confusion of "statecraft" and "politics." In our Flemish view of grassroots socialism, we also associate these terms with power and we considered people's power incompatible with government. Murray explained the distinction aptly in his work, *Urbanization Without Cities*.[6]

He notes that statecraft continues to engage the State and is no different from it. Statecraft utilizes state violence to control the "regulative apparatus of society" (e.g. legal and ordinance, professional legislators, armies, police forces, and bureaucracies). "Statecraft acquires a political aura when so-called 'political parties' attempt, in various power plays, to occupy the offices that make state policy and execute it," he writes, emphasizing that conventional political parties are in no way derivative of the body politic or constituted by it. They are, in fact, replications of the State when they are in power. On the other hand, politics is an organic phenomenon, an expression of community, "just as the process of flowering is an organic activity of a plant." Politics requires rational discourse, public empowerment, practical reason, and is, in essence, a participatory activity.

The Story of Belgium: Brussels, Wallonia, and Flanders

I am a Flemish Belgian. That identity has important implications for my political engagement. Because of my native language—Flemish, a variant of Dutch—I hardly come into contact with my French speaking compatriots in Brussels and Wallonia.

Belgium is a small but densely populated country (11.5 million inhabitants across 30,000 km²) in the center of Western Europe with powerful neighbours: Germany, France, England, and the Netherlands; in the past it usually functioned as a battlefield for all kinds of rivalries. Belgium has a complex political structure with a federal government but also with regional governments (Flanders, Wallonia, and Great Brussels) and community governments (based on languages: Flanders/Brussels, Wallonia/Brussels and the German East cantons), each having their own powers. Flanders is the Dutch-speaking northern part of Belgium (with 58% of the population), Wallonia is the French-speaking southern part of Belgium (32%). The small German-speaking cantons in the east (75,000) were annexed to compensate for the war damage of World War I.

The Belgian capital Brussels (10% of the country's population) occupies a special position: initially a Flemish town on the Flemish side of the language-border, it became, in the course of the last century, a French-speaking city (only a minority of 10% are Flemings). When Belgium became independent in 1830, it adopted French (the lingua franca on the continent at those times) as the official national language for government, universities, the army, etc. Only in the course of the twentieth century, pushed by a strong Flemish nationalist movement, Dutch became recognized as a second official language (later on, German became the third one). "Flemish"—a mosaic of regional dialects—was relegated to the everyday language of the lower classes. The ruling elite (including its Flemish members) spoke French. The schooled Flemish middle classes were mostly bilingual with limited possibilities of social promotion. They pioneered a right-wing resentful nationalism which fights for confederalism and sometimes separatism. The right-wing party N-VA (National Flemish Alliance) is now the largest political party in Flanders (33%), side-by-side with the neofascists of VB (Flemish Interest, 6%), who are as racist as they legally can be.

Moreover, the (language) border between Flanders and Wallonia is amplified by a socio-political fracture. Wallonia was the first industrialized region on the continent with a combative working class and a dominating Socialist Party (side by side with the communists of the Parti du Travail who even now have twelve MPs). Flanders, on the contrary, was mainly a rural area with many small-scale farmers and middle-classers who were dominated by a distinct conservative Catholic Party, later on replaced by the center-right Christian-democrats. These Christian-democrats dominated Belgian politics—in an alternated coalition with social-democrats or liberals—until recently when they were surpassed by the Flemish nationalists. Meanwhile the economic balance between Flanders and Wallonia changed: Wallonia lost its old industrial equipment and Flanders prospered—centered around the harbour of Antwerp. In that period the Christian trade union (1.7 million members)—a defender of a capitalism "with a human face"—became more important than the socialist anticapitalist trade union (1.3 million members). In any case, the Belgian working class has resisted neoliberalism pretty well and is one of the most organized workforces in the world.

Initially the Belgian territories were called the "Southern Netherlands" because, together with the "Northern Netherlands," we constituted one country ruled by the Spanish Habsburgs (the famous emperor Charles V and his son Philip II). After the religious wars in 1648, the northern protestant Dutch Republic was established but the southern Netherlands remained in the hands of the Catholic (Austrian) Habsburgs till their annexation to France by Napoleon's armies. When Napoleon was defeated in 1815, both of the Netherlands were contracted again as a buffer against revolutionary France. But a coalition of discontented Catholic clergy and French-speaking old nobility and liberals provoked a popular revolt against the

Dutch-speaking protestant king in the Hague. In 1830, a new constitutional monarchy was established: independent Belgium.

As a result of this history, many progressive Flemish movements and activist groups look to the Netherlands for information (books, magazines, and internet), contacts (most Dutch cities are within an close reach of 100–150 km or less), and political support, rather than in Brussels or in Wallonia (except for important national demonstrations or interesting lectures). Comrades in Wallonia and Brussels look for inspiration and support in the northern part of France (Paris is only 250 km away). Of course, this cultural and political dualism impedes collaboration and the development of a strong Belgian libertarian movement.

After the Fall of the Wall: The Search for a Breeding Ground for Social Ecology

Initially I was very impressed by Murray's social ecology, but I soon realized that his political theory—libertarian municipalism—was the crucial cornerstone of his worldview. It was outlined in his book, *The Rise of Urbanization and the Decline of Citizenship* (1987), later retitled *Urbanization Without Cities: The Rise and Decline of Citizenship*.[7] When we want to clean up the heaps of rubble created by global capitalism, then we need to establish a political movement which is able to develop new social institutions and a new political culture. In Murray's words: "Social ecology would be obliged to embody its ethics in a politics of libertarian municipalism, in which municipalities conjointly gain rights to self governance through networks of confederal councils, to which towns and cities would be expected to send their mandated, recallable delegates to negotiate differences. All decisions would have to be ratified by a majority of the popular assemblies of the confederated towns and cities."[8]

At first, I tried to introduce Bookchin's social ecology with emphasis on libertarian municipalism in the Dutch-speaking region of Belgium via lectures and articles in Flemish and Dutch magazines, brochures, and book contributions. The anarchist tradition in the Netherlands is long and solid. But Murray's approach, with his emphasis on collective education, developing local roots and lasting engagement with a short term strategy ("democratize the republic") and long term strategy ("radicalize democracy")—collided with the dominating ethical-individualist and subcultural variants of anarchism. In Belgium, the situation was different: the traces of a more or less influential anarchist movement disappeared during World War I and the remains contributed to the establishment of the Belgian Communist Party. The budding new anarchism of the 1960s and 1970s was marginalized by the self-confident attitude of the many Marxist-Leninist sects who monopolized the radical left scene until the fall of the Berlin Wall in 1989. Besides the absence of a historical tradition and their quantitative weakness,

Flemish anarchists were strikingly hostile to organization and indifferent to theoretical renewal (i.e. no intellectual waffling, direct action now!). Of course, Murray's proposal to participate in local elections also aroused much suspicion. Only in the city of Ghent did Flemish anarchists succeed in laying the foundations of a lasting presence.

To my surprise, there was also a positive response from some disoriented Marxists and communists who were searching for a theoretical and political renewal. This happened against the historical background of an imploding east European state socialism, a triumphant neoliberal, free market ideology, and the political shift to the Right of the social democrats, who chose socially adjusted liberalism (i.e. the "Purple" third way—a combination of the socialist "Red" and the (economically) liberal "Blue"). In Flanders—not in Wallonia—these events were combined with the shock of "Black Sunday." On November 24, 1991, the neofascists of the Flemish nationalist party, Flemish Interest (Vlaams Belang) scored extraordinarily well in the national elections with a scarcely concealed racist campaign: "Our own people first" (a slogan derived from another slogan of the French Front National). Their parliamentary seats increased from 3 to 17. For the first time since World War II, when many Flemish nationalists collaborated with the German occupier in exchange for vague promises of Flemish autonomy, the "brown pest" reared its ugly head again. In those politically turbulent times, I could regularly publish articles in the Flemish Marxist Magazine and organize lectures for the circles of the Frans Masereel Fund, a former cultural organization of the Communist Party. One of the first translations of a Bookchin article in Flanders was "The Left that Was: A Personal Reflection," published in a communist magazine.[9]

But I felt more affinity with the Flemish Green Party (Groen) that already had a small electoral breakthrough at the start of the 1980s in Flanders' biggest city, Antwerp. (Later on the party would become professionalized, comparable with its German sister party, Die Grünen, upon which Murray once set his hopes. It evolved from a lucid and principled organization to a more "realistic," pragmatic one.) In spite of this evolution, it is a mistake to put the party on par with all the other status quo political parties. It was to the party's great merit to cherish typical libertarian ideas such as direct democracy, decentralization, human scale organizations, and unity in diversity (instead of unity by hierarchy), etc. I took the view that at best a dialogue with green theory and practice would remain possible; at worst we could appeal to the conscience of the Greens, referring to the deep gap between their political principles and reality.

By choosing the parliamentary route, the Green party risked nestling itself in the sphere of statecraft, contrary to a libertarian politics. But in the traditional political and ideological climate of mainstream conservatism, I took the view that a more or less scrupulous green party could make small breaches in the dominant business-as-usual style of politics, by which bottom up initiatives gasping for breath could squeeze some extra oxygen. Examples are government measures that could delay imminent disaster, preventing our social and ecological basis corroding to such an extent that catastrophic authoritarian scenarios would become widely acceptable. We also thought about measures toward political decentralization in order to empower municipalist initiatives.

For these reasons I argued for a mutual openness between the Green party and municipalist projects. The party cannot stop cherishing libertarian ideals. Otherwise, it would slide off into the vague Centre and lose the meaning of its existence. But the municipalists cannot survive on a diet of principles and ideals alone. They are confronted with real issues which must be addressed with practical solutions. This involves a considerable dose of pragmatic readiness to compromise, in the course of which some support from the Green party would be welcome. Moreover, there is also an element of conjuncture: in periods of stagnancy, statecraft possesses an unassailable aura, resulting in the diminshing of municipalist initiatives; but in the rare periods of revolutionary upheaval, libertarian politics advances with the intention to banish statecraft to the dustbin of history once and for all. So the openness mentioned above does not exclude friction and even open conflict.

I have written these words in the past but I maintain my statements to the present day. In the last few months, I published a long three-part article on libertarian municipalism in *Oikos,* the theoretical magazine of the Flemish Green Party, Groen. I think that green politicians everywhere in Europe—not only in Belgium and the Netherlands—realise that the huge social transformations we need cannot be achieved in parliament alone, but that they need support from the power of the street and the power of counterinstitutions (municipalities, the commons) built by municipalists.

The New Millennium: Times of Disillusion and Reorientation

At the end of August, 1998, I participated with my compatriot, Rafa Grinfeld, and the Dutchman, Peter Zegers, in a well organized but poorly attended international conference on libertarian municipalism in the Portugese capital of Lisbon. The occasion was to discuss the recent publication of Janet Biehl's book, *The Politics of Social Ecology: Libertarian Municipalism.*[10] She defined libertarian municipalism as a revolutionary, yet realistic, political path for green parties to follow.

But the majority of participants—syndicalists, urban activists, community organizers, etc.—interpreted libertarian municipalism in their own way or used it piecemeal to set up social alternatives. Some interpretations were clear misunderstandings. I think of the Spanish *Confederación General del Trabajo* (CGT) members who used libertarian municipalism to broaden their field of action from the workplace to the sphere of production (public transport, health care, education, etc). But others wanted to use libertarian municipalism as an inspiring compass— which indicates the direction but not the detailed road to get somewhere—to strengthen their anticapitalist resistance and to offer a strategic perspective to their struggles. Sometimes, only first steps could be realized, depending on contextual conditions. Most of the participants did not expect to literally apply the political precepts of libertarian municipalism to the real world. A literal application of libertarian municipalism presupposes a revolutionary situation (think about Syria in 2012) which was totally absent in the decade following the fall of the Berlin Wall. Therefore, Murray considered the conference as a missed opportunity and he retired to his office to write the remaining parts of his *The Third Revolution*.[11] In those years, Janet Biehl reverted to her former social democratic identity.

For me, the 1998 conference was disillusioning and not the renaissance I was hoping for. Out of my personal experiences of discussing libertarian municipalism in Flanders and the Netherlands, I did not believe in the creation of a new organization based around members who are tried and tested in the ideas of social ecology and libertarian municipalism. Others, mainly in Scandinavia and also in the Netherlands, did. I refer in this context to the detailed *Principles & Bylaws* of the Demokratisk Alternative (Oslo, 2000) and the less-detailed *Uitgangspunten & Statuten* of the Confederaal-Basisdemocratisch Project (Amsterdam, 2001–2). The Dutch project had a short life, but the Oslo chapter of Democratic Alternative still ran for office in the local elections of 2007, with disappointing results: 200 votes in a city where half a million people have voting rights. Democratic Alternative cofounder, Sveinung Legard, had the courage to draw lessons from this electoral disaster. In 2013, he wrote:

> One lesson… is that it is not enough to mobilize around the idea of direct democracy. Most people will try to figure out whether it will lead to a better life for themselves and their fellow citizens, and not just judge it on its merits of being inclusive or participatory…. In one sense, direct democracy is an end in itself, but it is also a means to achieve social improvements. Another seminal problem was that the people in the street did not know us from before. Previously, Democratic Alternative in Oslo had mainly been active in the anti-globalization movement and was known on the leftist activist scene where we had promoted social ecology and communalism. Most of those activists were involved in other parties and found it more meaningful to campaign for them than for us. If non-activists are going to support you in an election, they have to know you and trust that you will do a solid job once elected. This trust can only come through longterm engagement in issues

which are important for "ordinary people" and the disadvantaged—and not through ideological battles on the Left....

A practical advice, therefore, is for social ecologists to forget a little bit about discussions with others on the Left, distance themselves a little bit from the activist scene, and instead seek to build a reputation among people who are not already organized.

I could not state it better than Sveinung. Ideological battles on the Left are, for the most part, a loss of energy and provoke a repulsive reaction of non-ideological activists who are in the first place motivated by the elaboration of their own local projects. Even in a region as conservative as Flanders, you can easily find ten leftist sects each with 10 or 20 members.

I rather believe in the establishment of a loose network of libertarian municipalists which can organize open study groups and conferences but which does not function as a vanguard. Such a network can support exemplary local initiatives (as in other countries: Spain, Rojava, Chiapas, etc.) and propose constructive solutions to obstacles in the development of municipalist movements.

The Second Birth of Libertarian Municipalism

In connection with the death of Bookchin in the summer of 2006, I wrote two obituaries, one on the site of the green magazine *Oikos*, the other for the Flemish Marxist Magazine. Six years later, I again took up the thread of libertarian municipalism (or communalism). Meanwhile, I worked together with mainly ex-Trotskyist activists in a loose organization, Socialism21, created in the wake of the antiglobalization movement. It called itself libertarian ecosocialist, symbolized by the colours black, red, and green. In 2015, Socialism21 published a reader entitled, *The Earth or Capitalism: Toward a Social-Ecological Society,* with many translated articles by Johny Lenaerts and one by myself about democratic confederalism in Turkish and Syrian Kurdistan. It was Johny who had given me the Dutch translation of Janet Biehl's speech, "Bookchin, Öcalan, and the Dialectics of Democracy," written for the conference *Challenging Capitalist Modernity: Alternative Concepts and the Kurdish Question*, Hamburg, February 3–5, 2012).[12] For the first time, I heard about the libertarian turn in the PKK (the Kurdistan Workers' Party; *Partiya Karkerên Kurdistanê*) and I was surprised to read about the progress of communalist institutions and practices in the Middle-East. This unexpected Kurdish Spring revived a political theory seemingly destined to become a footnote in Leftist history. Communalism turned out to be a feasible concrete utopia and not the political fantasy of an old revolutionary. Yet I want to add some critical considerations.

Democratic confederalism in Rojava is a kind of "disaster socialism," to use a term coined by Naomi Klein, whereby a long existing resistance movement grasps the opportunities created by the weakening of the central state and the indifference or noninvolvement of local and international powers. Those powers will put an end to the political experiment as soon as it becomes an obstacle for their own strategic interests. What can the international municipalist movement do with that? The democratic confederalist experiment is a light in the darkness of the Middle-East but it should not be idealized: in the existing situation of scarcity and war, the military and political wings of the Kurdish movement have authority over civil society, which is the actual heart of bottom-up democracy and socialism from below. Will civil society be strong and dynamic enough to claim back its authority in a more normalized political situation? Also, is it possible for a traditionally hierarchical vanguard movement to transform itself in the course of a decade to an exemplary libertarian socialist structure with a balanced ecological, feminist, pluralist, and grassroots socialist program?

We do not propose an equivalent of Orwell's *Homage to Catalonia* (1938) to give us a truthful picture of the Kurdish utopia (the basis for a title of a recent Flemish book about Rojava), but for the time being it deserves at least the benefit of the doubt and thus also our critical support.[13]

A second remark concerns the renewed interest for municipalism in the countries of the West. Well-known urban protest movements, such as the Occupy movement, spontaneously flourished in the wake of the financial crisis of 2009, but soon faded away. The dominant diagnosis was that they did not create a lasting alternative. Maybe communalism could fill this political gap? Murray constructed his political theory with elements drawn from radical American and European political history. His libertarian municipalism was, in the first place, aimed to be applied in the Western urban context of post-scarcity. Thanks to the Kurdish Spring, libertarian municipalism has received a much broader political resonance and ideological respectability. We can make use of these successes to raise municipalism as a possible strategic compass for a much needed social, ecological, and political transformation. But this has to be done in a cautious way.

Since the financial crash of 2008, the political and ideological wind has turned. Neoliberalism has lost some of its feathers and parliamentary democracy has lost much of its legitimacy. The political consequences have been mixed. On the one hand, many people are seeking security under the wings of authoritarian leaders: from Trump in the US, Erdoğan in Turkey, Bolsonaro in Brazil, Le Pen in France, Wilders and Baudet in the Netherlands, and De Winter and Van Grieken in Flanders. On the other side, we observe a resurrection of interest for variants of participative and direct democracy and postcapitalist alternatives ("the commons").

But these are not in the form of theoretical constructions or great metanarratives. Active citizens are mainly focussed on local and very specific projects to enhance the quality of life of their neighbourhood and environment. Critical analysis, demonstrations, and direct action are not explicitly excluded—I refer in this context to the recent, very hopeful climate demonstrations by young students everywhere in Europe (initiated in Sweden and Flanders). But these are insufficient—for one plays a waiting game (do the responsible authorities lend their ear to our demands?) and the initiative is left in the opponent's hands. For this reason, many citizens engage themselves in many "small revolutions" which enable them to think for themselves, to act, and to experiment. And this is a good thing: the humiliating feeling of dependence on private or public institutions is challenged by engaging in social and political projects based on mutual aid and conviviality. This can be the breeding ground of a new culture of political participation which demonstrates how each step of repairing and renewing the social fabric is a step in the right direction. Each initiative to empower a neighbourhood, street, or district is an end in itself, even when the next step toward greater political impact is not yet realized. No time is wasted.

Political ideas which aim for a radical and global transformation, as communalist ideas do, have a function in this process. That is also the reason why we invest much energy and time in translating Murray's essays and books. These theories can act as a general political compass and a narrative source of inspiration from which ideologically concerned activists can draw the power to carry on their engagement, with the understanding that this power does not translate itself directly into an unambiguous, concrete agenda of action. Communalism can provide inspiring ideas to guide us in the ongoing struggle between statecraft and grassroots politics. But a war cannot be waged exclusively on the precepts of a political theory alone—the dialectics of practice will also come into play (mindful of the Zapatista motto of "asking as we walk"). The most inspiring example of such a revolutionary path that is making a comeback is the many Spanish municipalist movements in control of local governments since their electoral victory in 2015. These municipalists do not want to realize a good government policy to the benefit of their citizens; on the contrary, they want to return the political power back to the citizen. In the course of which they have to compromise between the Scylla of a hostile and conservative political system and the Charybdis of citizen apathy.

Besides, one has to take into account the fact that each country and region, across the world, has its own historical background, political culture, opportunities, and obstacles which colour and shape their particular quests for grassroots political organization. Consequently, in spite of the impossibility of the full realization of our objective (such as described in Murray's political writings), undisputable steps can be taken toward a more decent and dignified society. To guide us as far as possible in this search is the best we can expect of a political theory that tries to open our minds and senses for the rich possibilities of a participatory and post-capitalist future.

The author, Roger Jacobs, would like to thank his friend Rafa Grinfeld (Antwerp)—indefatigable networker of communalism in Belgium—who corrected his imperfect English, and Johny Lenaerts (Louvain)—translator of Murry Bookchin (and many other anarchists) and networker in Flanders and the Netherlands—who supported the writing of this contribution, but "would have written it in a different way."

NOTES

1. Murray Bookchin. *Ecologie en anarchisme* (Utrecht: Anarchisties Kollektief Utrecht, 1977).

2. Murray Bookchin. *Post-Scarcity Anarchism* (London: Wildwood House, 1971); Murray Bookchin. *Toward an Ecological Society* (Montreal: Black Rose Books, 1980).

3. Murray Bookchin. *The Ecology of Freedom: The Emergence and Dissolution of Hierarchy*, (Montreal: Black Rose Books, 1991).

4. Ludo Martens. *Un autre regard sur Staline* (Another View of Stalin) (Antwerp: EPO, 1994).

5. Roger Jacobs. *Toward a New Social Movement*, 1978.

6. Murray Bookchin. *Urbanization Without Cities: The Rise and Decline of Citizenship* (Montreal: Black Rose Books, 1992).

7. Bookchin (1992).

8. Murray Bookchin, Eirik Eigland (ed.). *Social Ecology and Communalism* (Chico, CA: A.K. Press, 2007).

9. Murray Bookchin. "The Left That Was: A Personal Reflection," *Green Perspectives* 22, (November1991): http://social-ecology.org/wp/1991/04/the-left-that-was-a-personal-reflection/

10. Janet Biehl. *The Politics of Social Ecology: Libertarian Municipalism* (Montreal: Black Rose Books, 1998).

11. Murray Bookchin. *The Third Revolution*. 4 volumes. (Vol. 1, New York: Bloomsbury Continuum, 1996; Vol. 2, London: Cassell; 1998; Vol. 3, New York: Bloomsbury Academic and Professional, 2004; Vol. 4, New York: Bloomsbury Academic and Professional, 2005)

12. Janet Biehl. "Bookchin, Öcalan, and the Dialectics of Democracy," New Compass (February 16, 2012): http://new-compass.net/articles/bookchin-öcalan-and-dialectics-democracy

13. Ludo De Brabander. *Het Koerdisch Utopia* (The Kurdish Utopia) (Belgium: EPO, 2017).

The Social Ecology Education and Demonstration School (SEEDS): A Brief History

Bob Spivey

IN THE SUMMER of 1988, I attended a month-long program at the Institute for Social Ecology (ISE) held on the campus of Goddard College in Plainfield, Vermont. With activists of varying ages from all over the world, and classes in such areas as bioregional agriculture, ecofeminism, ecotechnology, community health, and social theory, it was a utopian and "socioerotic" experience that has nourished my activism since that time.

Soon after I met my life partner, Beverly Naidus, an internationally known artist and pioneer of socially-engaged art. We were invited to create a course that we called Activist Art in Community, which we co-taught at the ISE roughly every summer from 1990–2000.

I did my best to work as a social ecologist within various social movements and community organizing projects, initially in the Los Angeles area where Beverly was living until 1992, and then in Western Massachusetts. In 2003, Beverly accepted a tenured position at the University of Washington–Tacoma, and we travelled with our young son from Massachusetts to the Puget Sound in Washington state, living initially on Vashon Island.

While living on Vashon, Beverly and I, together with a small group of activists, created the Social Ecology Education and Demonstration School (SEEDS) in 2005. The ISE, with its comprehensive response to the ecological response, continues to serve as an inspiration and model for SEEDS.

The mission of SEEDS is to prepare participants to be creative change agents at both the community level, and as part of movements that are national and international in scope. Through workshops, consciousness-raising art actions, and demonstration projects, we aim to highlight the complex interrelationships of ecological processes and social institutions, and develop visions, strategies, and practical resources toward building a society where humans may live more in harmony with each other and with the natural world. The core insight of a social ecology is the recognition that the project to dominate the natural world for the benefit of a few stems from a long history of systems of domination and oppression. We must therefore work to overcome all forms of injustice and oppression, as well as foster the skillful application of ecologically sound technologies and counter-institutions.

SEEDS gained status as a 501c3 non-profit organization in 2007. Since then, we have offered workshops on ecological land use and food systems, community health, ecofeminism, anti-oppression, and alliance-building among predominantly white communities with communities of colour. SEEDS organized weekend workshop programs in 2007 and 2009.

ISE co-founder Dan Chodorkoff, along with long-time staff and faculty members Brian Tokar and Grace Gershuny traveled to Washington State to present at these workshops, which also featured presentations by local ISE alum Lloyd Strecker and Bill Aal.

SEEDS members developed a Green Map of Vashon, and SEEDS received a grant to assist in the development of Eden Reframed, a permaculture and soil-restoration demonstration project incorporating "story hives" from Vashon farmers and gardeners within a beehive-like sculpture in the center of the circular garden structure. SEEDS also developed Theater of the Oppressed presentations around issue of racist treatment of workers at a particular company on Vashon.

In the 2009 build up to the UN climate convention in Copenhagen, SEEDS helped to create educational climate justice actions in Seattle in collaboration with a number of other community groups. These actions included a presentation and workshops on climate justice, direct action against Chase Bank and Bank of America, and a theatre presentation in Westlake Plaza that encouraged participants and observers to envision a "town meeting" where citizens would themselves be empowered to make binding decisions to lessen the worst consequences of rapid climate change. Alliance building has been invigorated with an increasing SEEDS focus on climate justice.

With the lives of key members pulling them in different directions, SEEDS activities have been at a low ebb for a number of years. However, SEEDS has recently been asked to join with the Puyallup Tribe and other local organizations in a project to vision and work toward a fossil-free port in Tacoma, Washington, where Beverly and I moved in 2016.

The Role of Social Ecology in the *Gilets Jaunes* Movement in France

Theo Rouhette

If the question had merely been how best to elaborate a theory, we should have said that theories, as theories, are not of so much importance [...] The people do not fling themselves into the unknown without some positive and clearly formulated idea to serve them, so to speak, as a springboard at the starting-point. As for this starting point, they must be led up to it by life itself.
— PYOTR KROPOTKIN[1]

DEDICATING HIS LIFE as a grassroots activist, historian and social theorist, Murray Bookchin has been a central contributor to the left ecological currents from the 1960s onward. Throughout the 20 books and numerous pamphlets he published, Bookchin formulated the theory of social ecology, which stands on the thesis that domination of nature is a consequence of the domination of humans by humans. The destruction of the natural world, far from being a historical necessity, is a byproduct of social modes of organization based on hierarchies and domination within human societies. Based on such a diagnosis, he developed a revolutionary agenda aiming to provide an alternative to a self-destructive capitalism:

> [Libertarian municipalism] is an effort to work from latent or incipient democratic possibilities toward a radically new configuration of society itself — a communal society oriented toward meeting human needs, responding to ecological imperatives, and developing a new ethics based on sharing and cooperation.[2]

A few years after Bookchin's passing away in 2006, social ecology is experiencing resurgence both in theory and in practice, under a variety of forms. In this context, it is becoming increasingly important to define key terms associated with his thought, such as communalism and municipalism. Both are indeed being used interchangeably despite emerging nuances, particularly in the francophone context. This trend illustrates the growth of a spectrum of divergent political trajectories referring to the same principles of social ecology, which can result in a certain confusion when first approaching the thought of Murray Bookchin.

In this article, the term "communalism" will be used to designate the revolutionary process of abolishing the forms of domination orchestrated both by the capitalist market and the modern nation-state in order to implement a communal society organized as a confederation of free communes. Bookchin initially named this political program of social ecology "libertarian municipalism," only to shift later in his life towards emphasizing the historical term "communalism." These ideas have indirectly contributed to the formation of a radically ecological, feminist, and emancipatory society in Kurdistan, Northern Syria.[3] The Rojava Revolution of 2012 provided a refuge to many people fleeing war zones in Syria, and established democratic confederalism, a societal alternative developed by Abdullah Öcalan and directly inspired by the readings of Bookchin.

The term "municipalism" will, in turn, be used to point at the programmatic approach intending to democratize local politics through the exercise of municipal power by citizen assemblies. In Europe, municipalist movements have won several elections, particularly in Spain following the Indignados movement of 2011. Cities like Madrid, Barcelona, Zaragoza, and Cadiz have created a coalition of the *ciudades de cambio*, ("cities of change") following their victories in 2015, despite the electoral setback of this municipalist wave in 2019. On the initiative of Barcelona en Comú, the global municipalist movement gathered in June 2017 for the Fearless Cities Summit, with the goal to radicalize democracy, feminize politics, and stand up to the far right.[4]

In the French context, both communalism and municipalism have gained popular support, as the historic idea that the nation-state can defend citizens and public goods from the predation of companies and banks is being eroded by the numerous cases of complicity of political institutions with the industrial and financial system. The growing influence of these radical libertarian ideas within the Left offers new spaces for a renewed political praxis akin to that advocated by social ecologists. The relevance and role of communalism in the *gilets jaunes*, or the yellow vests movement, that started in November 2018, will be the focus of this article; it will attempt to determine how and why Bookchin's ideas found a fertile ground to materialize in France, leading to the birth of an embryonic radical municipalist movement.

First of all, a significant number of publications have recently been translated and published in french, dramatically increasing the readership of Bookchin's ideas in francophone countries of Europe. In 2017, the book *Un Autre Futur pour le Kurdistan? Municipalisme libertaire et confédéralisme démocratique* written by

Pierre Bance, was published by the editor AutreFutur. His biography, written and edited by Janet Biehl, was translated in 2018 by Elise Gaignebet, entitled *Écologie ou catastrophe, la vie de Murray Bookchin* and prefaced by Pinar Selek for the publisher L'amourier. A compilation of several texts from Murray Bookchin, entitled *Pouvoir de détruire, pouvoir de créer. Vers une écologie sociale et libertaire* was published in 2019 by the publisher L'échappée, with a preface from Daniel Blanchard. Lastly, in October 2019 a compilation of texts entitled *Murray Bookchin et l'écologie sociale libertaire* was edited by Vincent Gerber and Floréal Romero and published by La passager clandestin; while Floréal Romero wrote in the same year *Agir ici et maintenant. Penser l'écologie sociale de Murray Bookchin,* published by Les editions du Communs.

Furthermore, in February 2020, the *Institut d'Ecologie Sociale et de Communalisme* (IESC) was created as a logical prolongation of the international initiatives promoting social ecology, such as the Institute of Social Ecology (ISE) originally founded by Bookchin in 1974. The fundamental principles of the IESC include the fight against all forms of domination, a radical critique of capitalism, the confederation of assemblies in direct democracy, and economic self-organization. The IESC hopes to become a hub for francophone social ecologists by gathering documents, organizing training and research, and promoting mutual aid between collectives and other European institutes, such as the Transnational Institute of Social Ecology (TRISE).

These publications and the creation of the IESC demonstrate the theoretical interest for social ecology in the contemporary ecological and political context. This interest is both a cause and a consequence of the recognition by citizens and activists of the relevance of radical municipalism—in other words, Bookchin's ideas are still alive and thriving.

In France, and similarly to many of the countries shaken by popular uprisings 2018 onward, the context of this emergence is marked by the so-called "crisis of representative democracy." Past governments have crystallized within a growing part of the population the understanding that the republican institutions, characterized by hyper-presidentialism and a centralized bureaucracy, were profoundly anti-democratic and unable to answer the current socio-ecological emergencies. The sterile competition between neoliberalism and the far right in the 2017 presidential election, marked by the largest abstention in decades, led to a widespread anti-establishment sentiment. While this mass depoliticization by the liberal-authoritarian system serves the interests of the state apparatus and its associated ruling class, it also contributes to reinforce the popular consciousness that a counter-power able to challenge the nation-state and the neoliberal status quo is necessary.

Therefore, the orchestrated apolitism pushing citizens away from state institutions has turned into a desire for radical political change. A 2016 poll from the newspaper *Le Monde* evaluating the on-going crisis of representative democracy found that more than 40% of the population would like to see an alternative to the actual system.[5] In the poll, this alternative was presented as participative and horizontal, relatively close to council communism, with institutions organized through the principles of direct democracy and libertarian forms of socialism.

This desire to institute an alternative to the dead end of republican institutions, designated by Bookchin as statecraft, is correlated to a growing recognition of the human scale as a promising site for the establishment of emancipatory politics.[6] This renewed active public life would start both from below and from the locality. This political diagnosis, so defining of Bookchin's communalist project, is also a key characteristic of the libertarian branch the *gilets jaunes* movement, which shook up French politics since November 2018.

The *gilets jaunes* protests started from a tax revolt in November 2018 and quickly evolved into a general and popular mobilization against the government. Initiated by an opposition against a carbon tax raising the price of oil which would have hurt the popular classes of rural areas, the movement quickly enlarged its scope to include demands for fiscal justice, an increase in low-salary jobs, and the protection of public services.

The sites of struggles reflect the paramount importance for the movement of face-to-face meetings: the spontaneous occupation of roundabouts led to mass blockages and allowed people from all parties, ages, and social classes to gather and socialize. Testimonies regularly mention the psychological suffering resulting from social isolation and the happiness of expressing, sharing, and building solidarity on roundabouts through mobilization, effectively inventing new means of being a citizen in a fragmented society. The re-appropriation of space was extended in the *maison du peuple* (people's house) that served as a base to experiment conviviality and organize direct actions. Seen through the lens of social ecology, the forms of struggle deployed by the movement constitute the premises of a renewed citizenship, occurring through the spontaneous germination of solidarity, collective education, and social relationships:

> True citizenship and politics entail the on-going formulation of personality, education, a growing sense of public responsibility and commitment that render communing and an active body politic meaningful.[7]

Quickly, the movement categorically rejected all forms of representation by potential leaders, all political parties, and any form of mediation. Instead, they opted for self-organization through social media and online platforms, bypassing any intermediaries for mobilization and negotiation, unions as much as any other institutionalized actor. The central ethos of the movement became characterized by democratic self-government, organizational autonomy on roundabouts, and the decentralized coordination of local groups, while more than 80% of the French population supported the movement at its peak.

The popular uprising that started from a tax protest, in a few months, had therefore stimulated political sociality in roundabouts and rejected all forms of representation. The weekly protests, occurring every Saturday, took place from mid-November 2018 to mid-March 2020, for a total of 70 actions only halted by the forced confinement caused by the COVID-19 crisis. It is throughout this fertile and heated period of mobilization that the *gilets jaunes* movement adapted a libertarian and municipalist approach, both unconsciously and explicitly, based on using face-to-face meetings as strategic sites for collective emancipation.

Yet, in addition to the spontaneity of this anarchistic development, the early phase of the movement reveals the influence of Bookchin's ideas in one determinant location. Commercy is a municipality of 6,000 inhabitants in the Meuse department where citizen assemblies were formed and where the long series of *assemblée des assemblées* (assembly of assemblies, aka. ADA) was initiated. Before the *gilets jaunes* movement, a collective called "La qu'on vive," for "Here where we live," was created in Commercy, through which libertarian municipalism was introduced and discussed. One student indeed presented to the collective the communalist agenda and the revolutions of Chiapas and Rojava. Enthusiastic, the collective then strived to establish libertarian municipalism in Commercy until the *gilets jaunes* uprising started, stimulating the political scene of the commune. On November 17, 2018, the first day of the national uprising against the carbon tax, 500 people blocked the city centre and a flag with "*municipalisme libertaire!*" was floating on a roundabout at the entry of Commercy.[8]

The *gilets jaunes* of Commercy called for the establishment of local citizen assemblies everywhere in the country. Their slogan was nothing less than "Power to the people, by the people, and for the people," and the call proudly affirmed: "Long live direct democracy, no need for regional representatives." The *gilets jaunes* of Commercy organized the first assembly of assemblies of the movement, which gathered 350 people from 75 delegations in January 2019. The ADA received support from diverse libertarian movements, including the Zapatistas of Chiapas and the Kurds of Rojava. The final call from this ADA clearly stated the necessity to organize "democratically, autonomously and independently." Four other ADAs have been organized since then: St Nazaire (44), Montceau-les-Mines (71), Montpellier (34), and Toulouse (31).

Additionally, the citizens' assembly of Commercy has, in parallel, organized the first "Commune des Communes," or Commune of Communes, in January 2020, one year after the first ADA. This first gathering of the *communes libres et initiatives municipalistes* (free communes and municipalist initiatives) from all over the territory allowed activists involved in the emerging network to meet and exchange around key topics: their respective political stories and achievements, the differences between communalists and municipalists (in their respective approach to the municipal elections, discussed below), the relations to inhabitants and local parties, the strategies to build dual power, etc. Several delegations have participated in an event that gathered around 200 participants.

While there were reasons to doubt the overall radicalism of the movement prior to these events, they have firmly established a growing libertarian orientation within the movement; while it simultaneously maintained its core demands for social justice and the protection of public services. Not only did these events follow a form of confederal organization (as face-to-face assemblies of mandated and revocable delegations from local groups and assemblies) but the debates actively discussed libertarian municipalism as a strategy for the future of the movement. "*Fin du monde, fin du mois, même combat*" ("End of the world, end of the month, same struggle") became a slogan for the movement, explicitly linking social inequalities with ecological collapse.

In other words, while Bookchin ideas have had little influence in France until then, staying at the margins even within the alternative political culture, it has been adopted spontaneously and on its own initiative by a large and diverse population that has begun to put it into practice and to extend it into more permanent institutions. From this perspective, it clearly appears that the movement of the *gilets jaunes* has propelled libertarian municipalism as a key catalyst towards radical political changes, adequately fitting the revolutionary agenda of the most radical branch of the movement. It also demonstrates how the *gilets jaunes* situate themselves in a long historical tradition of communal autonomy and direct democracy to confront the nation-state and its repressive forces, a tradition marked by the various forms of freedoms investigated by Bookchin throughout his work, from *The Spanish Anarchists* (1977), to *The Third Revolution* (1996–1998).

Stimulated by reflections about the potentialities and challenges of a communalist agenda, the movement quickly moved from blockages and protests toward an institutionalization of popular assemblies and a confederal form of coordination. Proving wrong from the outset the idea that municipalizing politics could lead to parochial oppositions between territories, the spatial organization of the regional and confederal assemblies became a central topic of exchanges. The forms and diversity of the units forming the confederalist network were also discussed: should these organizations be solely composed of citizen assemblies, or could associations, cooperatives, and collectives also be part of these emerging political structures?

Furthermore, the *gilets jaunes* movement became a broad and diverse social force demonstrating in the process of struggle a popular convergence unseen since the uprisings of 1968. Months of struggles have however shown that the convergence *between* movements can be confronted by concrete obstacles, such as class discrimination. The relation between the "green" and the "yellow" movements exemplified this, as *gilets jaunes* supportive of environmental protests and global climate marches saw very few "greens" joining their sites of protests. In other words, strong factors of division persist and prevent the convergence of fragmented movements into one movement, such as class prejudice or the split between "revolutionaries" and "moderates." Overcoming these challenges would require elaborating a collective program with minimum and maximum goals able to unite the various fronts of protest against all forms of domination and to develop a shared vision with other movements, such as the feminist and migrant movements (e.g. black vests, *gilets noirs).*

Another key issue of concern raised in assemblies centered on the relation between local sites of power, such as city halls, and diverse sites of counter-power, including but not limited to popular assemblies and *zones à défendre* (ZAD). One spontaneous idea expressed by the vests that is an important aspect of libertarian municipalism is the clear distinction made between local elections and electoral pursuits on higher administrative levels. One key organizer from the ADA of St. Nazaire noted that the debates on the second ADA focused on two complementary strategies: taking power through municipal elections and building counter-power through parallel institutions. These reflections have been key determinants of the strategies of the movement with regards to the municipal elections, held every six years in France and that (partially) took place in March 2020.[9]

In the continuity of the *gilets jaunes* movement and the popular defiance toward representation, the year preceding the municipal elections has witnessed the emergence of hundreds of "citizen" and "participative" electoral lists for the municipal elections. While the *gilets jaunes* movement has undoubtedly stimulated the creation of such lists, they are characterized by a diversity of objectives and relationships to political parties that suggest that other factors have influenced their emergence. The name of the lists usually include similar concepts—like "common," "together," "collective," or "assembly"—and reflect a shared desire for an autonomous fabric of local politics by ordinary citizens.[10] According to the platform Action Commune, which gathered on its tool "La Boussole Démocratique" more than 400 participative lists all over France,[11] 55.4% of the lists originated from a pre-existing structure (mostly cooperatives, associations, AMAPs, and *gilets jaunes* local groups) while 68.8% were not supported by political parties. Candidates within those lists represented 1.4% of the total candidates of the elections.

The differences between the participative lists, despite a high context-dependency, allow distinguishing three broad categories. First, there are lists generally related to *gilets jaunes* assemblies explicitly carrying a communalist agenda: that is, conceiving victory in the election is only a means to achieve decentralization of power and the creation of a confederation of free communes. Commercy stands as the typical example of this category, but others have followed the electoral path from a communalist approach, such as the collective "Faire Commune" in Paris. The other category gathered the municipalist lists, more influenced by the Spanish municipalism than libertarian municipalism per say, despite explicit references to Bookchin in certain cases. These lists promote the democratization of decision-making institutions through the use of participatory tools to transform local politics. Here, Saillans constitutes a historic precursor for such lists.[12] Lastly, less easily identifiable are the numerous lists which present themselves as "*citoyenne*" and "democratic" but that are still linked to political parties, the latter quickly realizing the electoral potential of the growing popularity of participatory democracy. This "citizen washing" is an explicit strategy of the presidential majority party and to a lesser extent of the plurality of divided left parties. "L'Archipel Citoyen" in Toulouse, "Poitiers Collectif" in Poitiers, or "Decidons Paris" are good examples of such lists, supported by green parties (e.g. EELV) or left-wing parties (e.g. France Insoumise, NPA).

The coronavirus crisis has caused a historic abstention in the first round of the election, participation dropping to an unprecedented 40% in 2020. That the government maintained the election provoked a legitimate widespread polemic: organizers and voters indeed caught the virus during the first round held on the 16th of March, some even dying as a consequence. Despite the associated biases and uncertainties, results in key municipalities can testify to the relative success of the three categories described here. First of all, according to the review from Action Commune, 66 participative lists out of 405 lists have won the election for a total approximating 2,000 elected citizens. This doesn't only include small towns and villages, as proved the victories in medium-scale and strategic cities like Poitiers, Chambéry, and Rezé aptly prove.

This concretizes the democratic wave that has shaken the country, compared to the last election of 2014 back when Saillans was the only example. Many of the victorious lists have won through alliances with other political parties, creating complex mixes of citizens, ecologists, socialists, and communists. However, both in Commercy and in Saillans, the participatory lists have lost in the first round. In Commercy, the *gilets jaunes* have gathered 9.76% of the votes, way behind the dominant right-wing party. In Saillans, the opposition list won by just 18 votes, with 51.05%. Looking at lists supported by parties, the list "l'Archipel citoyen" in Toulouse lost the city with more than 48% of the votes after an intense campaign.

The 2020 election was marked by a historic victory of ecology. The ecological party, EELV, has indeed won 7 of the 40 largest cities in France: Grenoble,[13] Strasbourg, Bordeaux, Annecy, Besançon, Lyon, and Tours, as well as the powerful metropolis of Lyon. Counter-intuitively, both the participative lists and the green parties have benefited from the coronavirus and the resulting confinement: pragmatically this provided the time necessary to create alliances, and opened up the public space for the promotion of both ecology and localism through the unexpected but concrete example of a viral epidemic.

It is, however, too ambitious to draw clear political conclusions from the municipal elections given the impact of the virus crisis. What remains certain is that beyond the electoral moment, the defeated communalist lists, such as the *gilets jaunes* of Commercy, will continue to gather in popular assemblies, to build popular counter-power to the elected *conseil municipal,* and contribute to the federation of similar initiatives in the territory. Such a post-electoral approach remains more case-specific concerning the defeated municipalist lists, given the higher importance attributed to the elections themselves. On the side of electoral victory, much hope rests upon the success of the 23 participative lists that have won, such as the communalist list in Ménil-la-Horgne, situated close to Commercy, as the form and content of their democratic institutions will undoubtedly have a major influence on the degree of popular support for the emerging movement in the coming years.

Any municipal initiatives will nevertheless face the attack from the central government who has been weakening the power of mayors, already restricted by the *communauté de communes* that reduce the jurisdiction of isolated municipalities—a fact that has severely hampered the municipalists of Saillans from 2014–2020. These institutional attacks to the local scale can be interpreted as an explicit recognition by the State of its strategic importance for radical social movements, keeping in check their transformative potential. Nevertheless, the results of the first round of the election have confirmed the birth of a new political force large enough to develop its own internal differentiation—between the communalist and municipalist trends—as participants from the Commune of Communes have reported.[14]

Despite this breakthrough, minor in comparison to the Spanish municipalist wave of 2015, it is evident that most political agitation will take place outside the city halls and local institutions. Back to the strategy of establishing counter-powers to statecraft, the fragility of most of the *maisons du peuple* of the *gilets jaunes* and the repression of street protests demonstrate the brutality of the repressive state apparatus that these sites of counter-power must inevitably confront. Yet, the victory of the ZAD in Notre-Dames-des-Landes, after a long occupation against an airport project in the North West of France, proves that counter-institutions can hold their promises and become sites for communalist experimentations in the most radical sense. The formation of citizen councils acting as counter-powers to city halls could catalyze the evolution towards a dual-power situation in certain localities, a process boosted by the confederal dynamic born out of the Commune of Communes of Commercy. These developments, to be watched closely, are completed by various experimentations in smaller villages and ecovillages imple-menting alternative economics based on the commons, which could increasingly inspire new forms of collective production and exchange. Parallel to those sites, the various associations and collectives at the core of the municipalist movement have created multiple digital platforms both connecting the territorial actors together and diffusing publications and toolkits on municipalism. Several initiatives can be highlighted here, from the municipalist collective of Saillans "La Belle Démocratie," to the platform "Action Commune" and the collective "La commune est à nous."

Only a synergistic combination of those diverse strategies, with various degrees of radicality, could progressively erode governmental power and successfully implement new institutions of social and political life. The influence of Bookchin's ideas in the largest social movement of the past decades in France, which catalyzed the growth of radical municipalism, is highly visible and precious in this context. An influence that has been implicit and intuitive at times, and explicit at other times. The collective "Faire Commune," in their analysis of the Commune des Communes, explains how Bookchin's theories served as arbitrators, as participants mobilized his ideas to argue and counter-argue during the debates.[15] Like other concrete forms of freedom in the world, from Chiapas to Rojava, these social movements, citizen platforms, and emancipated societies then feed back to the realm of theory by providing precious insights from praxis.

◐   ◑   ◐

Social ecologists therefore have many reasons to be enthusiastic about the unfolding of the *gilets jaunes* as discussed in this article. In a context of increasingly frequent crisis within the global dynamics of capitalism, and rampant chauvinistic nationalism, social ecologists still have a lot to contribute in their interaction with contemporary social movements. The communalist/municipalist movement emerging in Europe should be conceived as a form of "collaborative theory building," experimenting on strategic sites through transformative and pre-figurative politics.[16] In this creative trial-and-error process, other aspects of Bookchin's thought could greatly expand the constructive radicalism of the movement.

First, when analyzing the linkages between the social and ecological crisis, Bookchin, following many radical thinkers before him, pointed out to the growth imperative of capitalism as a core condition *sine qua non* of its reproduction and expansion. In this regard, social ecologists should further propagate the idea that only a democratic critique and alternative to the grow-or-die paradigm will be able to coherently tackle the ecological crisis. In the realm of ideas, it amounts to confronting the governmental environmentalism that has badly failed in the last decades, as demonstrated by Roussopoulos;[17] and in the realm of reality, it amounts to promoting an economic confederalism—based on federations of producers and consumers working towards a cooperative and rational economy focused on the management of the commons. The economic form of communalism would go beyond collective property of the means of production to encapsulate the union of production and consumption based on bioregional features of a given territory.

Second, in opposition to the techno-skepticism of certain ecological tendencies, the role of technology is also a promising arena where contemporary social movements can further benefit from the insights of social ecology. Rather than its negation, they could strive to develop the emancipatory potentialities of technology.[18] In the continuity of revolutionary movements, like the Egyptian uprising during the Arab Spring, the *gilets jaunes* have showed how social media platforms could be turned into liberatory tools for militants' self-organization. The insights on the necessary re-appropriation of technology, designed to fit the rational needs of human-scaled communities, could be a major strategy for communalist initiatives to build territorial economic autonomy.

Third, the emerging forms of citizenship and sociability resisting the orchestrated atomization of society, as seen in the roundabouts of the *gilets jaunes*, could be catalysed by a historical investigation and (re)actualization of the Greek concept and practice of *paideia*, so central in the theoretical articulation of social ecology.[19] The methods of popular education and the re-appropriation of public spaces fulfilling the role of a contemporary *agora* would serve at least two purposes: strengthening the theoretical core of the movement, and fighting the widespread sense of powerlessness that prevent so many citizens from believing in their ability to change their societies.

This discussion of the *gilets jaunes* has presented only a glimpse of what could be the kind of mutualism between the social ecology of Bookchin and the next spontaneous and popular movements that will inevitably arise in the coming decade. While Murray Bookchin developed his theories throughout the second half of the past century, the 2020s may indeed witness social ecology becoming a major contributor to the emergence and establishment of a societal alternative to the rule of capitalism and the resulting ecological collapse. As stated by Italian anarchist Malatesta: "Everything depends on what people are capable of wanting." Assembleist movements, directed towards direct democracy and radical ecology, give to Bookchin's program a new resonance. In France, his ideas are vibrating in different sites of struggles, contributing to new forms of freedom, and leading to the infancy of a young but dynamic communalist movement. Let us hope that this radical agenda will continue to guide new generations of protesters, activists, researchers, and citizens towards a renewed ecological humanism and the liberation of human societies from all forms of domination.

NOTES

1. Pyotr Kropotkin. "The Paris Commune," *Freedom Anarchist Pamphlet Number 8*, (London: Freedom Press, 1971), 10.

2. Murray Bookchin. "Libertarian Municipalism: An Overview," *Green Perspectives* 24, (1991).

3. Michael Knapp, Anja Flach, Ercan Aybago. *Revolution in Rojava : Democratic Autonomy and Women's Liberation in Syrian Kurdistan,* (London: Pluto Press, 2016).

4. Barcelona en Comú. *Fearless Cities: A Guide to the Global Municipalist Movement*, (New Internationalist, 2019).

5. Le Monde. "Les Français, la démocratie et ses alternatives," (2016).

6. The distinction between politics and statecraft is developed at length in Chapter 6 of: Murray Bookchin. *Urbanization Without Cities: The Rise and Decline of Citizenship*, (Montreal: Black Rose Books, 1992).

7. Bookchin. *Urbanization Without Cities,* (1992).

8. François Bonnet. "À Commercy, les «gilets jaunes» expérimentent la démocratie directe de l'assemblée populaire," *Mediapart,* (2019).

9. At the time of writing (April 2020), the second round of the elections has been delayed to further notice, probably in June 2020, due to the crisis of the coronavirus. Nonetheless, the first round of the election led to the confirmed elections of 30,000 mayors out of the 35,000 communes of France.

10. Pierre Sauvetre. "Prendre les mairies ou fédérer les communes? Municipales, municipalisme et communalisme," (AOC media, 2020).

11. The lists are self-declared: members have to register themselves on the platform. Additionally, candidates and citizens can evaluate the participatory nature of the lists of their municipalities.

12. Saillans, a rural village of 1200 inhabitants, experienced a small revolution when a citizen collective opposed to a supermarket construction won the municipal election with the goal of transforming in hall into a "people's house." The inhabitants set up an "administrative board" that was open and transparent, in sharp opposition with the previous mayor, and administered tasks through a dozen "action-project groups" and participative commissions. Inhabitants that were heavily involved in the citizen collective and then city hall expressed the benefits but pitfalls of this new approach. Popular education was identified as a key factor of success in the communication of the agenda the initial collective was defending. Some inhabitants noted however that active involvement is a time consuming activity. Saillans is now a well-known example of democratization of a municipal council through elections.

13. In 2014, the election of Eric Piolle in Grenoble promised an authentic renewal of local politics through a radical green-red alliance of numerous unions and grassroots associations. Since the 1960s Grenoble has been the laboratory of diverse municipalist experiments. However, the new municipal team quickly disappointed the inhabitants, as the promises of "participative democracy" were betrayed. According to local activists the only thing that changed is a hypocritical discourse hiding the same-old practices, punctuated by the closure of public services, including 2 libraries, police repression, and a power cut for a local refugee squat. The example of Grenoble demonstrates that the demand for radical change in municipal institutions can always be instrumentalized by opportunistic electoralism; and that coming from local social movements and popular associations doesn't protect from this drift.

14. Collectif Faire Commune. "Première Commune des communes à Commercy: retour d'expériences" (esquisse collective, 2020).

15. Collectif Faire Commune. "Première Commune des communes à Commercy: retour d'expériences" (esquisse collective, 2020).

16. Bertie Russell. "Beyond the Local Trap: New Municipalism and the Rise of the Fearless cities," *Antipode*, Vol. 51. No. 3 (2019), 989–1010.

17. Dimitrios Roussopoulos. *Political Ecology: Beyond Environmentalism*, (Porsgrunn: New Compass, 2015).

18. Murray Bookchin. *Post-Scarcity Anarchism* (Oakland: AK Press, 2004).

19. Murray Bookchin. *Urbanization Without Cities: The Rise and Decline of Citizenship* (Montreal: Black Rose Books, 1992).

Murray Bookchin in Italy

Selva Varengo

THE WORKS OF Murray Bookchin, who had been interested in ecological issues since 1952, first arrived in Italy in 1974. This occurred when the anarchist monthly *A Rivista* published *Tecnologia e rivoluzione libertaria*, later republished by the magazine *Volontà*. Since the first translation in 1974, *A Rivista* has continued to publish translations of Bookchin's articles and numerous comments and reflections; now, if you enter "Bookchin" into its search engine, you will get almost three hundred results.

The introduction of Bookchin's thought in the Italian-speaking world occurred through anarchist and libertarian circles. It was a stimulating discovery. His proposal to combine ecological and social questions was profoundly innovative and perfectly responsive to a growing ecological sensibility in politically radical spheres.

In 1975, the famous Feltrinelli publishing house published *I limiti della città*, the Italian translation of *The Limits of the City* with an introduction by architect, Gianni Scudo. Afterwards, a series of translations of Bookchin's articles, totalling nearly 50, were published mainly by the Italian anarchist presses. Bookchin's thought influenced not only libertarian anarchists, but also various elements of Italian radical ecology movements.

In Italy, there are translations of about a dozen of his books, produced by several Italian publishers. In particular, *Le Edizioni Antistato* (Antistato Editions) of Milan, which later became *Elèuthera editrice* printed his most important titles, convincing us of the importance of Bookchin's reflections on contemporary anarchist thought. Beginning in the 1970s, Bookchin developed a close relationship with the Italian anarchist archive, *Centro Studi Libertari—Archivio Giuseppe Pinelli*; however, the bonds between the two were sundered in the last decade of Bookchin's life by increasing political differences. Still, this rupture has not prevented comrades of the *Centro Studi* to define him as one of the most acute and influential libertarian thinkers of the twentieth century, and to brandish Bookchin's aphorism on the top of their website: "If we do not do the impossible, we shall be faced with the unthinkable."

Alongside these early translation initiatives, it is necessary to highlight Bookchin's many visits to Italy, where he attended various meetings and conferences.

His participation in the 1984 International Anarchist Meeting in Venice is particularly noteworthy, as are his visits to many other Italian cities like Milan, Carrara, Bordighera, San Giorgio di Nogaro, Pisa, etc.

The Italian interest in Bookchin was also demonstrated by the development, over the years, of social ecology and ecofeminist groups. Especially significant was the experience in Friuli, Italy, and the website *ecologiasociale.org*, active until 2007 and reborn in 2018 as *ecologiasociale.info*.

With rare exceptions, we have not succeeded in developing a real social ecology movement in Italy. However, all this activity has stimulated theoretical analyses over many years, and continues to do so. There are, in fact, at least a dozen graduate theses on Bookchin's thought in Italy and about 50 articles and essays presenting or analyzing his thinking from a political, philosophical, urbanist, or historical point of view.

There are three monographs dedicated to him. In chronological order, the first is my text *La rivoluzione ecologica* (Milan, 2007), in which I present the political thought of Murray Bookchin through the transversal reading of his texts and thematic analysis, emphasizing the originality of Bookchin's thought, especially with his proposal to organically incorporate ecology into libertarian thought. In 2011, Ermanno Castanò, in his *Ecologia e potere* (Milan, 2011), conducted a critical reading of the texts of Bookchin, highlighting his affinities with the thought of Merleau-Ponty. The latest volume is *Anarchia verde* (Lecce, 2016), by Marco Piracci, which is dedicated to a close comparison of the social ecologist ideas of Murray Bookchin and with the anarcho-primitivist ideas of John Zerzan.

In the last few years, a renewed interest in Bookchin's thought has emerged. This interest is certainly linked to the appearance of democratic confederalism in Kurdish Rojava, and to Kurdish leader Abdullah Öcalan's interest in Bookchin's thought.

The most recent book, in chronological order, is the Italian translation of *The Next Revolution*, an anthology edited by Debbie Bookchin and Blair Taylor, published by Verso Books in 2015, and released in Italy in 2018 by the publishing house BFS. The volume sparked a lively debate, still ongoing, mostly for Bookchin's trenchant judgments of the anarchist movement in the posthumous articles published therein.

The social ecology of Bookchin, beyond its latest pro-institutional drifts, can certainly still contribute to the practices of radical political ecology as well as to anarchism. Many of its elements remain insightful when assessing the causes of the ecological crisis and numerous Italian ecological activists are aware of this school of thought. Social ecology exerts a strong, often unconscious, influence on popular movements in Italy; this is evident in ecological/anti-industrialist movements like the *No TAV* (High Speed Train), *No TAP* (Trans Adriatic Pipeline), *No MUOS* (Mobile User Objective System), *No Terzo Valico* (third pass in lower Piedmont). I write this essay in the wake of the latest climate demonstration led by millions of young people in 196 countries, all responding to the call of Greta Thurnberg; in Italy, alone, a million students marched in 182 cities and towns. In this light, Bookchin's teachings about the need for radical system change, and the need for citizen-led direct democracy, are as timely as ever. To act against climate change in a capitalist economy, or in any system based on the logic of infinite growth, is simply impossible. Certainly, it is important to reduce consumption, limit gas emissions, and change lifestyle, but these efforts are insufficient if not accompanied, as Bookchin wrote, by a great cultural and political movement capable of radically changing the system and overthrowing age-old institutions of domination. For too long, the legacy of freedom has remained all too silent in the history of mankind.

BIBLIOGRAPHY OF BOOKCHIN'S WORKS IN ITALIAN

BOOKS BY BOOKCHIN IN ITALIAN

I limiti della città, (Milano: Giangiacomo Feltrinelli Editore, 1975).

Spontaneità e organizzazione, (Carrara-Torino: Edizioni del Centro Documentazione Anarchica, 1977).

L'anarchismo nell'età dell'abbondanza, (Milano: La Salamandra, 1979).

L'ecologia della libertà. Emergenza e dissoluzione della gerarchia, Milano: Antistato, 1984; (Milano: Elèuthera, 2017).

La crisi della modernità, (Bologna: Agalev Edizioni, 1988).

Per una società ecologica, (Milano: Elèuthera, 1989).

Democrazia diretta, edited by Salvo Vaccaro, (Milano: Elèuthera, 1993).

L'idea dell'ecologia sociale. Saggi sul naturalismo dialettico, edited by Salvo Vaccaro, (Palermo: Ila Palma, 1996).

Ecologismo libertario, (Lecce: Bepress, 2012).

Tecnologia & liberazione, (Lecce: Bepress, 2017).

La prossima rivoluzione. Dalle assemblee popolari alla democrazia diretta, (Pisa: BFS, 2018).

ESSAYS, ARTICLES, AND INTERVIEWS BY BOOKCHIN

"Tecnologia e rivoluzione libertaria," in *A Rivista,* no. 31 (1974).

"Tecnologia e rivoluzione libertaria," in *Volontà,* (1974).

"Potere di distruggere, potere di creare," *Centro documentazione anarchica,* (1976).

"Oltre i limiti del marxismo," *An.Archos,* no. 2 (1979): 59–86.

"L'autogestione e la nuova tecnologia," *Interrogations,* no. 17–18 (June 1979): 212–230.

"Comment, progetto per un giornale," *A Rivista,* no. 75 (June/July 1979): 20–23.

"Il marxismo come ideologia borghese," in *A Rivista,* no. 81 (March 1980): 33–41.

"Cara ecologia. Lettera aperta al movimento ecologista," in *A Rivista,* no. 85 (August/September 1980): 36–40.

"Il futuro del movimento antinucleare," *Volontà*, no. 3 (July/September 1980): 65–73.

"Reagan, la rabbia del ceto medio," in *Volontà*, no. 1 (January/March 1981)

"Utopismo e futurismo," in *Volontà*, no. 3 (1981): 75–83.

"Io sono nato...," in *A Rivista*, no. 93 (June/July 1981): 18–19.

"Fabbrica, scuola di potere," in *A Rivista*, (1981–1982): 97.

"Sociobiologia o ecologia sociale?" in *Volontà*, no. 1 (January/March 1982): 70–86.

"Sociobiologia o ecologia sociale?" in *Volontà*, no. 3 (July/September 1982): 10–29.

"La crisi ecologica: le sue radici nella societá. Problemi e soluzioni," transcript of the speech held in Carrara, October 1984, edited by Circolo Culturale Anarchico of Carrara; in *Umanità Nova*, no. 37 (November 1984): 4–5.

"1984 e il ruolo della memoria. A proposito di George Orwell," in *A Rivista*, no. 120, (June/July 1984): 27–34.

"L'armonia perduta, speech at the International Anarchist Meeting in Venezia, 24–30 September 1984," in *A Rivista*, no. 121, (August/September 1984): 11–18.

"L'anarchismo: 1984 ed oltre," in *Volontà*, no. 3, (July/September 1984): 77–101; speech at the International Anarchist Meeting, Venezia, (September 1984): 24–30.

"Al di là del ghiaccio. L'alternativa verde," *Umanità Nova*, no. 4 (February 1984): 4.

"Introduzione" for the Italian translation of *The Ecology of Freedom* (May 1984).

"Ecologia della libertà, interview," in *Oblum*, Milano, (May/June 1985)

"Agricoltura, mercato, morale," in *A Rivista*, no. 132 (November 1985): 30–36.

"Tesi sul municipalismo libertario," in *Volontà*, no. 4 (1985): 14–30.

"L'America secondo me, interview of Rossella Di Leo," in *A Rivista*, no. 134 (February 1986): 19–24.

"La guerra civile spagnola: Cinquant'anni dopo," in *Volontà*, no. 4, (October/December 1986).

"Noi verdi, noi anarchici, transcription by Alison Leitch of a video-speech at the International Conference organized by the Greens in Pescara, (September 1986): 19–21," in *A Rivista*, no. 141 (November 1986): 9–12.

"Ecologia sociale e pacifismo," in *A Rivista*, no. 144 (March 1987): 15–18.

"Libertà e necessità nel mondo naturale," in *Volontà*, no. 2–3 (1987): 7–37.

"Non sottovalutiamo la specie umana," in *Volontà*, no. 2–3 (1987): 125–175.

"Sociale non profonda," in *A Rivista*, no. 153 (March 1988): 32–39.

"Che cos'è l'ecologia sociale," in *A Rivista*, no. 153 (March 1988).

"Ecologia sociale perché," in *A Rivista*, no. 159 (1988).

"Prefazione," in *L'ecologia della libertà*, third edition, Milano: Elèuthera, (1989)

"Per una società ecologica," in *A Rivista*, no. 166 (August/September 1989).

"Società, politica, stato," in *Volontà*, no. 4 (December 1989): 39–56.

"L'uomo, tiranno," interview in *Panorama*, (April 9, 1989): 170–171.

"No all'eco-business," interview of Salvo Vaccaro, *L'ora*, Palermo, (January 30, 1990): 7.

"La politica radicale nell'età del capitalismo avanzato," *Quaderni della società civile*, Palermo, (February 1991).

"La proposta federativa," in *Volontà*, no. 2–3 (February/March 1991): 129–135.

"Occhio al bioregionalismo," letter to *A Rivista*, no. 185 (October 1991): 40–41.

"Municipalismo libertario. La mia proposta," in *A Rivista*, no. 187 (December 1991/January 1992): 14–20.

"Una politica municipalista," in *Volontà*, no. 1 (1992): 241–251.

"Democrazia diretta, come," in *A Rivista*, no. 202 (August/September 1993): 31–36.

"L'unico e l'umano," in *Volontà*, no. 2–3 (September 1994): 59–82.

"La via del comunitarismo," in *Volontà*, no. 4, 1994, 33–54.

"Comunalismo perché," *A Rivista*, no. 215, February 1995, 25–31.

"Municipalismo libertario perché?, speech at the conference on Libertarian Municipalism, Plainfield, Vermont, 26 August 1999," *A Rivista*, no. 258.

"Tesi sull'ecologica sociale in un periodo di reazione," *Antisofia 3: Viaggio nella modernità*, Eterotopia/Mimesis (2004).

"Il capitalismo e la crisi ambientale," in *L'ecologia come giustizia e libertà. Scienza e pace nell'era della crisi globale*, Roma: Nonluoghi Libere Edizioni (2009).

BIBLIOGRAPHY ON BOOKCHIN IN ITALIAN

Castanò Ermanno. *Ecologia e potere. Un saggio su Murray Bookchin*, (Milano: Mimesis Edizioni, 2011).

Piracci Marco. *Anarchia Verde. Murray Bookchin e John Zerzan a confronto*, (Lecce: Bepress 2016).

Varengo Selva. *La rivoluzione ecologica. Il pensiero libertario di Murray Bookchin*, (Milano: Zero in Condotta, 2007).

Janet Biehl. *Dallo Stato nazione al comunalismo. Murray Bookchin, Abdullah Öcalan e le dialettiche della democrazia*, (Chiomonte: Tabor edizioni, 2015).

ESSAYS AND ARTICLES ON BOOKCHIN

AA. VV., "Dossier Murray Bookchino. 'L'ecologia della libertà,'" in *A Rivista*, no. 320 (October 2006): 27–44.

AA. VV., "Per una società ecologica/Dossier Murray Bookchin," in *A Rivista*, no. 413 (February 2017): 103–116.

AA.VV., "Murray Bookchin 1921–2006, Bollettino del Centro Studi Libertari," *Giuseppe Pinelli*, no. 28, 5–9.

Berti Francesco, "Anarchismo e municipalismo: un matrimonio difficile," in *A Rivista*, (1993).

Berti Francesco, "Prefazione in M. Bookchin, L'idea dell'ecologia sociale. Saggi sul naturalismo dialettico," *Palermo:* Ila Palma (1996).

Berti Giampiero, Prefazione in S. Varengo, *La rivoluzione ecologica. Il pensiero libertario di Murray Bookchin*, Milano: Zero in Condotta (2007).

Biehl Janet, "La strana coppia," in *A Rivista*, no. 381 (June 2013): 91–96.

Bookchin Debbie, Venturini Federico, "Bookchin: l'eredità vivente di un rivoluzionario americano," in *r/project*, (March 2, 2015).

Bookchin Debbie, "Come le idee di mio padre hyear aiutato i curdi a creare una nuova democrazia," in N. Santi e S. Vaccaro, *La sfida anarchica nel Rojava*, Pisa: BFS (2019).

Borselli Simone, "Il dibattito su A," in *A Rivista*, no. 320, (October 2006).

Caccia Beppe, "Un ecologista sociale del ventunesimo secolo," in *il manifesto*, no. 190 (August 13, 2006): 13.

"Bookchin e la sinistra europea: l'incontro mancato," in *A Rivista*, no. 320 (October 2006).

Cannillo Alessandra, "Dall'atomismo sociale alla società ecologica. L'etica di Murray Bookchin," in *Rivista internazionale di filosofia e psicologia*, vol. 2, no. 1 (2011): 18–31.

Castanò Ermanno, "Eco-anarchismo. Cronaca di un incontro al buio," *Antasofia no. 3. Viaggio nella modernità*, Milano (2004).

Cerundolo Luisa, "La tradizione libertaria americana e l'ecologia sociale radicale di Murray Bookchin," in *Annali Dipartimento Scienze Stroiche e Sociali*, Lecce (1988): 167–187.

Cossutta Marco, "Per un anarchismo attualista. Murray Bookchin: dall'ecologia sociale al municipalismo libertario," in *Tigor: rivista di scienze della comunicazione e di argomentazione giuridica*, year 6, no. 2 (July-December 2014): 61–70.

Creagh Ronald, "Da Rocker a Bookchin. Note sul pensiero libertario americano contemporaneo," in R. Rocker, *Pionieri della libertà. Le origini del pensiero liberale e libertario negli Stati Uniti*, Milano: Edizioni Antistato (1982).

De Toni Paolo, In ricordo di Murray Bookchin, *Germinal*, no. 101–102 (November 2006): 32–33.

De Toni Paolo (Gruppo Ecologia Sociale Friuli), "L'anarchismo di fronte alla catastrofe climatica," in *Umanità Nova*, (September 30, 2014).

Donini Elisabetta, "Liberare l'uomo dal dominio della natura. Una ristampa di Bookchin," *La nuova ecologia*, no. 42, (September 1987): 74.

Donno Antonio, "Il radicalismo negli Stati Uniti degli anni '80: l'anarco-ecologismo di Murray Bookchin," *Il Protagora*, no. 9–10 (January/December 1986): 49–64.

Ferbi Silvia, "Un grande utopista contemporaneo," in *A Rivista*, no. 7 (2006).

Ferbi Silvia, "Ecologia sociale, municipalismo libertario e democrazia diretta: Murray Bookchin e l'espropriazione della politica da parte dello stato," *Collegamenti Wobbly*, no. 2, (July/December 2006): 145–157.

Fernandez Benjamin, "Murray Bookchin, ecologia o barbarie," in *Le monde diplomatique*, (August 1, 2016): 3.

Gallo Claudio, "Bookchin: nella democrazia radicale tutti possono cambiare il mondo," in *La Stampa*, (April 4, 2018).

Gallo Claudio, "Così i curdi siriani hanno abbandonato Marx per mio padre," in *La Stampa*, April 22, 2016.

Matteo Maria, "L'utopia del signor Vitali," in *A Rivista*, no. 206 (February 1994).

Padoan Dario, "Città e municipalismo libertario," in *A Rivista anarchica*, (1993).

Paterna Stefano, "La sfida dell'ecologia della libertà," in *La Città Futura.it*, (March 12, 2015).

Pricolo Vincenzo, "La democrazia dei post-moderni," *Il Giornale*, (January 7, 2002): 20.

Pucciarelli Mimmo, "Il 'mio' Murray," *A Rivista*, no. 423 (March 2018).

Romiti Maria Teresa, "Ecologia sociale," *A Rivista*, no. 93 (June/July 1981): 16.

Scalzone Lucia Martini, Introduzione in *M. Bookchin, The Modern Crisis. La crisi della modernità*, Bologna: Agalev (1988): 5–13.

Schibel Karl-Ludwing, Ritorna "L'ecologia della libertà," in *A Rivista*, no. 224 (February 1996): 24–25.

Schibel Karl-Ludwing, "Un grande se n'è andato: Murray Bookchin," in *Libertaria*, no. 4, (October/December 2006): 72–75.

Scudo Gianni, Introduzione in *M. Bookchin, I limiti della città*, Milano: Feltrinelli (1975): 5–12.

Silvestri Giulio, "Bookchin: un municipalista libertario," in *Rivista indipendenza*.

Sini Peppe, "Oltre ogni dogmatismo," in *La non violenza è in cammino*, no. 1391, (August 18, 2006).

Toesca Pietro M., Ritorna "L'ecologia della libertà" Vol. 2, in *A Rivista*, no. 224, (February 1996): 24.

Ughetto Claudio, "Recensione di Democrazia diretta," in *Diorama Letterario*, no. 249 (January 2002).

Vaccaro Salvo, "Recensioni: Murray Bookchin, L'ecologia della libertà," in *Umanità Nova*, no. 37, 1964, (November 18, 1984): 2.

Vaccaro Salvo, "Non mitizziamo Bookchin," in *Volontà*, no. 2 (April/June 1986): 115–117.

Vaccaro Salvo, "Ancora Bookchin," in *A Rivista*, no. 163 (April 1989): 30–31.

Vaccaro Salvo, "Dalla controcultura all'ecologia sociale. 1921–2006: Murray Bookchin," in *Umanità Nova*, no. 30, 1986, (October 1, 2006: 8.

Vaccaro Salvo, Prefazione in *Murray Bookchin, Democrazia diretta. Idee per un municipalismo libertario*, Milano: Elèuthera (2015).

Varengo Selva, "Con Bookchin sottobraccio," in *A Rivista*, no. 347 (October 2009).

Varengo Selva, "Il ritorno di Murray," in *A Rivista*, no. 355, estate 2010.

Varengo Selva, "Murray Bookchin e l'ecologia sociale," in *Etologia ed etica*, Roma: Aracne (2012): 219–231.

Varengo Selva, "La società ecologica," in *Etiche dell'ambiente. Voci e prospettive*, Milano: LED (2012): 245–263.

Varengo Selva, Seniga Martino, e Bookchin Debbie, "Bookchin e l'anarchismo. Dibattito," in *A Rivista*, no. 424 (April 2018): 49–55.

Vigilante Antonio, "Politica del desiderio. Aldo Capitini e Murray Bookchin," in *Educazione aperta. Rivista di pedagogia critica*, no. 4 (estate 2018): 131–166.

Sandro Moiso, "Murray Bookchin: una nuova prospettiva per il XXI secolo," in *Carmilla*, February 22, 2018.

Claudio Gallo, "Bookchin: nella democrazia radicale tutti possono cambiare il mondo," in *La Stampa*, April 4, 2018.

Reflections on the Future of Social Ecology: Conclusion

Yavor Tarinski

AS A REVOLUTIONARY FIGURE, Murray Bookchin was never interested in confining his thought within the walls of academia. On the contrary, his writings were a highly potent and clear-minded political intervention in burning social issues. For a thinker of his rank, Bookchin's legacy for the 21st century is nothing less than a quantum leap in the development of a revolutionary politics for the grassroots transformation of society.

As demonstrated in this book, the theoretical body of social ecology is very rich, offering one of the most coherent libertarian alternatives to capitalism and statecraft. But nonetheless, for many years, it remained on the margins of radical thought. Anarchists and autonomists distrusted its insistence on the need for the creation of democratic horizontal institutions in municipalities, considering it as a kind of reformism. Many on the Left, on the other hand, were skeptical of social ecology's attack on all forms of hierarchy and bureaucracy. While traditional political tendencies kept their distance from these ideas, social ecologists found it difficult to reach people beyond the activist scene.

All this changed with two major events, as demonstrated by many of the essays in this anthology: the Rojava Revolution and the rising municipalist wave in Europe. The first demonstrated in practice what a version of Bookchin's libertarian municipalism (the political dimension of social ecology) might actually look like. The second showed the importance of creating and strengthening grassroots institutions here and now, without waiting for a great revolution. These two tendencies were both inspired by Bookchin's ideas and the theoretical body of social ecology.

Furthermore, contemporary social movements in general are increasingly beginning to experiment with some of these ideas. The French Yellow Vest movement is a stark example, with it being organized along democratic confederalist lines. In Greece, as well, local ecological initiatives all over the country have begun efforts at similar confederalization of their struggle. It seems that social ecology and Bookchin's thought have been embraced by an increasing number of social and political movements. It is for this reason then, that there must be dialogue among social ecologists about what must be avoided and what must be pursued in terms of theoretical work.

The Question of Class

One strand of critique of Bookchin's thought is his supposed de-emphasizing of the role of economic class analysis. John Clark, among others, makes this criticism, suggesting that "Bookchin seems to have naively equated the obsolescence of the classical concept of the working class with the obsolescence of class analysis."[1] This critique implies that social ecologists should return to a more traditional class-centered approach.

Bookchin, however, has always insisted that we cannot ignore class interests by completely absorbing them into trans-class ones.[2] It is not that we should overlook social inequalities, but if we place class analysis at the center of our political projects, we risk missing other more ancient aspects of domination.[3] For this reason, Bookchin sought to reinvigorate not the identity of the proletariat, which was mostly an economic category, but that of the citizen—as a self-managing and competent agent who democratically participates in the shaping of society. Bookchin challenged all forms of domination and promoted the direct democratic management by all people of the various aspects of public life.

It is precisely this empowerment that makes social ecology so attractive to a greater number of activists and social movements. Feminists, ecologists, and other social movements are increasingly realizing the need for people to collectively and rationally undertake the direct management of all spheres of social life. It is what makes Bookchin's thought so revolutionary and topical today. A retreat to a more class-centered analysis would lose much of this appeal, but more importantly, it would make social ecology much less dangerous to the status quo and its web of intertwined forms of domination.[4]

Which Municipalism?

Social ecologists must be on the lookout for another danger—with all the excitement from the rising municipalist wave in Europe, we must be careful to not equate every form of municipalism with Bookchin's thought and social ecology in general—otherwise, we risk stripping it of its content. Laura Roth from the international committee of Barcelona en Comú warns that, by municipalism, different people may mean different things: there are those who simply advocate for stronger local self-administration; while others intend it as more of a political strategy that prioritizes the local level over other levels.

Bookchin's work emphasizes a libertarian dimension of municipalism—one that offers a unique perspective to international social movements beyond parochial localism or neoliberal globalism. So far it has appeared as a suitable grassroots political agenda for the 21st century, and its revolutionary potential should be nurtured.

Bookchin himself was aware since the 1990s of a certain strand of left-wing politicians who, in his words, "were prepared to blur the tension [...] between the civic realm and the state, in order to gain greater public attention in electoral campaigns for gubernatorial, congressional, and other state offices." He was aware that this equation of libertarian municipalism with a mere "tactic" or "strategy" would eventually drain it of its revolutionary content.

When Bookchin spoke of municipalism, he meant the effort to transform and democratize cities by submitting local governments to popular assemblies and knitting them together in confederations.[5] In short, he meant nothing less than bringing power back to the people. All those who fight for a democratic and ecological future should delve into this legacy and be wary of those who try to exploit its rising popularity in order to reach positions of power. The municipalist initiatives that can be placed within this paradigm are those that will be initiated by social movements, run using participatory procedures, and who will strive to constantly empower the citizenry; not those merely introducing mild labour- and migrant-friendly reforms. In the end, libertarian municipalism is not about giving a helping hand to those in need, but actually vesting them with real decision-making power in the management of society.

Creating Grassroots Institutions

One point, addressed by Bookchin and social ecologists, on which we should put emphasis, is the need to create grassroots democratic institutions, expressed in the project of libertarian municipalism. Unfortunately, this is a topic that is still being viewed with certain hostility by anarchists, who at times go so far as to blame the formation of local assemblies for obstructing insurrections,[6] while leftists often see it as nothing more than another tool for strengthening partisan politics.[7]

Bookchin strongly disagreed with such opinions, arguing that no rationally formed society can exist without institutions, and without such it will simply dissolve.[8] So he insisted that the road towards a democratic and ecological society navigates, not beyond, but through the participatory formation of new decision-making bodies that will empower the citizenry and challenge the domination of statecraft and capitalist relations.[9]

As demonstrated by some of the essays in this anthology, social movements that take into serious consideration Bookchin's ideas about grassroots formation of institutions have shown in practice how fruitful this approach is. Recep Akgün, in his essay *Bookchin and the Kurdish Movement in Turkey,* demonstrates how the

Kurdish movement, when embracing a strategy based on the immediate formation of democratic institutions, managed to deepen their scope, approach, and worldview. The Yellow Vests in France, too, have embraced a similar trajectory, as demonstrated by Theo Rouhette in his *The Role of Social Ecology in the Gilets Jaunes Movement.* In both these contemporary cases we see how the contours of libertarian municipalism help social movements build long lasting democratic structures beyond statecraft and capitalism, as in the case of the Kurdish movement, or help social struggles prolong their temporality and infuse local communities with a democratic culture, as with the Yellow Vests. In a world where an increasing number of people refuse to participate in electoral politics, trust in statecraft and capitalism is diminishing. It is of vital importance for the people themselves to create democratic institutions that will remake society along more egalitarian and ecological lines, and not let it descend into barbarism.

Castoriadis for Social Ecologists

Social ecologists can find an important source of inspiration and ideas in the works of Greco-French philosopher Cornelius Castoriadis. Although there was a major break between him and Bookchin, most evident in the latter's resignation letter from the journal *Democracy and Nature*,[10] there are more commonalities in the thought of these two great thinkers than they would have liked to admit.

Castoriadis, like Bookchin, places direct democracy at the heart of his political project. The ancient Athenian *polis* is a major source of inspiration for both thinkers, without overlooking its many problematic aspects. By carefully studying it, Castoriadis reached the conclusion that democracy cannot be viewed simply as a set of participatory procedures. Instead, it is a distinctive political system, where people obtain an active civic culture—or what the ancient Athenians called "*astynomos orgè*" (passion for law-making)—and directly participate in the management of society.

Furthermore, their views on ecology as a deeply political issue was also a point of convergence. Castoriadis argued that ecology is all about people collectively setting natural limits to their activities.[11] This, he insisted, has nothing to do with science, since the latter is not about self-limitation. Instead, ecology is a deeply political matter requiring democratic deliberation on how humanity will use its technology and what relations it will have with the planet.

Despite their political similarities, Bookchin accused Castoriadis of being post-modern in his philosophical approach, especially for using the concept of the "social imaginary." This did not do justice to the latter, because he is definitely no postmodernist thinker.

What Castoriadis refers to as the "social imaginary" are the meanings that each society creates to define what is "real," "possible" etc.[12] In this sense nothing is predetermined, and it is up to societies to institute themselves in such a way as to create different sets of significations. We have actually seen this in practice in the experiences of the Zapatistas and Rojava: when a direct democratic form of societal self-management was implemented, older worldviews like patriarchy and pseudo-mastery over nature were widely replaced with more progressive ones, like feminism and ecological stewardship.

In this sense, Castoriadis' philosophy can prove very helpful for those fighting for social change because it suggests that there is nothing unalterable in the human condition. People can act monstrously or empathically in accordance with the way they structure society. History is, according to Castoriadis, a human creation.[13] And there is a constant clash of different antithetical sets of meaning. For example, in the nihilistic desert of capitalist consumerism, the far-right advances authoritarianism and domination, while democratic social movements strive towards equality and cooperation. The participation or passivity of each one of us will determine the meaning and content of social life in the future. In this sense, Castoriadis' philosophical approach is a deeply revolutionary call to action, in contrast to a postmodern academic watering down of theory. And as such, it has much to offer to social ecologists.

Conclusion

As social ecology expands its reach, it increasingly influences, and is being influenced, by other political ideas, which undoubtedly is a good thing. This is the nature of dialectics. Within the theoretical body of social ecology one can detect feminist, indigenous, enlightenment, and other influences, which gives it a multi-faceted approach and makes it accessible for people from different parts of the planet, as we have seen in this book.

But we must be careful to not let its coherence become diluted by the incorporation of incompatible aspects of other theoretical tendencies. Otherwise we run the risk of infusing social ecology with relativism and turning it into yet another postmodernist caricature, something which Bookchin himself described as reactionary.[14]

This does not mean that we should aspire to some kind of theoretical "purity." On the contrary, theoretical and practical influences are of vital importance for a theory to remain vibrant and attuned to the times. But such influences should bear similar revolutionary democratic potential as does social ecology. This book, with all these wonderful authors, presents us with the ways in which Bookchin's legacy, and the social ecological school of thought he helped establish, spreads across the globe and crosspollinates with local theoretical tendencies and social movements, enriching a plethora of revolutionary practices. And this is the very goal of social ecology: communities knitting the project for a democratic and ecological society into their own context, culture, and traditions, thereby creating the foundations of what the Zapatistas call: "a world where many worlds fit."

NOTES

1. Andrew Light (editor), *Social Ecology After Bookchin* (New York; The Guilford Press 1998), 150.

2. Murray Bookchin, *The Next Revolution: Popular Assemblies & the Promise of Direct Democracy* (New York; Verso 2015), 89.

3. Bookchin, *The Next Revolution,* 43.

4. Laura Roth, "Which municipalism? Let's be choosy," Open Democracy, January 2, 2019, https://www.opendemocracy.net/en/can-europe-make-it/which-municipalism-lets-be-choosy/.

5. Bookchin, "Libertarian Municipalism: An Overview," The Anarchist Library, from *Green Perspectives,* October 1991, https://theanarchistlibrary.org/library/murray-bookchin-libertarian-municipalism-an-overview.

6. The Bosnian Experiment with Direct Democracy, 2014, CrimethInc., May 13, 2016, https://crimethinc.com/2016/05/13/feature-born-in-flames-died-in-plenums-the-bosnian-experiment-with-direct-democracy-2014.

7. Jordi Argelaguet, "Promoting internal party democracy: a selling point, a serious danger, or aredundant exercise?" https://ecpr.eu/Filestore/PaperProposal/e40858ee-579c-47a6-b443-73df4dceaee5.pdf.

8. Murray Bookchin, "What is Communalism? The Democratic Dimension of Anarchism," Inclusive Democracy, September 18, 1994, https://www.inclusivedemocracy.org/dn/vol3/bookchin_communalism.htm.

9. Janet Biehl, "Bookchin's Libertarian Municipalism," *Revista Cadernos de Campo,* No. 26, (Jan./June. 2019), 63-78, http://oaji.net/articles/2020/4826-1589377036.pdf.

10. Murray Bookchin and Janet Biehl: "Advisory Board Resignation Letter" in *Democracy and Nature,* Vol.3, No.3, 1997.

11. Cornelius Castoriadis: The Rising Tide of Insignificancy (unauthorized translation, 2003), 109–123

12. John B. Thompson, "Ideology and the Social Imaginary: An Appraisal of Castoriadis and Lefort," *Theory and Society,* Vol. 11, No. 5 (Sep., 1982), 659–681, https://www.jstor.org/stable/657343.

13. Cornelius Castoriadis, *History as Creation* (London: Solidarity, 1971).

14. Damian White, Murray Bookchin's New Life, *Jacobin Mag,* July 11, 2016, https://www.jacobin-mag.com/2016/07/murray-bookchin-ecology-kurdistan-pkk-rojava-technology-environmentalism-anarchy/.

ACKNOWLEDGMENTS

I WANT TO ACKNOWLEDGE Dimitrios and Nathan for their initial vision in bringing this anthology to fruition; the staff of Black Rose Books for their ongoing support and guidance, and the Milton Parc community of Montreal for providing spiritual nourishment and camaraderie during the compilation of the book.

I would also like to acknowledge the passionate support of Ioanna Maravelidi and the social ecologists from the Athens-based digital journal Aftoleksi. A big thank you to all the translators who converted our foreign authors' contributions into English, as well as the copy editors and proofreaders who helped refine the language: Caitlin Kindig, Aidan Gilchrist-Blackwood, Samuel Helguero, Laura Wenzel, Esten Steflik-Fabec, Nicola Morry, Rosalie Acutt, Claudia McDonnell, and Lachlan Zeitz. Also to my friends and life companions who stood by me while I devoted time to this effort. And of course to acknowledge my deep gratitude to all the contributors who continue to promote Murray's vision in their daily lives and work.

BIOGRAPHIES

Editor

YAVOR TARINSKI is a writer and social movement activist, a member of the Administrative Board of the Transnational Institute of Social Ecology (TRISE), a bibliographer at Agora International, and editor at the Greek libertarian journal, *Aftoleksi*. He is the author of *Direct Democracy: Context, Society, Individuality* (2019), *Short Introduction to the Political Legacy of Castoriadis* (2020) and *Common Futures: Social Transformation and Political Ecology* (coauthored with Alexandros Schismenos, 2021). He is also the editor of the Bulgarian books *The Direct Democracy of the 21ˢᵗ Century* (2013) and *The Project of Autonomy* (2014).

Contributors

JEAN-FRANÇOIS FILION holds a masters degree in sociology from the Université Laval, as well as a PhD in philosophy from the University of Paris I (Panthéon-Sorbonne). He is an associate professor at the Sociology Department of the University of Québec in Montréal (UQAM), as well as author of *Dialectical Sociology: Introduction to the Work of Michel Freitag* (Nota Bene, 2006).

JANET BIEHL is an author, editor, and graphic artist who, for more than two decades, has worked ceaselessly to develop and popularize the theory and politics of social ecology, in collaboration with Murray Bookchin. Along with other major works, she wrote the biography *Ecology and Catastrophe: The Life of Murray Bookchin* (Oxford University Press, 2015) and edited *The Murray Bookchin Reader* (Black Rose Books, 1999). She was a founding member of TRISE.

BRIAN MORRIS is an emeritus professor of anthropology at Goldsmiths College at the University of London. He is a specialist on folk taxonomy, ethnobotany and ethnozoology, and on religion and symbolism. He has carried out fieldwork among South Asian hunter-gatherers and in Malawi, and studied the Ojibwa. His writings include the books *Bakunin: The Philosophy of Freedom* (1993), *The Anarchist Geographer: An Introduction to the Life of Peter Kropotkin* (2012), *Pioneers of Ecological Humanism* (2012), and the forthcoming *Anthropology and Dialectical Naturalism: A Philosophical Manifesto* (Black Rose Books, 2021).

EIRIK EIGLAD lives in Porsgrunn, Telemark, Norway. In the early 1990s he joined the antimilitarist, environmentalist, and antiracist movement and was radicalized as a social ecologist. As a movement activist, writer, translator, and editor he has been involved in a range of left-libertarian projects in Norway; organizing seminars, actions, protests, and conferences. He is the author of the book *Communalism as Alternative* (2014). He was a founding member of TRISE.

GIORGOS PAPAHRISTODOULOU has worked as a journalist for many years and participated in the two-year struggle for self-management and defense of the local public radio of Ioannina (2013-2015). He was a member of the editorial boards of the journals *Contact* and *Babylonia*. He has participated in self-organized initiatives for the defense of the commons and public spaces in the city.

JASON TONEY is an editor, researcher, and activist based in Montréal. He is editor of the anthology, *Take the City! Voices of Radical Municipalism* (2020). He works with Black Rose Books and the Karl Polanyi Foundation.

NIKOS VRANTSIS has studied political science and has completed his master's degree in political theory and philosophy at Aristotle University of Thessaloniki. He writes on public spaces and has studied the architectural conditions of democracy.

PETER PIPERKOV is an activist, economist, and former PhD student in political economy at the UNWE in Sofia, Bulgaria. He is cofounder of Indymedia Bulgaria. He is also editor of the anthology *Asking We Walk: Life After Capitalism* (Anarres, 2010) and currently a member of social center Fabrika Autonomia in the city of Sofia. He has a Bachelor of International Economic Relations and Accountancy, and a Masters of Public Finance. He is a member of TRISE.

KOSTAS PAPOULIS He has studied economics and contributed essays to several anthologies about alternative solutions to the Greek economic crisis. Papoulis is a long-term participant in democratic and ecological movements.

RAMAZAN KAYA is a political activist in Turkey, member of the Green Party. He writes for ecological newspapers and journals in his country. He is author of *The Ecological Movement and the Green Party in Turkey* (2011).

GEORGI KONSTANTINOV was born in 1933 in the city of Blagoevgrad, Bulgaria, and is one of the most prominent figures of contemporary Bulgarian anarchism. He was sentenced to death by the Stalinist regime in the country twice, once for bombing Stalin's statue in 1953, and again for fleeing the country in 1973, but was granted pardon in both cases. He served 10 years at the Belene labor camp—one of the most monstrous gulags of Bulgaria's communist regime. Nowadays, he remains devoted to his radical ideas, and has authored numerous essays and books on anarchism.

STAVROS KARAGEORGAKIS teaches Greek history at a high school, and environmental philosophy in several university philosophy departments in Greece. He has authored and translated many books on social ecology and anarchism. He is a member of the editorial board of the Greek social ecology journal, *Eutopia*.

NIOVI CHATZINIKOLAOU is an English teacher in a private language school. She is also a translator. She holds a Master of Science in environmental education and she is an activist for climate justice and animal rights.

COSTAS DESPINIADIS is a writer, publisher, translator and editor, and the founder of the Greek publishing house and journal, Panopticon. He has translated 25 books and dozens of essays by Arendt, Shelley, Goldman, Thoreau, Huxley, Kropotkin, and Proudhon, among others. His own essays and books have been translated into French, German, Spanish, and English, including *The Anatomist of Power: Franz Kafka and the Critique of Authority* (Black Rose Books, 2019).

ALEXANDROS SCHISMENOS holds a Doctor of Philosophy and has authored four books in Greek and several articles regarding social autonomy and political philosophy. He has participated in social and ecological movements since the late 1990s. He is a member of TRISE.

HAWZHIN AZEEZ is a Kurdish academic, activist, poet, and intersectional feminist from southern Kurdistan (northern Iraq). She holds a PhD in political science and international relations, majoring in post-conflict reconstruction and nation-state building. She is cofounder of *The Middle Eastern Feminist* and was the co-chair of the Rojava-based NGO Hevi Foundation, which is currently working on the ground across to build libraries, schools, and universities.

RECEP AKGÜN is an assistant professor in the Department of Sociology at Karamanoglu Mehmetbey University in Turkey. He studied philosophy at Istanbul University and received a masters degree from the Institute of the Middle East at Marmara University in Istanbul. He completed a PhD in sociology at Middle East Technical University, Turkey.

WOLFGANG HAUG is a German anarchist publisher and publicist. He led the Trotzdem Verlag publishing house and was editor of the anarchist magazine *Schwarzer Faden*. He has worked as a journalist for German outlets, as well as for publications from other parts of the world, such as the London-based *Freedom Newspaper*, the US magazine *Green Perspectives* with Murray Bookchin, and the London-based journal *Democracy and Nature* with Takis Fotopoulos.

DIMITRIOS I. ROUSSOPOULOS has been a lifelong political activist, writer, publisher, community organizer, and public speaker, living in Montréal. He is also a cofounder of the Transnational Institute of Social Ecology (TRISE). He began his activist life as a leader in the Canadian anti-nuclear campaign and peace movement and has since been a pioneer in social movements for housing rights, urban ecology, community control, and radical municipalism. He has also been at the forefront of radical political publishing which he continues to do at Black Rose Books.

EVE OLNEY, PHD works across multidisciplinary research practices as an independent researcher, activist, creative producer, and educator. She is a member of the urban activist group, Urban React (Greece) and the collaborative commoning project Living Commons (Ireland). Her work is published and exhibited across art, architectural, and sociopolitical activist forums. She is a member of TRISE.

ROGER JACOBS holds degrees in philosophy and human ecology. He has worked for 15 years at the Centrum voor Basiseducatie in Hasselt, Belgium. He is coauthor of several books. He has also published numerous articles for books and journals on social ecology and emancipatory education. He is a member of TRISE.

BOB SPIVEY is Board Member of the Institute for Social Ecology and cofounder of Social Ecology Education and Demonstration School (SEEDS), Vashon Island, Washington, USA.

THEO ROUHETTE is an ecologist and activist from the south-east of France. He has a background in biodiversity and ecosystem science. Since 2014, his activism has been focused on social ecology and related themes such as direct democracy and ecological justice, especially climate and water issues. He is a member of the TRISE Administrative Board.

SELVA VARENGO holds a PhD in European cultural studies as well as a Master's Degree in Philosophy. She is the author of *La Rivoluzione Ecologica: Il Pensiero Libertario Di Murray Bookchin* and *Pagine anarchiche: Petr Kropotkin e il mensile « Freedom » (1886-1914)*.

ALSO AVAILABLE FROM **BLACK ROSE BOOKS**

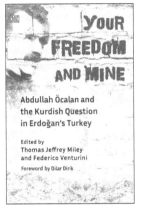

**Your Freedom and Mine:
Abdullah Öcalan and the Kurdish
Question in Erdogan's Turkey**
978-1-55164-670-1 cloth
978-1-55164-668-8 paper
978-1-55164-672-5 ebook

**Take the City:
Voices of Radical Municipalism**
978-1-55164-729-6 cloth
978-1-55164-727-2 paper
978-1-55164-731-9 ebook

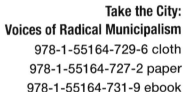

**Villages in Cities: Community Land Ownership,
Cooperative Housing, and the Milton Parc Story**
978-1-55164-688-6 cloth
978-1-55164-687-9 paper
978-1-55164-689-3 ebook

**Political Ecology:
System Change Not Climate Change**
978-1-55164-653-4 cloth
978-1-55164-651-0 paper
978-1-55164-655-8 ebook

CPSIA information can be obtained
at www.ICGtesting.com
Printed in the USA
BVHW040037160321
602609BV00007B/72

9 781551 647098